Director's Guide to Best Practices

*Examples from the Nature and
Environmental Learning Center Profession*

Second Edition

by
Norma Jeanne Byrd

Association of Nature Center Administrators

**ANCA Headquarters
c/o Aullwood Audubon Center
1000 Aullwood Road
Dayton, OH 45414
937-890-7360
www.natctr.org**

**Made possible with a grant from
the Institute for Museum and Library Services**

This publication is designed to provide accurate, authoritative information in regard to the subject matter covered. It is sold with the understanding that the publisher and the author are not engaged in rendering legal, accounting, or other professional service. If legal advice or other expert assistance is required, the services of competent professionals should be sought.

Director's Guide to Best Practices © 2006 Second Edition
Published by Association of Nature Center Administrators
c/o Aullwood Audubon Center, 1000 Aullwood Road
Dayton, OH 45414
937-890-7360
www.natctr.org

Originally published as **The Nature Center Handbook** © 1998
Director's Guide to Best Practices © 2000
Association of Nature Center Administrators, Dayton, OH

Use of works by other authors has been granted with permission of the publishers. See the following pages.

Cover art: Charley Harper
Cover design: Biltmore Press, Asheville, NC
Printing: VictorGraphics, Inc., Baltimore, MD
Production and editorial assistance: Patti Martino, Robert Mercer
Publication assistance: Larry Brown, Tim Sandsmark, ANCA
Text layout and design: Norma Jeanne Byrd, Patti Martino

Printed on recycled paper.

ISBN 10: 0-9702976-2-9
ISBN 13: 978-0-9702976-2-4

About the Cover

Cincinnati, Ohio artist Charley Harper generously donated the use of his artwork, *Mystery of the Missing Migrants* for the cover of *Director's Guide to Best Practices*. The following excerpt is from his book, *Beguiled by the Wild*.

> *At age three, Charley Harper fell head-first from the second-story window of the family farmhouse onto a stump, which was unaffected by the crash. He was too, his parents thought, until a few years later when he announced that he wanted to be an artist.*
>
> *Unlike traditional super-realistic wildlife art, his is flat, simple and funny. He doesn't put all the details in — he tries to leave them out. He distills reality and calls it minimal realism, adding, "When Audubon painted a bird, he had to count all the feathers in the wings. I just count the wings."*

Mystery of the Missing Migrants

For centuries, the neo-tropical migrants in this picture have shuttled between winter homes in the tropical rainforest and nesting sites in our woodlands. Now their populations are plummeting. Why? Habitat destruction. Down There? Up Here? Is your favorite songster in this flock? Each April, I listen anxiously to the dawn chorus for the return of my favorite, that world-class flutist, the wood thrush. Are silent springs forthcoming? Remember the canary in the coal mine?

Charley Harper

From *Beguiled by the Wild* by Charley Harper (1994). Flower Valley Press, Gaithersburg, MD. Used with permission of the artist and the publisher.

About the Author

Norma Jeanne Byrd landed her first nature center job on Sanibel Island, Florida after the no-name storm of 1977. The storm flooded much of the island including the grounds of the new nature center at the Sanibel-Captiva Conservation Foundation. She waded through water above her knees and climbed a railing to apply for a job there. A staff member remarked, "I don't know who she is, but hire her! Anyone that determined should work here!"

It was the beginning of a career that includes starting two native plant nurseries in south Florida, being one of the founders of the Florida Native Plant Society, directing fundraising for several nonprofit organizations including The Nature Conservancy, directing stewardship at three Florida natural areas, and consulting with numerous environmental organizations. As the director of a popular coastal nature preserve on Jupiter Island, Florida, she faced the challenges and rewards of being an administrator.

Norma Jeanne writes from her home in Palm Beach Gardens, Florida.

TABLE OF CONTENTS

Chapter 2: Strategic Planning

Chapter 3: Boards

Chapter 4: Staff

Chapter 5: Fundraising and Development

FOREWORD

My first day on the job as a director of a new nature center was in 1975. I had graduated from college just a few days before. As I walked around the site, I realized I was clueless. I knew something about nature, more about environmental education, and a little about planning, but nothing, literally nothing, about how to develop or run a nature center.

I picked up a rock and tossed it into the pond. Ripples. Circles of growth expanding from a core. Experience becoming knowledge. It suddenly occurred to me, watching the ripples, that I knew exactly what to do as a new director.

NOT!

After a few more rocks and a few more years, I am still learning. Most of us in this profession are trained in some other discipline, and we have all tossed rocks into the pond. I do wish that on that first day I had known of someone to talk to, and had something to refer to. Today, the members of ANCA are the "who" and the book Director's Guide to Best Practices is the "thing."
Corky McReynolds, ANCA President 1997-1999

Most of us can relate to Corky's words. They sure hit home with me because I was pretty green, so to speak, to the challenges and opportunities of being a nature center director when I took my first director's job. I was lucky because the "who," ANCA, was there for me and in 1995 I attended the first ANCA Summit at Treehaven in northern Wisconsin. It was truly an invaluable experience.

Then came the "thing"- this wonderful book which has special meaning for me because I was fortunate enough to be one of the "rookie reviewers" for the first printing of this publication many years ago when it was entitled *The Nature Center Handbook: A Manual of Best Practices from the Field*. We represented a primary target audience for the book- directors with five years experience or less. We were tasked with helping to ensure that the content was addressing our needs as those fairly new to the field.

Recognizing that leaders from other organizations in addition to nature and environmental centers could greatly benefit from this book, the title was changed in the revised second edition to *Director's Guide to Best Practices: Examples from the Nature and Environmental Learning Center Profession.*

Now in its third printing, the purpose of the book has not changed and it is still invaluable for new and seasoned directors alike. It draws from the experience of administrators and experts in the field and delivers the best practices to develop your leadership skills no matter where you work.

There were many who had the vision, dedication and belief in producing this book and a big thank you goes to all of you, especially to:

- Institute of Museum and Library Services (IMLS) who funded the project that resulted in printing the first edition of this book published in 1998.
- The many veteran and rookie reviewers and former ANCA board members who gave your talent, knowledge and commitment to creating this book while still leading your own organizations. Thank you for your dedication to our profession.
- Norma Jeanne Byrd, the author of *Director's Guide to Best Practices,* for her passion and the excellent work she did to write the original book and each revision.

Now more than ever we need good strong leaders who model the best practices contained in this book. This is the essence of ANCA – that we learn from each other, share what we know, and strive to be even better directors. This book will help you get there.

Tim Sandsmark, President 2005-2007
Association of Nature Center Administrators

Director, Lookout Mountain Nature Center and Preserve
Golden, Colorado

INTRODUCTION

Director's Guide to Best Practices

Director's Guide to Best Practices: Examples from the Nature and Environmental Learning Center Profession is a resource for anyone who wants to be a better director. This book contains practices, tips, techniques, and examples from administrators and other experts in the field, and covers five essential areas - leadership, strategic planning, boards, staff, and fundraising.

The Association of Nature Center Administrators (ANCA) developed *Director's Guide to Best Practices* for busy leaders with many roles and responsibilities. It is a source book for those new to their jobs and provides inspiration and challenge to even the most experienced directors.

History

The demand for a national professional network for nature center administrators prompted the founders to create ANCA in 1989. They recognized the need to develop peer relationships and ways to share knowledge, expertise, successes, and failures with others in the profession. ANCA meets that demand by providing products and services to its members including the quarterly *Directions* newsletter, the annual Summit, and professional consultation.

ANCA members consistently express the need for professional development and training in leadership and business administration to help them become better directors. At ANCA's annual strategic planning session in 1996, the idea for *Director's Guide to Best Practices* emerged. This book demonstrates ANCA's commitment to its mission.

Mission

ANCA promotes and supports best leadership and management practices for the nature and environmental learning center profession. Adopted June 6, 2000.

Creating *Director's Guide to Best Practices*

The wide pool of knowledge, practical experience, and wisdom of directors from large and small nature and environmental learning centers guided this book's development from beginning to end.

It began with a survey sent to ANCA members in early 1997. The survey asked members to prioritize a list of issues of greatest concern that had been identified in earlier ANCA surveys, at ANCA Summits, and at other local and national meetings. The top five issues from the survey became the five topic chapters of the book.

Directors also participated in creating the book outline and recommended sources for books, people, and other resources. Interviews with 30 environmental center directors and conversations with numerous others produced a collection of shared recommendations and individual experiences.

Research into the published works of acknowledged experts on each topic came next. Numerous works are cited throughout the book and included in the references. Be sure to use these excellent sources for even more detailed information.

A series of recommended best practices for organization leaders emerged from the collective wisdom of directors and other experts. In all, directors from 23 states and 40 different facilities reviewed and commented on the chapter drafts and evaluated the book's effectiveness to bring this resource to you.

The end result is *Director's Guide to Best Practices, Examples from the Nature and Environmental Learning Center Profession.*

This book contains the current thinking in the field in an easy-to-use format. It is designed for busy directors. Use it for a quick reference or to thoroughly explore a chapter topic. Read it cover to cover. Share it with your board, staff, and colleagues. Make use of the ideas it contains and assess your organization with this book as a guide.

Don't let it sit on a shelf.

Audience for the Book

Leaders, administrators, and managers of any organization will find guidance and inspiration in the *Director's Guide to Best Practices*. Although ANCA's original focus was directors with less than five years experience, the tools, tips, and techniques in this book apply to administrators everywhere. Whether seasoned or new to the field, this book is for you.

Director's Guide to Best Practices also will appeal to those who aspire to become organization directors. The best practices can help prepare ambitious new leaders for this challenging role.

Definitions

The word "director" refers to the person who bears ultimate authority and responsibility for achieving an organization's goals. A director's primary responsibilities include management of an organization, its programs, personnel, finances and marketing. In most cases, it also includes managing facilities and physical resources. Other titles for this role include:

- Administrator: an individual who provides the vision and leadership to carry out the administration and development of an organization's mission, goals, and objectives.
- Chief executive officer: the highest ranking executive responsible for organizational operations.
- Executive director: a person who manages or directs an organization.
- Leader: the person who leads, directs, or guides an organization.

Peter F. Drucker in *The Effective Executive* says the ability "to get the right things done" is what makes an effective director. This may involve doing what others overlooked and avoiding those things that are unproductive.

That's what *Director's Guide to Best Practices* will do for you: help *you* get the right things done.

*From *The Effective Executive* by Peter F. Drucker © 1966, 1967 HarperCollins Publishers, Inc., New York.

Tips for Using the Book

Director's Guide to Best Practices is arranged for easy use. Each chapter begins with introductory and general information specific to the chapter topic. Each chapter also contains:

- Checklist of Recommended Practices;
- Recommended Practices;
- References;
- Other Resources;
- Appendix;
- Contacts; and
- Reviewers.

Use the **Checklist** found at the beginning of each chapter for a quick reference. It is designed to help you assess yourself and evaluate your programs. The **Recommended Practices** contain detailed information on each topic to guide your work.

Look for the following symbols throughout the book:

- *Bullets* indicate key points of information.
- ❑ *Check boxes* indicate recommended actions.

Shaded Boxes

Shaded boxes contain tips from other directors, techniques that have worked successfully elsewhere, or information adapted from other published, knowledgeable sources. Don't skip these!

The General Appendix at the end of the book includes useful resources that apply to many different aspects of leading and operating a successful organization.

Acknowledgments

Running an organization is a collaborative effort, and so was the production of this book. Each of the following organizations and people contributed to the book's creation.

Institute of Museum and Library Services

The Institute of Museum and Library Services (IMLS) awarded ANCA a $50,000 grant in 1996 to produce *The Nature Center Handbook*, the predecessor to *Director's Guide to Best Practices*. We are enormously grateful for IMLS's generous support.

ANCA Members

In conjunction with IMLS, ANCA's board members contributed hundreds of hours as an in-kind match to the IMLS grant. ANCA also funded this revised edition.

ANCA members contributed in many ways, and especially by expressing the concerns directors share. The advice and suggestions of ANCA members in surveys, Summit attendance, and in discussions with each other have made the book richer and of use to all. Your enthusiasm and commitment to the nature and environmental learning center profession contributes greatly to keeping the field exciting and rewarding.

Reviewers

Some people volunteered extra time for the challenging job as one of 40 reviewers for the book. This exceptional collection of people offered their tremendous experience to the rest of the profession. We thank you for your dedication to this project.

The first group of reviewers included directors with nature or environmental learning center experience ranging from more than five to nearly 30 years in the field. Through interviews and comments on the drafts, these directors helped shaped the content and substance of the book. Other professionals also offered their knowledge and experience to enhance the book's quality.

Thank you for contributing your ideas, suggestions, experiences, materials, and time to review the drafts. This book is possible because of you.

The reviewers include:

Carolyn Chipman-Evans, Brent Evans, Ken Finch, Anne Harper, Tracy Kay, Charity Krueger, Corky McReynolds, Robert Mercer, Judy Miller, Cindy O'Connor, Rich Patterson, Corky Potter, Lee Reading, Marcy Rogge, Jack Shea, Bo Townsend, Ken Voorhis, Doug Weeks, Pat Welch, and Jim Yaich. Thanks also to Steve Bass, Dave Catlin, L. Wayne Clark, Libby Dorn, Richard Haley, David Heil, Deb McRae, Larry Perkins, Larry Pickens, and Mike Riska for their involvement.

The second group of reviewers represented a primary target audience for the book -- directors with five years experience or less. These reviewers evaluated the drafts to make sure the content addressed the needs of directors more recent to the field. When the project began, their experience ranged from a few months to nearly five years as nature center directors.

Their comments and suggestions helped ensure each chapter covers issues thoroughly without leaving out important information along the way. We thank you for your valuable contributions that will make the book useful for all directors.

These reviewers are:

Andy Brown, Lynn Corliss, Peggy Hunt, Greg Lee, Bob Marye, Carl Palmer, Tim Sandsmark, Christine Turnbull, Robert Venner, and Brian Winslow.

Our sincere thanks also go to:

- National Audubon Society for co-sponsoring the IMLS grant proposal;
- Charley Harper for donating the beautiful artwork on the cover, *Mystery of the Missing Migrants*. Thanks also to Bill Hopple and the Cincinnati Nature Center for making this connection to Charley possible.

Other Authors

This resource book is a compilation of directors' experiences and the knowledge borrowed from other experts in the field. Numerous resources are cited and attributed in the book. To each of these authors whose works I have referenced and shared, thank you for your contributions.

A Final Note

I am grateful to the following people for making this book possible. A special thank you goes to:

- ANCA president Tim Sandsmark for his belief in the book which contributed greatly to its success and usefulness to directors.
- Former ANCA presidents Corky McReynolds and Pat Welch. Corky's guidance and leadership and Pat's enthusiasm inspired me to become involved with ANCA and contribute to the field of leadership.
- Larry Brown who attended to the important work of gaining publishers permissions and coordinating the printing of this 2006 edition.
- Bob Mercer who carefully reviewed and edited every chapter to make sure we got it right the first time out, producing a top-notch, high quality book.
- Patti Martino who assisted with initial production and design and brought great talent, good humor and endurance to the creation of this book.
- Joe Rosselot, my husband, for his love and support.

Norma Jeanne Byrd
July 2006

CHAPTER 1: LEADERSHIP

*The true function of an artful leader is empowering, mentoring and inspiring others
from a place of honor and respect.*

Angeles Arrien, *The Warrior: Living the Four-Fold Way*

What is Leadership?

In *The Five Practices of Exemplary Leadership,* James M. Kouzes and Barry Z. Posner define leadership as "a relationship between those who aspire to lead and those who choose to follow" (p. 1). Mastering the dynamics of this relationship and mobilizing others toward shared aspirations is the key to becoming a successful leader.

Kouzes and Posner's research consistently identified five practices and 10 commitments common in extraordinary leadership achievements. **See Table, *The Five Practices and Ten Commitments of Exemplary Leadership,* p.3.**

Also, see Appendix A, *Attributes of Leadership Among Environmental Education Administrators,* p. 21.

Organization Leadership

Leadership is a director's primary responsibility. To achieve the organization's mission, an administrator inspires and motivates others to work as a team. A director must also possess and develop certain qualities to build the trust, confidence and support of those involved with the organization.

An executive director brings leadership to every dimension of the organization's operation, directing multiple people and tasks for a common goal. A successful organization is one where the mission is fulfilled, clients are reached through programs and services, and sufficient funding is attained to achieve the organization's goals.

The director is not the only leader. Leadership may be found and developed through staff, board members, and volunteers. The director cultivates, develops, and consistently demonstrates his or her own leadership skills and abilities while encouraging leadership development in others. Others will follow strong leaders and adopt the attitudes and behaviors they demonstrate.

In a essay titled *Leadership: Management's Better Half*, leadership consultant John H. Zenger identifies six behavioral dimensions of leadership. Leaders:

- Create values through communication;
- Develop responsible followers;
- Inspire lofty goal accomplishment;
- Model appropriate behavior;
- Focus attention on important issues;
- Connect their group to the outside world (Zenger, 1986).

The Institute for Conservation Leadership developed a profile of an executive director in *A Sourcebook for Executive Directors* (ICL, p. 3). The profile lists necessary skills in fundraising, planning, personnel, time management, delegation, conflict management and more. It also lists personal traits such as being caring, sensitive, reliable, humble, and open. **See p. 4.**

For some, these expectations may seem to conflict with each other. Can a director work long hours every week and be relaxed and open? Some people can but others feel deprived of important time with family, friends, and interests outside of work. Each person must find a balance that brings challenge and fulfillment, at least most of the time.

Leadership is an ongoing process learned through experience, mentoring, and training. Use the practices to analyze your strengths, weaknesses, and areas to be improved. Share the practices with staff and board members to help develop their knowledge and skills. Then carry on with the important and always challenging responsibilities of leading your organization.

The Five Practices and Ten Commitments of Leadership

Model the Way	Find your voice by clarifying your personal values.
	Set the example by aligning actions with shared values.
Inspire a Shared Vision	Envision the future by imagining exciting and ennobling possibilities.
	Enlist others in a common vision by appealing to shared aspirations.
Challenge the Process	Search for opportunities by seeking innovative ways to change, grow, and improve.
	Experiment and take risks by constantly generating small wins and learning from mistakes.
Enable Others to Act	Foster collaboration by promoting cooperative goals and building trust.
	Strengthen others by sharing power and discretion.
Encourage the Heart	Recognize contributions by showing appreciation for individual excellence.
	Celebrate the values and victories by creating a spirit of community.

From "The Five Practices of Exemplary Leadership" by James. M. Kouzes and Barry Z. Posner (p. 12).

Profile of an Executive Director

☐   Skilled in financial management and fund raising.
☐   Constant grasp of issues.
☐   Perfect delegator.
☐   Supervisor, trainer, and teacher extraordinaire.
☐   Willing to work 50-70 hours per week.
☐   Efficient time and work load manager.
☐   Brilliant strategist and visionary.
☐   Totally reliable.
☐   Caring and sensitive.
☐   Thick-skinned.
☐   Fluent writer.
☐   Expertise in personnel and administrative law.
☐   Humble.
☐   Completely confident.
☐   Exemplary communicator.
☐   Skilled conflict manager.
☐   Relaxed and open.
☐   Willing to change.

Source: *A Sourcebook for Executive Directors, Fourth Edition.* **1995. Produced by the Institute for Conservation Leadership, a non profit training, facilitation and consultation organization serving the environmental community. Institute for Conservation Leadership, 6930 Carroll Avenue, Suite 420, Takoma Park, MD 20912. www.icl.org.**

Checklist of Recommended Practices

I.   Lead the Organization

☐   Practice 1   Believe in the Organization's Purpose and Mission
☐   Practice 2   Enlist Others to Create a Shared Vision
☐   Practice 3   Work Strategically Toward the Organization's Vision
☐   Practice 4   Take Risks and Encourage Change
☐   Practice 5   Learn to Manage Change

II.   Lead Others

☐   Practice 6   Choose to Lead Others
☐   Practice 7   Build a Team
☐   Practice 8   Develop Effective Communication Skills
☐   Practice 9   Demonstrate Interest, Care and Concern for People
☐   Practice 10   Build Partnerships and Network with Others

III.   Develop Personal Leadership

☐   Practice 11   Lead by Example
☐   Practice 12   Participate in Lifelong Learning
☐   Practice 13   Seek Balance Between Work and Personal Life
☐   Practice 14   Acknowledge Weaknesses and Work to Improve Them
☐   Practice 15   Know When it is Time to Leave

Recommended Practices

I.   Lead the Organization

Practice 1

Believe in the Organization's Purpose and Mission

Commitment to the organization's mission, strong personal and organizational values, and passion for the organization's purpose are essential qualities in a director. In order to lead and inspire others, the director's role requires belief in and understanding of the organization's overall purpose. **See Strategic Planning Chapter**.

Leadership Qualities: Credibility

"... more than anything, people want leaders who are credible. Credibility is the foundation of leadership."

James M. Kouzes and Barry Z. Posner, *The Leadership Challenge*, p. 32-33.

Practice 2

Enlist Others to Create a Shared Vision

To create a desired future, commitment to the mission and passion for the organization's purpose alone are insufficient. It must be accompanied by the ability to inspire a shared vision.

The director is a guiding force for creating the vision but doesn't have sole responsibility (McReynolds, 1994, Vol. 4, No. 3). Enlisting others in a shared vision requires a leader to "listen deeply to others, discover and appeal to a common purpose, and give life to a vision by communicating expressively so people can see themselves in it" (Kouzes and Posner, p.148). **See Strategic Planning Chapter.**

Practice 3

Work Strategically Toward the Organization's Vision

Working strategically enables the director to concentrate on organizational goals by enlisting the support of others to achieve the vision and mission. Involvement with professional organizations such as ANCA provides opportunities to learn from and involve others in the work of your organization and its mission.

Without strategic steps, the numerous activities and responsibilities of the director's role will constantly pull attention and focus away from the vision (Herman and Heimovics, p. 78). **See Strategic Planning Chapter.**

Leadership Qualities: Initiative

Initiative is a motive that drives effective leaders to take a proactive rather than a reactive approach to their work.

Edwin A. Locke, *The Essence of Leadership* (p. 19-20).
Reprinted by permission of Lexington Books.

Practice 4

Take Risks and Encourage Change

Successful directors enjoy the challenges and risks of their positions. They also actively promote the concept of change. The role of an administrator is to "continually encourage the process of change, while accepting that it can be stressful, requiring reflection, energy and time" (McReynolds, 1994, Vol 4, No. 3).

Successful directors foster risk-taking by setting high goals but not so high that people feel frustrated. By raising the bar gradually and offering coaching and training, leaders build skills in people while helping them achieve goals at each new level (Kouzes and Posner, p. 207).

Risk taking involves relying on others, placing trust in their strengths and abilities, encouraging them to take risks and accepting that they may not always be successful. A successful leader celebrates small wins (Kouzes and Posner, p. 208-209) and stands behind staff when they fail.

Practice 5

Learn to Manage Change

Change is inevitable in organizations and life. To make change an ally rather than an enemy, learn to surrender to change rather than fight it (Pritchett and Pound, p. 4).

In *A Survival Guide to The Stress of Organizational Change*, Price Pritchett and Ron Pound list 15 "basic mistakes" that can sabotage anyone's ability to adapt to change. Mistakes include "Expect Somebody Else to Reduce Your Stress," "Try to Control the Uncontrollable," "Pick the Wrong Battles," "Try to Eliminate Uncertainty and Instability" and 11 others (Pritchett and Pound, p. 5-34). The survival guide offers sage advice to counter these behaviors plus tips for ways to reduce stress. **See Contacts, p. 33.**

New directors enter at a time of change and often find themselves in a "honeymoon" period where everything they do is accepted and praised. They worry about what will happen when the honeymoon is over.

Know that change will occur and plan for it. Make the most of your strong points, work to improve your weaknesses, and build a team with expertise to complement and enhance each other's skills.

---

15 Steps to Lower Stress

1. Invest 30 minutes in vigorous physical exercise, 3-5 times per week (assuming your doctor doesn't have a problem with that). Work up a sweat.
2. Learn relaxation techniques.
3. Cut down on caffeine.
4. Eat right.
5. Meditate. Get still. "Center."
6. Develop better time management habits.
7. Play. Have fun. Recharge.
8. Get plenty of sleep.
9. Smile more. Laugh. Use humor to lighten your emotional load.
10. Count your blessings — daily. Make thankfulness a habit.
11. Say nice things when you talk to yourself.
12. Simplify.
13. Set personal goals. Give yourself a sense of purpose.
14. Forgive. Grudges are too heavy to carry around.
15. Practice optimism and positive expectancy. Hope is a muscle — develop it.

From *A Survival Guide to The Stress of Organizational Change* by Price Pritchett and Ron Pound (p. 35). Used with full permission of Pritchett Rummler-Brache. All rights are reserved.

II.   Lead Others

Practice 6   **Choose to Lead Others**

Effective leaders must want to lead (Locke, p. 21), prefer a
leadership role and accept the responsibilities that come with
leading others. Good leaders are made by those who follow them;
without followers, there is no leader. **See Appendix B, *Thirty
Methods of Influence*, p. 33. Also, see Boards and Staff Chapters.**

Leadership Qualities: Energy and Enthusiasm

Energy is necessary for leaders to sustain a high achievement drive and get
ahead in their organizations. Working long, intense work weeks (and many
weekends) over a span of many years — a work pattern common among
leaders — requires that an individual have a high level of physical, mental,
and emotional vitality. A leader's visible display of energy enthusiastically
communicates the vision and helps to increase employees' commitment to it.

Edwin A. Locke, *The Essence of Leadership* (p. 17).
Reprinted by permission of Lexington Books.

Practice 7   **Build a Team**

Actively involving others in the institution's goals and activities is
a crucial component to achieving the organization's vision.
Individuals with a common purpose and shared goals will generate
a team that works together to accomplish great things. Successful
directors create teams by involving board members, staff,
volunteers, community members, colleagues, consultants and
others in the organization.

A director understands team dynamics and demonstrates these
concepts through practices that promote team processes. The
director fosters teamwork and shared ownership by facilitating
collaborative visioning, planning and goal setting through positive
group interaction, participation and team motivation.

A leader works to strengthen individuals and the team by creating
an atmosphere of trust, respect and dignity. Strengths and
weaknesses are recognized and supported. By nurturing self-
esteem, building strengths and empowering others, a director forms

a strong, loyal and cohesive team and helps develop new leaders. **See Boards Chapter, p. 75. See Staff Chapter, p. 135.**

Cross-trained staff members are an advantage to any organization. When team members learn the duties and responsibilities of their positions in addition to functions of other positions, they develop a more complete knowledge of the organization. During times of change or transition, team members with multiple skills and institutional knowledge can carry it through difficult times and prevent crisis. **See Staff Chapter, p. 135.**

Leadership Qualities: Flexibility and Adaptability

To handle and foster change, leaders must be flexible... flexibility refers to the ability to adapt to changing circumstances; it does not refer to being indecisive.

Edwin A. Locke, *The Essence of Leadership* (p. 31).
Reprinted by permission of Lexington Books.

Leading the Team

An interview with Pat Welch, Executive Director
Pine Jog Environmental Education Center, West Palm Beach, FL
by Corky McReynolds, Ph.D.
Director, Treehaven Education and Conference Center, Tomahawk, WI

Editor's Note: This interview is from a series conducted with executive directors about their experiences for Director's Guide to Best Practices.

CM: There is a great deal of talk and confusion about teams. Our colleague Charity Krueger advises to build a team early and rebuild continually. How have you built teams at Pine Jog?

PW: By dictating that we will have teams!

CM: Excuse me?

PW: I mean, I believe it is important enough to push into the culture, to stretch, to work hard at trying.

CM: How are teams used at Pine Jog?

PW: We had to ask ourselves what kind of teams fit our culture. Four questions have guided our teams:
    1)   What information do we need?
    2)   Who needs to be involved?
    3)   Who needs to make the final decision?
    4)   Who needs to be informed of the decision?

    We have an educational team that sets criteria and guidelines for our programs. They had to ask themselves the questions to guide the program chain, and decide on the level of decision-making.

CM: Now that you have created specific teams for specific purposes, what have you learned so far?

PW: Teams can't spin off without being well-grounded. Teams need specific responsibilities, training and coaching. They need to be well-prepared or they will be set up for failure.

CM: What problems have you experienced?

PW: We evolved very quickly from thinking that all decisions needed to involve all. Even little decisions like where the Coke machine should be. Now we are pulling back to make decisions that can be made at the lowest common denominator.

CM: What advice do you have for a new director?

PW: Teams are a powerful way to empower staff. Do it! There are lots of benefits.

Practice 8   **Develop Effective Communication Skills**

Effective communication with people both inside and outside the organization is essential to be a successful director. Skills for effective communication include common sense, fairness, respect, openness and trust (McReynolds, 1994, Vol. 4, No. 4).

Communication with community members, business leaders, politicians, members, donors and colleagues requires these skills along with preparation, knowledge and self-confidence. Well-planned meetings are important to aid productive and effective communication. **See Boards Chapter: Practice 8, p. 96; Appendix L, *Checklist for Conducting More Effective Board Meetings,* p. 126; and Appendix M, *The Action Agenda,* p. 127.**

Plan meetings with team members (board, staff and volunteers) so that regular contact occurs that is appropriate and productive. Frequent but brief meetings with individuals and teams can help foster openness and trust. **See Staff Chapter, Practice 6, p. 153-156; and Practice 9, p. 157.**

Retreats are an effective way to bring team members together for a longer, more focused meeting. **See Strategic Planning Chapter, Appendix E, *How Do I Use Retreats in the Planning Process?,* p. 67.**

Good communication begins with listening. Simply listening "to what other people have to say and appreciating their unique points of view demonstrates your respect for others and their ideas" (Kouzes and Posner, p. 249) Other communication skills for directors include giving clear instructions, being responsive to questions and suggestions, and keeping people well informed. **See Staff Chapter, Practice 9, p. 157.**

See General Appendix, Appendix A, *The Art of Collaborative Negotiating, p. 299).*

> **Leadership Qualities: Maturity**
>
> Maturity is " ... the balance between courage and consideration. If a person can express his [or her] feelings and convictions with courage balanced with consideration for the feelings and convictions of another person, he [or she] is mature."
>
> **Stephen R. Covey, *Principle-Centered Leadership* (p. 61).**
> **Reprinted with permission.**

Practice 9

Demonstrate Interest, Care and Concern for People

Executive directors are interested in people's lives, in understanding why they do what they do, in motivating and inspiring them, and in demonstrating how people can work together cooperatively in a positive manner. People oriented directors have deep concern for others, are open-minded, tolerant and able to relate to many different types of people. In addition, these directors are approachable, easy to get along with, capable of giving good advice and have a sense of humor (McReynolds, 1994, Vol. 4, No. 4).

See Appendix B, *Thirty Methods of Influence,* p. 33 and Staff Chapter, Section II: Build Strong Relationships, p. 153-167.

> **Leadership Qualities: Trust**
>
> "Without trust you cannot lead. Without trust you cannot get extraordinary things done. Individuals who are unable to trust others fail to become leaders, precisely because they can't bear to be dependent on the words and work of others. So they either end up doing all the work themselves or they supervise work so closely that they become over controlling. Their obvious lack of trust in others results in others' lack of trust in them."
>
> **James M. Kouzes and Barry Z. Posner, *The Leadership Challenge* (p. 244).**

Practice 10

Build Partnerships and Network with Others

Directors recognize the importance of developing relationships and cooperative partnerships with others outside the focus of the organization's mission. Being aware of the different, as well as similar, concerns of other people and organizations provides opportunities to involve and engage new partners in your work. Community organizations, businesses and civic groups are prime sources.

Agencies and organizations that share similar missions and goals with your institution are excellent sources for sharing information, resources, and people. Partnership possibilities exist with universities, schools, federal, state and local agencies, and non-governmental organizations to name a few.

Networking and collaboration often leads to strong personal and professional relationships. The Association of Nature Center Administrators was established for this very purpose.

III. Develop Personal Leadership

Practice 11   **Lead by Example**

It is the director's responsibility to lead by example, demonstrating commitment and values by being a role model to others. Consistency between words and actions is challenging and essential. Teach others by example and become a role model for the standards staff and volunteers are expected to follow. This is a highly effective form of training (Locke, p. 71-72).

See General Appendix: Appendix B, *Self-Test on Individual Ethics*, p. 302, Appendix C, *Building Opportunities for Ethical Reflection*, p. 304 and Appendix D, *Steps to Take When Faced With an Ethical Challenge*, p. 306.

Leadership Qualities: Integrity and Honesty

Integrity includes but goes beyond honesty. Honesty is telling the truth — in other words *conforming our words to reality*. Integrity is *conforming reality to our words* — in other words, keeping promises and fulfilling expectations. This requires an integrated character, a oneness, primarily with self but also with life.

Stephen R. Covey, *The Seven Habits of Highly Effective People* (p. 195-196). Reprinted with permission.

Practice 12   Participate in Lifelong Learning

Directors view themselves as constant learners and are able to use that learning in the context of their profession (McReynolds, 1994, Vol 4, No. 2). Reflective thinking is an important element of lifelong learning as directors learn from their experiences and from their mistakes. Those organization leaders who request frequent feedback can identify their skill development needs more easily.

Participation in on-going training and self-development to improve skills and knowledge is necessary for directors, staff and other valued members of the organization team. **See Staff Chapter, Practice 12, p. 164.**

Leading and Learning

**An interview with Charity Krueger, Executive Director
Aullwood Audubon Center and Farm, Dayton, OH
by Corky McReynolds, Ph.D.
Director, Treehaven Education and Conference Center, Tomahawk, WI**

Editor's Note: This interview is from a series conducted with executive directors about their experiences for Director's Guide to Best Practices.

CM: Research indicates leaders are continual learners. How have you applied learning to your leadership of Aullwood?

CK: Leadership keeps evolving. What I focus on now, I would not have focused on when I started. I have learned to become more community focused. I have also learned the organization is ever changing, such as staff personalities. I also now realize that everything working consistently all the time is expecting too much.

CM: How have you applied learning to your personal and professional life?

CK: Learning is the ability to put things in perspective. My greatest fear is not having enough energy, so I have learned to conserve my energy and pace myself.

CM: What advice do you have for new center directors?

CK: Don't think you have to know it all. Provide for yourself and your staff opportunities to grow. Above all, build a team early and learn to keep rebuilding the team.

Practice 13   ## Seek Balance Between Work and Personal Life

Maintaining the balance between work and personal life is essential for a successful director. Directors are drawn to the challenge of leading the organization which can result in excess work and little time away from job responsibilities.

Staff and volunteers look to the director to be a role model both at work and in life. While there are times when the demands of the job require extra time and energy, it is equally important to take time off to enjoy other parts of life.

> **D**o not burn yourselves out. Be as I am - a reluctant enthusiast ... a part-time crusader, a half-hearted fanatic. Save the other half of yourselves and your lives for pleasure and adventure. It is not enough to fight for the land; it is even more important to enjoy it. While you can. While it's still here. So get out there and hunt and fish and mess around with your friends, ramble out yonder and explore the forests, encounter the grizz, climb the mountains, bag the peaks, run the rivers, breathe deep of that yet sweet and lucid air, sit quietly for a while and contemplate the precious stillness, that lovely, mysterious and awesome space. Enjoy yourselves, keep your brain in your head and your head firmly attached to the body, the body active and alive, and I promise you this much: I promise you this one sweet victory over our enemies, over those desk-bound people with their hearts in a safe deposit box and their eyes hypnotized by desk calculators. I promise you this: you will outlive the bastards.
>
> Edward Abbey

Practice 14   ## Acknowledge Weaknesses and Work to Improve Them

Learn to recognize your strengths and weaknesses so you may work to improve them. One way is to seek input from staff and board members who work most closely with you. Be open to feedback from others and work to honestly evaluate yourself. Seek peer input through participation in professional organizations such as ANCA. Encourage the board to review and evaluate your performance. **See Boards Chapter, p. 85.**

Be sure to see the General Appendix, Appendix E, *Core Competencies,* p. 307, developed for executive directors. Use this for self-evaluation or to request input from others.

Practice 15

Know When it is Time to Leave

A sign of great leadership and strength in a director is knowing when it is time to leave. It is hard for many people to recognize when another director is needed to carry on or advance the work of an organization. A director who is fully vested in the organization and its success may find separating from it to be very difficult.

Each director brings unique skills and talents to the organization. But organizations are dynamic, living institutions that respond and adapt to changing conditions in the environment. The skills a director brings to his or her role this year may not be the same skills needed in five years. Directors should expect to learn new skills to keep up with the changing needs of the organization.

Some directors choose to leave when they feel their talents are needed elsewhere. Others leave when forced by the board of directors. No matter when it occurs, planning for your departure is important.

Prepare the organization for your departure at all times by building the strengths and abilities of the team -- your board, staff, and volunteers. Cross-train team members so they are knowledgeable about all aspects of the organization. Share information and see that the organization carries on with you as its leader or with the leadership of another.

Leadership Qualities: Self-confidence

Self-confidence is evident through liking oneself and people, being willing to adapt to the situation at hand and knowing one's strengths and limitations. Limitations are viewed as opportunities to learn.

Corky McReynolds, *Attributes of Leadership.*

Chaos and the Strange Attractor of Meaning

These ideas speak with a simple clarity to issues of effective leadership. They bring us back to the importance of simple governing principles: guiding visions, strong values, organizational beliefs — the few rules individuals can use to shape their own behavior. The leader's task is to communicate them, to keep them ever-present and clear, and then allow individuals in the system their random sometimes chaotic-looking meanderings.

This is no simple task. Anytime we see systems in apparent chaos, our training urges us to interfere, to stabilize and shore things up. But if we can trust the workings of chaos, we will see that the dominant shape of our organizations can be maintained if we retain clarity about the purpose and direction of the organization. If we succeed in maintaining focus, rather than hands-on control, we also create the flexibility and responsiveness that every organization craves. What leaders are called upon to do in a chaotic world is to shape their organizations through concepts, not through elaborate rules or structures.

Margaret J. Wheatley
Leadership and the New Science

References

Arrien, Angeles. *The Warrior: Living the Four-Fold Way.* Compact disc. Oakland, CA: Wisdom Circles, 1996.

Covey, Dr. Stephen R. *Principle-Centered Leadership.* © 1990 Stephen R. Covey. Salt Lake City, UT: Franklin Covey Co. Used with permission from Franklin Covey Co., (800) 654-1776.

_____ *The Seven Habits of Highly Effective People.* © 1989 Stephen R. Covey. Salt Lake City, UT: Franklin Covey Co. Used with permission from Franklin Covey Co., (800) 654-1776.

Herman, Robert D. and Heimovics, Richard D. *Executive Leadership in Nonprofit Organizations.* New York: Jossey-Bass, Inc., a subsidiary of John Wiley & Sons, Inc., 1991.

Kouzes, James M. and Posner, Barry Z. *The Leadership Challenge*, 3rd Edition. San Francisco: John Wiley & Sons, Inc., 2002.

_____ *The Five Practices of Exemplary Leadership.* San Francisco, CA. Pfeiffer, an imprint of John Wiley & Sons, Inc., 2003.

Locke, Edwin A. and Kirkpatrick, Shelley. *The Essence of Leadership.* New York, NY: Lexington Books, 1991. By permission. Lanham, MD: University Press of America.

McReynolds, Corky (Charles E.) *Attributes of Leadership Among Environmental Education Administrators.* Printed in *Directions*, Volume 4, Nos. 2, 3, 4, 6. Dayton, OH: Association of Nature Center Administrators, 1994-95.

Pritchett, Price and Pound, Ron. *A Survival Guide to The Stress of Organizational Change.* Plano, TX: Pritchett Rummler-Brache, 1995.

Rusmore, Barbara, Berthoud, Heather, Russell, Dianne, and Schechtman, Mike. *A Source Book for Executive Directors, Fifth Edition.* Takoma Park, MD: Institute for Conservation Leadership, 1997.

Wheatley, Margaret J. *Leadership and the New Science.* San Francisco, CA: Berrett-Koehler Publishers, Inc., 1994.

Zenger, John H., *Leadership: Management's Better Half.* San Jose, CA, AchieveGlobal, Inc. (formerly Zenger Miller, Inc.), 1986.

Other Resources

Drucker, Peter F. *Managing the Non-Profit Organization.* New York, NY: HarperCollins Publishers Inc., 1990.

_____ *The Effective Executive.* New York, NY: HarperCollins Publishers Inc., 1993.

Vaill, Peter B. *Managing as A Performing Art.* San Francisco, CA: Jossey-Bass Inc., Publishers, 1989.

Wheatley, Margaret J. and Kellner-Rogers, Myron. *A Simpler Way.* San Francisco, CA: Berrett-Koehler Publishers, Inc., 1996.

Appendix A

Attributes of Leadership
Among Environmental Education Administrators

by Corky McReynolds, Ph.D.
Director, Treehaven Education and Conference Center, Tomahawk, WI

*This is a summary of a doctoral dissertation by Corky McReynolds which was printed in ANCA's newsletter, **Directions** in 1994-1995. His work was the first study on leadership among nature center and environmental education center administrators. Reprinted with permission.*

OVERVIEW
Reprinted from *Directions*, March/April 1994, Volume 4, #2.

The study of leadership has exploded into a phenomenon as organizations, either large or small, private or public, try to gain advantage or at least keep up with the ever-increasing rate of change. The leadership literature is saturated with books by practitioners, researchers and consultants; commercially available assessments; and expensive training opportunities. All of these resources can in some way be useful for the nature center administrator, but there have been no studies attempting to discover a sense of leadership within our profession.

Nature and environmental education centers, like other organizations, are facing challenging times, rapid social changes, scary threats and exciting opportunities. The literature soundly supports the importance of leadership in the corporate business community and formal educational institutions, but what is leadership in the context of the nature/environmental center and does it really matter?

Nature/environmental centers face mounting program, staff, fiscal and facility challenges to meet current and future services. Nature centers have had to become more "business-like" and, in one sense, are small businesses with educational missions. Nature center administrators are challenged with providing the leadership necessary to guide their centers into a successful future, but few directors have received formal training in management/business skills or leadership development.

The purpose of this study was to establish a foundation of the attributes of successful nature center directors for effective leadership. Attributes are defined as "essential qualities" and may include management-oriented competencies, skills and/or leadership abilities to successfully direct a nature/environmental education center.

Little is known about the administrative/ organizational aspects of nature centers. Although nearly 1200 centers, of some kind or another, are listed in the Natural Science for Youth Foundation (NSYF) directory (1990), there is little available discussing centers as organizational entities. Peterson (1984) observed, "Environmental interpretive centers must be viewed as a business and managed with that in mind... centers should employ people who have the skills and background to operate the center in a business manner, making decisions that will keep the organization financially robust, not just for today, but over time" (p. 108-109). In 1989 NSYF sponsored blue ribbon panels on the profession. Simmons and Widmar (1989b) reported from those discussions administrators' top concerns included funding, marketing and public relations. Malcolm (1992) surveyed nature center administrators and noted those with particular administrative training favored those types of administrative responsibilities. Although few in number, the studies indicate that nature/environmental education centers do share common missions, common problems and common leadership opportunities.

Director's Guide to Best Practices

Appendix A continued

Summary of Methodology

A peer reputational study was used to select 20 center administrators from a larger list based on similar criteria. Minimum criteria were established to develop consistency among the selected centers and included: operating year-round, maintaining a site with acreage, maintaining a budget of at least $50,000, employing a full-time director (with two years at the center), one other staff, and serving school-age children. A master list of centers meeting the criteria was developed, followed by a peer reputational survey.

The survey allowed the center administrators to select their peers with effective center reputations, and reduced the number of eligible centers to a reasonable number for participation in the study. Visits to each of the centers were made and in-depth interviews were conducted. The interviews ranged from 2 ½ to 6 hours. Constant comparative analysis was used to form categories, themes and models from the data of original propositions (Strauss 1990). Propositions are individual statements derived from the interview data. Categories emerge from similar propositions while the related categories are linked to become conceptual themes. Major themes through further analysis have developed into a theoretical model.

Summary of Results

Eight major conceptual themes were constructed from 25 sub-themes, 118 categories and 635 propositions. Each of the eight conceptual themes will be described briefly here and further detailed in articles two and three of this series.

Passion for the Purpose. The center directors exhibited high intensity, strong beliefs and a clear understanding of the overall purpose for which they are striving. A strong sense of mission with values was a major category throughout the interviews. Directors considered their vocation as avocation and were influenced from the past through experiences and mentoring.

Living is Learning. Center directors view themselves as constant learners and are able to use that learning within the context of their profession. Directors engage in reflective thinking, understand the broader picture while juggling daily tasks and are proactive toward risk taking and change.

Vision is Vital. Center directors challenge the direction of the center, develop vision and recognize the vision needs of the organization. The director maintains the vision while performing in multiple levels of tasks to attain the vision.

Passion for the People. Center directors are people oriented and view themselves as serving with people through teamwork. Verbal and oral communication skills and connecting to the community are critical.

Methods of Management. Center directors recognize organization and management are important. They practice and seek new skills in planning, personnel, volunteerism, board management and politics.

Business is a Bonus. Center directors express a desire to develop stronger skills in business and finance. Constant challenges include fund raising and grant writing.

Program is Priority. Program considerations are given top priority in nature center development. Directors recognize and pursue high quality and service for the center's users.

Pride in a Profession. Center directors view their roles and position as a professional career and seek to achieve that kind of recognition. Concerns were expressed about the hardship of the profession on them as individuals and families. Professional development needs focused on people management, planning, business management, fund raising and computers. Networking was an expressed priority and actively pursued.

References

Malcolm, Diana. (1992). "Nature Center Administrators' Perceptions of their Job Responsibilities" *Directions* V., 2 , No. 5, January/February.

Simmons, Debora and Widmar, Ron. (1989b). Report #2, NSYF's blue ribbon report on nature centers' big concerns. *Natural Science Center News*, Natural Science for Youth Foundation, 4 (1), 9-12.

Strauss, Anselm and Corbin, Juliet. (1990). *Basics of Qualitative Research*. Newbury Park, CA: SAGE.

Appendix A continued
Peterson, Ervand. (1984). *Environmental interpretive centers of the United States: an ethnographic study*. Doctoral Dissertation, University of Michigan.

Natural Science for Youth Foundation. (1990). *Directory of Nature and Environmental Education Related Centers in the United States*. Atlanta, Georgia.

Part Two: Emerging Themes

Reprinted from *Directions*, May/June 1994, Vol. 4, #3

Themes in qualitative analysis are built from the ground up by connecting similar and recurrent conceptual themes. Categories are built from the grouping of individual statements. The major themes of this study emerged through the analysis of the interviews. Three overall themes predominated and were given the titles *Passion for the Purpose, Living is Learning*, and *Vision is Vital*.

Passion for the Purpose

Throughout the interview process the environmental center administrators exhibited high intensity, strong beliefs, and a clear understanding of the overall purpose for which they were striving. This passion for the purpose is built upon two broad sub-themes, Understanding the Self and Influences from the Past, that indicate these administrators have taken the opportunity to reflect on why they do what they do as a profession. The conceptual categories that compose the subtheme **Understanding the Self** are presented below.

Understanding the Self

Believing in the Purpose represents the foundation from which administrators operate - a desire to do something with significance, meaning, and purpose. As one administrator describes, *I fully believed in what the purpose was all about. That was very, very important to me because I never could have done it all these years if I hadn't believed that behind it there was some meaningful purpose.*

The leader must have a clear understanding and belief in the purpose of the organization; however, the belief in the purpose is not just the dominion of the director, but of all who are employed or associated with the center.

Sense of mission with high values describes the high values administrators perceive as important within the framework of a sense for the mission. A sense of mission is a belief in the organization's purpose and

is actualized into behavior: *...the directors have to have a sense of mission...I think you have to feel that way. You really have to feel that you are on a very important mission. The mission here is to demonstrate to people that humans are interdependent in the environment.* The high values associated with the sense of mission include perseverance, discipline, honesty, credibility, humor, enthusiasm and patience.

Attributes of service and compassion present directors' responses toward both others and themselves. The leader is open-minded and flexible, but stays focused on the mission, refusing to be pulled off center. One of the primary roles of the administrator is establishing a positive working atmosphere, which begins with trust. Trust is created by trusting; once established, it becomes mistrust only if the bonds that were built are broken.

Strong self-confidence is evidenced by the administrators' inward reflections and self-understanding. The director needs a strong self-confidence, which is evident through liking oneself and people, being willing to adapt to the situation at hand and knowing one's strengths and limitations. Limitations are viewed as opportunities to learn.

Passion for the Purpose also includes *Understanding Your Potential*. The directors' potential is related to the purpose of the center. Its realization is self-determined by a striving for excellence. Knowing more about yourself and your role revolves around discoveries that directors made about themselves as they matured in their profession. Comments included, "don't be afraid to push for what you believe;" "don't worry so much;" and "don't work seven days a week." Strengths are organization and creativity reflects a balance between having an ability to get things done and being creative. Vocation is avocation describes the tendency for center administrators' interests and careers to be one and the same. *I look at it - at my job - as a real avocation. I do, I'm an environmentalist seven days a week, twenty-four hours a day, not just when I am on the job.*

The second major sub-theme building towards Passion

Director's Guide to Best Practices

for Purpose was **Influences from the Past**. Nature center administrators reported the influence of mentors, including college professors, parents, supervisors, and peers. Mentoring fostered commitment to the environment and growth as an administrator. Past and present outdoor experiences have influenced a lifelong interest in the environment. Background and training in natural history and the ability to transfer learning from other training are also important.

Living is Learning
Center administrators view themselves as constant learners and are able to use that learning within the context of their profession. Two major sub-themes, **Life Experiences and Learning are Transferred to Practice** and **Proactive Towards Risk and Change**, support the theme *Living is Learning*.

Life Experiences and Learning are Transferred to Practice
Center administrators have the ability to view past experiences as important learning and are able to transfer them to nature center administration. The administrators reported a wide variety of work experiences, including running small businesses, working in state government, blue collar factory work, military experience, classroom teaching and principalship. These experiences appear unrelated to nature center administration, but for each administrator important learning occurred and was transferred to his or her role as a nature center director. From a broader perspective, everyday life experiences are learning opportunities. *What I find [is that] it is hard for me to go to anything and not have it turn around to be a beneficial opportunity for the center...even if it is looking in a waste container or a toilet paper dispenser in the bathroom, and saying that works better than ours.* Directors noted the ability to "think sideways" - keeping many thoughts and activities going at the same time, while retaining the broader view. Thinking sideways involves the administrator in active thinking about the center's multi-faceted operation and the director's complex roles. While maintaining the broad view, the center administrator also has the ability to organize tasks and priorities. Organizational ability is more than managing one's desk or duty schedule. It consists of seeing the future of the center and pursuing an overall plan. *I think one of my real primary goals is to keep us focused on a vision.*

Administrators engage in reflective and creative thinking about their roles, their centers' futures and complexity. Reflecting on personal limitations allows directors to fill those needs from other sources. Creative thinking and new ideas are not easy to explain. *They just jumped into my little mind and screamed. They just sort of happened, I guess.*

Proactive Towards Risk and Change
Center administrators reported enjoying the challenges and risks of their positions. In fact, pursuing challenges and taking risks are roles of the director. *I took the job because I was looking for some challenges in my life. If I had known there were going to be as many challenges as I have had, I probably would have done it again, but I think I would have looked at it more closely.* Center directors recognize leadership challenges and take action toward them. Providing leadership in risk-taking requires trusting others and drawing upon their strengths. The director is the proactive leader of the center, with a clear vision of the organization's purpose and a commitment to pursuing that purpose with all of one's resources. Effective decision-making includes the involvement of staff, board, and center stakeholders.

The center directors understand and promote the concept of change. Their role is to continually encourage the process of change, while accepting that it can be stressful, requiring reflection, energy, and time.

Vision is Vital
The third major theme derives from related categories focusing on the importance, establishment and meaning of vision to the center and oneself. Two sub-themes, Creating a Vision and Attaining the Vision, support **Vision is Vital**.

Creating a Vision
Understanding the center's reason for being and its philosophical foundation is a critical element in the creation of its vision and the directing of its resources. The director accepts the lead responsibility for articulating the center's vision, through reflection and organizational analysis, the vision of the center and for challenging the status quo.

Changing a mission statement to respond to future needs while maintaining the core reason for being is an important process for the director to continually examine. The director becomes the center's visionary. Directors are often viewed as the heartbeat, guiding force, or sometimes driving force of the organization.

Appendix A continued

While the director has a vital role in the creation, change, and implementation of vision, this does not necessarily include exclusive responsibility for establishing the vision. ...*seeing the future...here it starts from the bottom up*. Visioning for the future requires an understanding of the past. The framework for visioning consists of setting the direction, boundaries and mission. A mission is the over-arching goal, whose vision determines the strategy.

Attaining the Vision

The directors recognize the vision can only be attained through people who believe in it and have the skills necessary to implement it. Being a visionary is a strength but can be a weakness if the leader does not acknowledge the need for organization. *Visionaries alone are called futurists and oftentimes they are theorists, but visionaries with pragmatic follow-up are the doers.* Strategic visionaries have the ability to set a vision and see all the steps necessary to attain the vision. Attaining the vision involves the director in multiple levels of tasks depending on the center's size. The goal is to be more involved in higher level tasks with long-range implications for the vision and to spend less time in daily management tasks. A critical attribute of the director is recognizing the importance of other people and aligning them with a common vision. Teams are frequently used to effectively align resources while providing a good working atmosphere. *You have to have a good team to work with, to accomplish any project, because it can't just be one individual who accomplishes it.* However, teams require skill-building, open communication, and trust to work effectively. Attaining the vision requires shared responsibility, multiple levels of tasks, and teamwork.

The first three major themes presented from this study indicate that nature center administrators have a strong **Passion for the Purpose**. This passion stems from understanding oneself and one's role in the organization. Influences from the past enhance the directors' professional development. Directors view themselves as constant learners, who acquire and transfer new learning to the challenges facing their centers. Directors understand and accept challenges and are proactive toward risk and change. They guide the centers' vision and understand that it takes leadership to attain that vision. Leadership involves teamwork, resource alignment, and the organization of multiple levels of tasks. The director's role is to focus on higher level tasks

with long-range implications for the center.

Part Three: Emerging Themes
Reprinted from *Directions*, July/August 1994, Volume 4, #4

Passion for the People

The fourth theoretical theme presents the views of the directors about the critical importance of the people connected to the center and the attributes necessary to accomplish a center's vision with those people. The theme *Passion for the People* is derived from six supporting sub-themes: **Orientation to People, Serving as Leader with People, Communication is Critical, Connections and Cooperation, Connecting to the Center's Culture,** and **Connecting to the Center's Creation**.

Orientation to People

Directors in the study consistently express beliefs that one needs to be a "people person" to be an effective nature center administrator. Being people-oriented means having a deep concern about people and being able to relate to all kinds of people. *I think you need to be a 'people person.' By that, I mean you have to be able to relate to your staff as well as to your public.* Being a "people person" means having an interest in people's lives, and the reasons they do what they do. The effective director displays the kind of attitude and behavior that can excite and enthuse people about a center's vision. People skills means demonstrating cooperative behavior with others. An orientation towards people means being approachable and easy to get along with, giving good advice when asked, and having a sense of humor.

Credibility can be established by keeping people at the forefront. This provides the foundation on which the director develops and serves as leader for the organization.

Serving as Leader with People

The directors emphasize leading with people, not over them. As leader, the director enables the staff to be effective in their jobs by sustaining resources. The director is responsible for providing a positive working atmosphere by being honest and open. *My role is to help staff be successful by providing a good working atmosphere.*

The directors in the study describe their roles in a variety of ways, but consistently use action words, such as 'delegates,' 'coordinates,' orchestrates,' and 'team-leading.' A difficult but critical task is delegation. *I have been trying to delegate*

Director's Guide to Best Practices

more...have them look at their existing responsibilities and time lines to see if they want to do it, or what of their priorities should be shifted so that the new project should fit in. I don't believe in overloading the staff or dumping garbage on them. Delegation requires appropriate behavior by the director - which means giving credit, trust, guidance, and the responsibility to carry out the task. Delegation also means the acceptance of potential failure as long as that experience is viewed as a learning opportunity for the individual or team and for the center.

Serving as a leader with people means the director taking responsibility to enhance staff morale, while reducing the stress of staff. Success is often described as having a staff working as a team and maintaining a positive atmosphere within the center. *We were very fragmented when I started here, for a variety of reasons. That was very important to me, to get everybody working together as a team respecting everybody...*

Communication is Critical
Communication is critical to the success and effectiveness of the center, the director, and the staff. The directors view themselves as skilled in both verbal and written communications. *Certainly communications, and communication of both written and verbal skills, listening to the board, to the staff, to the volunteers. What are their expectations... being a good listener.* The directors utilize these communications skills to establish a communication system at the center. Systems vary from center to center, but each of the centers describing effective communications can clearly articulate factors necessary for success. Common traits of effective systems include common sense, fairness, respect, openness, and trust. The system is understood, whether it be weekly meetings, steering committees, or frequent one-on-one discussions.

Connections and Cooperation
Internal communications are matched in importance by the director's ability to communicate the center's vision externally in the community. Connections to the community are grounded in a genuine concern for and orientation to the people of the community. *We need to establish a presence in the community and give back to the community what it gives us...and the director sets the tone.* Making the right connections to the community often involves networking to find a point of contact, a bridge that can connect the center to the community. The directors express the critical need to establish connections early. *If I were to go to a new facility now, I would be much more aggressive about it. I would get out in the community a lot faster.* The community connection is an important function for the director to lead, while at the same time understanding and influencing the culture of the center.

Connecting to the Center's Culture
Culture is the values of an organization, the way things are viewed and acted upon. Understanding that an organizational culture exists, the director identifies and begins to reshape it into a new effort and a common vision....*in retrospect, I realize I really had to change a culture. You talk about corporate culture, I had to really change a culture, and changing culture is not easy....The culture was established by the past and its leadership so whatever occurred...was a mystery about resources.* A center's culture may be its strength or its weakness and the director must continually assess the center's strengths and weaknesses. People are consistently viewed by directors as a center's top strength.

Connecting to the Center's Creation
Many centers began as the dreams or causes of an individual or family. Others soon embraced the cause and the nature center was established.

Directors express a need to understand the history, the beginnings and the early culture of the center to assist them in understanding what and how change has occurred and its impact on the center's future. The directors soon discover the center is as much about people as it is about nature.

The remaining four major themes derived from the interviews are considered, to some degree, to be of lesser importance than the first four themes previously described. Less emphasis was placed by the directors on specific business or management skills than on themes such as passion for a purpose, people, vision and learning. The skills and attributes discussed by the directors regarding the following themes are important, but without passion, purpose and people, vision and continuous learning the directors would view themselves as less effective, if not unsuccessful, in attaining the vision of their respective centers.

Appendix A continued

Methods of Management and Business is a Bonus

Directors identify the need to have a sense of management and business. A sense of business means budgeting, scheduling and human interaction management, time management and marketing. Management practices include understanding different management styles and how to manage human resources. Personnel management is a source of concern. *...the most difficult is to handle personnel - personnel management....I would have been a little tougher, setting up certain expectations before we entered into a project to hold people a little more accountable.* The director accepts ultimate responsibility and accountability for decisions of the center....*it seems like you are called upon to use judgment constantly, making decisions and hopefully...my judgment, my ability is to make a good decision.*

Time management is a tool to assist the director in juggling numerous details while maintaining a view of the big picture.

Directors accept the need for planning, setting goals and reaching objectives. Planning processes differed among centers, but in all, planning was emphasized as a team function. *I think that is one of our greatest assets, that the staff have been a part of the planning and decision making process.*

The result of planning is enacted through staff, therefore effective staff management policies and procedures are viewed as necessary to maintain some sense of fairness and order in the organization. Management styles varied but were held in common by flattening the hierarchy, conducting performance appraisals, making decisions as a team and maintaining flexible job functions.

Volunteers were viewed as assets that are critical to a center, but without staff dedicated to volunteer management, they can become an unwieldy one.

Board management is a concern, challenge and reward for the nature center director. Communication among the board, staff and director is essential, but must be handled with great care. Understanding board/director roles is important for success....*the board is my boss, but at the same time, I have to be*

their leader...to direct them and I think you're most successful if you have that kind of good relationship.... Directors recognize there are internal board politics, and that significant organizational change is not possible without board leadership. A common tactic is for the director to take a lead role in working with the nominating committee to initiate a change in board membership.

Directors learn to use political survival tactics internal and external to the organization. *Use your skills of 'how does the other person think, foresee all the things they view as stumbling blocks'.* Directors recognize both that running a nature center is like running a small business and that one person cannot become proficient in all areas of business and finance. Specific legal, financial and computer management expertise can be the responsibilities of others, while the director is responsible for guiding the organization through writing a business and marketing plan, budgeting and planning. The director's role is to ensure that the business side of the center is in fact operated like a business using the best of structured tactics to keep the center in proper shape and spirit....*to me the center is an entrepreneurial experience, in the sense that we have to raise our own budget every year. I have to approach this as a business, a business with a vision and a philosophy.* The center's ability to stay afloat financially is utmost on the mind of the director. Constant search for new monies while attempting to hold onto existing funds is routine. Fund raising becomes a major job emphasis and a necessary skill. One of the bigger issues facing directors regarding fund raising efforts is its ethical or philosophical coexistence with the center's mission. The basic reason for fund raising is to provide the necessary financial support for a center to achieve its mission; however, the mission of a nature center is expressed through its programs, which should remain its top priority.

Program is Priority

The director provides the leadership to maintain the center's programs and services as first priority to its users.

Directors constantly seek ways to improve programs, grounding services in a knowledge of the audiences served and in the quality provided. *The quality of the program is the staying power for the organization.* In addition to a good working team and a positive working atmosphere, directors often identify the key to success through the quality of the programs and services

Appendix A continued

provided to the user. Growth, feedback, and behavioral change are also common criteria for measuring a center's success.

Pride in a Profession

Directors express a need to be recognized as professionals. While they take great pride in the profession, there is concern that recognition as professionals has yet to be achieved. *Our tremendous talents - our profession - haven't somehow amalgamated to make the optimum difference. We need the degree of professionalism and respect of the profession. That is an issue that the Association of Nature Center Administrators needs to address.* Networking was the approach commonly viewed as most effective in addressing professional development concerns. It is a tool that the directors wish they had had early in their careers.

Center directors are continually involved in a professionally complex role. The role of a center administrator can strain the balance between professional commitment and personal health. A common thread is the struggle against being over-extended and the concern over its impact on them as professionals and as people. *I try to approach a balance where I have a family life...and try to encourage my staff to have that also....I feel the profession is a long distance run, it's not a sprint, and you don't want to burn yourself out.* A strength of the director is the ability to balance the workload. A common weakness is the inability to say no, resulting in continual over-commitment. *You lose excellence when you are stretched too thin.* These professional and personal issues are real and would seem insurmountable if it were not for the extraordinary care and passion for the purpose that each center director believes and values.

The eight theoretical themes described in parts two and three of this series have been redeveloped into a conceptual model illustrating the interrelationships of the themes and sub-themes. The final article from the "Attributes of Leadership" study will present this model and discuss the implications of the study for future practices, professional development and research.

Part Four: TOWARD A MODEL

Reprinted from *Directions*, November/December 1994, Volume 4, #6.

The eight major themes and supporting categories discussed in the previous three articles in this series (see *Directions*, Vol. 4, Nos. 2, 3, & 4) have been reorganized into a conceptual model to illustrate the dynamic relationships of the research findings. The first phase of the model presents four conceptual groups (Fig. 1).

Personal Characteristics (PC) represent the inner core of the leader. The PC core represents the leader's highest values. The Administrative Functions (AF) are highly dynamic and may be altered, adapted and changed as new learning or new situations are experienced. The System View (SyV) represents the leader's broader vision, future direction and application of systems thinking. The SyV is forward thinking and incorporates the realization that neither the leaders nor organizational applications operate independently from one another. The Societal View (SoV) is the larger, global context within which the Personal Characteristics, Administrative Functions and Systems View are realized and practiced. The SoV is the "big picture," from which the leader derives mission, purpose and the desire to put the purpose into practice.

Each of the four conceptual groups of Attributes of Leadership are highly interactive. The most stable over time are Personal Characteristics, although constant new learning is taking place. For example, although a leader may change positions, the PC is likely to remain unchanged. The most fluid is the Administrative Function. The AF represents all the "things" a leader does, but new experiences affect how the leader implements administrative functions. The PC still serves as a foundation for the AF and guides one's practice.

SyV is dynamic, interacting with the idealist PC while tempered by the realities of AF. SoV represents a leader's personal mission and remains relatively stable over the course of a position or organizational changes.

Figure 2 presents the second phase of the model, illustrating its interconnectedness and dynamics of the conceptual groups.

Appendix A continued

Figure 1: Attributes of Leadership

Personal Characteristics (PC) Understanding the Self High Values Vocation as Avocation Attitude of Service/ Compassion Influenced from the Past Lifelong Learner Professional Development Pride in Profession	**Systems View (SyV)** Vision is Vital Enabling, Delegation, Coordination Team Broad View Thinking Politics
Administrative Functions (AF) Responsibilities Management Organization Planning Personnel Management Volunteerism Board Management Business Skills/ Marketing Financial Management Grant Writing/Fund Raising Responsibility/Accountability	**Societal View (SoV)** Passion for the People Passion for the Purpose

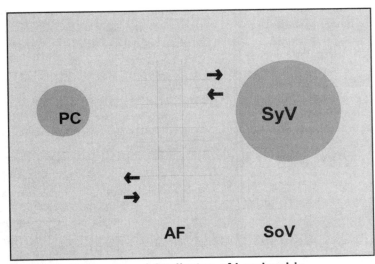

Figure 2: Dynamics of Attributes of Leadership

Appendix A continued

Implications for Practice

This study does not attempt to generalize its findings to the entire population of nature/environmental center directors. For example, it cannot conclude that all nature center directors must have a strong belief in a purpose or a past closely tied to outdoor experiences to be effective. The study does provide a commonality of findings that a group of directors collectively found to be important attributes of leadership within themselves.

The strength of the findings in this type of study is their transferability - insights one can gain into one's own situation. As a practitioner in the field of environmental centers, I discovered along the way of this research project a bit of irony. As the information became data, the data became themes and the themes became meanings, I openly expressed a sense of discouragement that I could never realize all of the leadership attributes I was discovering. I want to caution my colleagues not to expect to possess or excel in all of the attributes stated in the findings. Each of the findings represents a synthesis of twenty administrators, each with different backgrounds, levels of experience, training and situations. One person simply cannot excel in all of these areas of management, leadership or administration. Instead of generalizations, look for meanings and personal applications. The encouraging news to the practitioner is that each of the attributes can be incorporated at levels appropriate to each individual. Strengths can be enhanced, while limitations can be reduced. Kouzes and Posner's (1987) research focused on "personal best," a concept that is comparable to this study. Personal best represents the high standard of excellence at which personal practice can be aimed.

Reflections on Leadership: Reprise

Reprinted from *Directions*, January/February/March 1995, Volume 5, #1.

The four articles on the "Attributes of Leadership" in recent *Directions* represented a summary of a research project which began in 1989 and concluded in 1993. As the researcher and a practitioner in the field, the experience was the most rewarding of my career. The research included twenty site visits and in-depth interviews with nature/environmental

education center administrators from Vermont to Florida to California. The experience was a privilege to have met, to be involved, to explore, to view and participate in successes and challenges with each of the center administrators. Resulting from the experience was the challenge to connect meanings and patterns of relationships with hopeful insights into the professional lives of twenty extra-ordinary people. The year on the road to the centers was a privilege because I was able to think beyond the hurried life of everyday operations and into the visions and purpose of our profession. I thank each of the twenty participants for allowing me to peer in and through a slice of their life: David Hancocks, Kris Stevens, Robert Thomas, Tim Merriman, Mike Riska, Pat Welch, V. T. Dixon Gibbs, Tracy Kay, Charity Krueger, Joan Heidelberg, Jim Berry, Bill Rose, Mike Link, Jim Malkowski, Dick James, Larry Pickens, Sara Laughlin, Linda Liebes, Bob Nichols and Bob Mercer.

Discoveries

Through reflection on the research I am providing a distinction between major themes and minor themes. The major themes are Passion for the Purpose, Passion for the People, Vision is Vital and Living is Learning. These themes are global, broad view and involve the total being and perhaps as much of the heart as the head. The minor themes, such as Business is a Bonus and Methods of Management, are skill oriented themes. My concern is that we are so skill oriented in this society, spending billions on training, including leadership, that can be learned, but it cannot be practiced without belief and passion, the very attributes that make a successful leader. What really matters? Recently in *U.S.A. Today*, comments about Sears' new CEO included, *"He has the ability to form a vision and execute that vision. Sears didn't lack for retailers. It lacked vision."* The "learning" must come from the heart of the individual, the culture of the organization and the energy of a learning society.

In other words, all of the skill building is useless, or at least unused, until all of the entities are coalesced, beginning with the individual and one's desire. From the study most of the nature center administrators, when asked about professional development, indicated a desire to learn more skills such as computers, budgeting, personnel management and planning. Few indicated a desire to learn about leadership. This is disconcerting, although predictable. As a leadership researcher and author stated to me: "The positions you described are

Appendix A continued

much more complex than the managers we have studied." A typical nature center administrator has to do just about everything - or at least we think we do. All of the skills that one could ever imagine could be theoretically learned and practiced, but that would not necessarily guarantee a successful leader. The skills might make us better managers but not better leaders. Should we throw out skill building workshops? No! Engaging in new learning focused on our center can help us maintain or even enhance the efficiency of our current operations, or even help us prepare for our visions. It is the attributes of leadership, not skill enhancement, that propels our imagination beyond the daily toil into the challenges of attaining our vision. We should be looping our experiences into new learning while leadership, in its purest sense, empowers individuals and organizational capacity to successfully create and prosper through change.

Meanings

What does this all mean? Be encouraged that the patterns of attributes that emerged from this study are extraordinarily similar to other models in other fields. We can learn from each other. We can mentor new professionals. We can be honest with ourselves about our strengths and our limitations. We can constantly reflect on our motives and check those with our behavior. We need to share and remain open to each other and to those within our organizations. We need to recognize when it is time to "pass the baton." Our field has enormous challenges and, if you have basically agreed with the premise of this study, then leadership can affect many of those challenges.

The next stage of the research is to develop working case studies to assess the value and practice of leadership from the organizational perspective, not just from the administrators' perceptions. The case studies will involve leadership and team development, exercising real time analysis and strategy based on the previous research results, the assessed needs of the organization and effective adult learning theory. The developing model, tentatively titled LEADTEAM, will focus on organizational transformation rather than individually oriented content skill building. For example, a center may identify a need to learn more about program evaluation - a content skill - which can be learned in any number of venues. LEADTEAM will focus on the process to identify the content needs and development skills to effect change throughout the organization. Granted, this is an enormous stretch beyond the scope of the research. This is a concept that seems intuitive as I peer into the model of leadership and wonder how to put it into practice. I also hope there will be future graduate students to challenge the model, explore it further and create new ideas, for there is much to learn; but, alas, that in itself is the essence of leadership.

Communication

I encourage readers of *Directions* to rattle my bones with comments, offer tales of wonder or woe, or to critique successes and problems, so we can all learn together.

Director's Guide to Best Practices

Appendix B

Stephen R. Covey in *Principle-Centered Leadership* describes 30 ways to achieve a positive influence over others. These methods fall into three categories: 1) to model by example; 2) to build caring relationships; and 3) to mentor by instruction.

Thirty Methods of Influence

Example: Who You Are and How You Act
1. Refrain from saying the unkind or negative thing, particularly when you are provoked or fatigued.
2. Exercise patience with others.
3. Distinguish between the person and the behavior or performance.
4. Perform anonymous service.
5. Choose the proactive response.
6. Keep the promises you make to others.
7. Focus on the circle of influence.
8. Live the law of love.

Relationship: Do You Understand and Care?
9. Assume the best of others.
10. Seek first to understand.
11. Reward open, honest expressions or questions.
12. Give an understanding response.
13. If offended, take the initiative.
14. Admit your mistakes, apologize, and ask for forgiveness.
15. Let arguments fly out open windows.
16. Go one on one.
17. Renew your commitment to things you have in common.
18. Be influenced by them first.
19. Accept the person and the situation.

Instructions: What You Tell Me
20. Prepare your mind and heart before you prepare your speech.
21. Avoid fight or flight — talk through differences.
22. Recognize and take time to teach.
23. Agree on the limits, rules, expectations, and consequences.
24. Don't give up, and don't give in.
25. Be there at the crossroads.
26. Speak the languages of logic and emotion.
27. Delegate effectively.
28. Involve people in meaningful projects.
29. Train them in the law of the harvest.
30. Let natural consequences teach responsible behavior.

Overcoming Three Big Mistakes
1. **Mistake #1**: Advise before understand.
   Cure: Show empathy. Seek first to understand, then to be understood.
2. **Mistake #2**: Attempt to build/rebuild relationship without changing conduct or attitude.
   Cure: Show consistency and sincerity.
3. **Mistake #3**: Assume that good example and relationship are sufficient.
   Cure: Teach and talk about vision, mission, roles, goals, guidelines and standards.

Adapted from pages 119-129 of *Principle-Centered Leadership* by Stephen R. Covey. © 1990 Stephen R. Covey. Reprinted with permission from Franklin Covey Co.

Contacts

Center for Creative Leadership
P.O. Box 26300
Greensboro, NC 27438-6300
336-545-2810
336-282-3284 (fax)
info@leaders.ccl.org
www.ccl.org/leadership

Reviewers

Andy Brown, Battle Creek Nature Center, Prince Frederick, MD
Lynn Corliss, Center for Coastal Ecology, Beaufort, SC
Peggy Hunt, Pioneers Park Nature Center, Lincoln, NE
Tracy Kay*, Schuylkill Center for Environmental Education, Philadelphia, PA
Charity Krueger, Aullwood Audubon Center and Farm, Dayton, OH
Greg Lee*, Dodge Nature Center, West St. Paul, MN
Bob Marye*, Louisiana Nature Center, New Orleans, LA
Corky McReynolds, Treehaven Education and Conference Center, Tomahawk, WI
Robert Mercer, Silver Lake Nature Center, Bristol, PA
Carl Palmer*, Ogden Nature Center, Ogden, UT
Corky Potter, Shaver's Creek Environmental Center, University Park, PA
Lee Reading*, Joy Experiential Learning Center, Clarksville, OH
Marcy Rogge, Willowbrook Wildlife Center, Glen Ellyn, IL
Tim Sandsmark*, Greenway and Nature Center of Pueblo, Pueblo, CO
Christine Turnbull*, The Friends of Hunt Hill Audubon Sanctuary, Inc., Sarona, WI
Robert Venner, DeGraaf Nature Center, Holland, MI
Brian Winslow, Asbury Woods Nature Center, Erie, PA

* Former director

CHAPTER 2: STRATEGIC PLANNING

Creating a Desired Future

Strategic planning is a disciplined, consensus building process of creating a desired future for an organization and developing strategies to attain that future.

The process is *strategic* because it involves choosing how best to respond to rapidly changing circumstances in the organization's environment. Being strategic requires recognizing these choices and committing to one set of responses instead of another (CompassPoint, FAQ 2). **See Appendix A, *What is Strategic Planning?*, p. 63.**

Benefits of strategic planning include:

- Promotion of strategic thinking and action;
- Improved decision making;
- Enhanced organization responsiveness and improved performance;
- Direct benefits to the people of the organization (Bryson, p. 7).

Successful Strategic Planning

- Leads to action;
- Builds a shared vision that is values-based;
- Is an inclusive, participatory process in which board and staff take on shared ownership;
- Accepts accountability to the community;
- Is externally focused and sensitive to the organization's environment;
- Is based on quality data;
- Requires an openness to questioning the status quo;
- Is a key part of effective management.

Adapted from Strategic Planning, FAQ #2, *"What are the key concepts and definitions in strategic planning?"* Copyright © 1994-95. Support Center, San Francisco, CA. Used with permission. All rights reserved. This FAQ is no longer posted on the Internet. For current FAQs on strategic planning, visit CompassPoint Nonprofit Services (formerly Support Center) at www.compasspoint.org.

Types of Planning

The terms "strategic planning" and "long range planning" are frequently used interchangeably and are often misunderstood. These two types of planning are based on different assumptions.

Long range planning assumes that the future conditions are predictable. This type of planning is viewed as a periodic process that assumes current trends will continue. An organization using a long range planning process essentially would stay on course and develop a plan of action to accomplish goals over a period of several years (CompassPoint, FAQ #7).

In contrast, *strategic planning* assumes an organization must be responsive to an environment that is dynamic and hard to predict. Strategic planning is a continuous process that expects and responds to new trends, changes, and surprises. Strategic planning considers a range of possible futures and develops strategies based on current assessment of the organization's environment (CompassPoint, FAQ #7).

Master planning is a separate process essential for any land-based organization. A master plan shows the relationships between structures, land, people, and programs for a particular site. An ideal master plan is based on strategic and long range plans.

Strategic Planning in Your Organization

Strategic planning is an essential tool for any organization to use to develop a shared vision, strategies to achieve the vision, and a plan of action to guide the organization toward success. The process requires teamwork and improves communication, trust, respect and consensus among board members, staff, and other important members of your constituency.

Make strategic planning an on-going part of the organization's operations. This becomes easier once strategic thinking and action are incorporated into the institutional culture. Strategic planning will become the preferred manner of meeting the challenges and opportunities of running the organization.

Differences Between Strategic Planning and Operational Planning

Strategic Decisions	Operational Decisions
Future-oriented	Current-oriented
Fundamental, directional	Focus on implementation
Long term planning horizon	Short term planning horizon
Priorities to achieve over a several year period	Priorities to achieve in 1 year or less

From Strategic Planning, FAQ #6, *"What is the difference between strategic planning and operational planning?"* Copyright © 2000, CompassPoint, San Francisco, CA. All Rights Reserved. Used with permission.

Director's Role in Strategic Planning

Some directors may be expected to lead strategic planning without the benefit of experience. The process may seem challenging and overwhelming.

Your knowledge about strategic planning is essential but you don't have to know it all. When possible, bring in someone very familiar with the process to guide your steps. Learn about strategic planning from ANCA colleagues, others with experience, or from seminars and training programs. Trust your judgment and ability to work with your board, staff, and constituency. Listen to what they have to say about issues and priorities.

Use the following practices as a guide, not a formula. Enter the process at the place that best fits your organization. If your board is not convinced in the value of strategic planning or you and the staff lack experience in planning, start from the very beginning and work your way through.

Others may not need all the practices. Each organization and its board, staff, constituency, and director is different.

See Appendix B, *Strategic Planning Glossary*, p. 64.

Real Leaders

Strategic Planning Experiences

An interview with Bill Rose, Executive Director
Kalamazoo Nature Center, Kalamazoo, MI
by Corky McReynolds, Ph.D.
Director, Treehaven Education and Conference Center, Tomahawk, WI

Editor's Note: This interview is from a series conducted with executive directors about their experiences for Director's Guide to Best Practices.

CM: Almost seven years ago, the Kalamazoo Nature Center underwent an extensive strategic planning process. What were the outcomes?

BR: There were two levels of outcomes. First, as a new director, it was an opportunity to get together with staff and board - this was our first time to look at change and the first time the center had a vision. Second, the plan became the foundation that served toward creating a master plan and building renovation. Also, I learned early on in the process not every staff or board member could identify our mission.

CM: How is the strategic plan being used?

BR: It has given us something to relate to, allowing us to focus on things we had to do right away that was not dollar-driven. Increasing the nature center's outreach was one of those "act right away" items.

CM: How have you maintained momentum toward implementation?

BR: It is a leadership factor - to begin a new vision, to create a new culture. We need to continually articulate our vision, not as my plan, but as our plan. My role is knowing what our next step is, knowing that there are many paths, but a path is needed. Now we have come full circle. We have fulfilled much of it and it is time to do it again, to again ask what are our new opportunities.

CM: What advice do you have for a new director?

BR: Do it, make sure you do it, absolutely do it! The sooner the better - you can't keep on drifting. Be aware the process could be harmful unless it is done properly. Use an outside facilitator, give encouragement, because the implementation takes longer than you might expect.

Checklist of Recommended Practices

I. Prepare for Planning

- ❏ Practice 1   Assess if Organization is Ready
- ❏ Practice 2   Obtain Leadership Support
- ❏ Practice 3   Create a Strategic Planning Team
- ❏ Practice 4   Determine Who to Involve
- ❏ Practice 5   Design a Strategic Planning Process
- ❏ Practice 6   Identify the Driving or Key Question
- ❏ Practice 7   Identify Information Needs

II. Create the Plan

- ❏ Practice 8   Review, Revise, or Create an Organizational Mission Statement
- ❏ Practice 9   Develop a Statement of Values
- ❏ Practice 10   Establish an Organizational Vision of the Future
- ❏ Practice 11   Analyze the Organization
- ❏ Practice 12   Identify Strategic Issues
- ❏ Practice 13   Develop, Evaluate and Modify Strategies for Each Issue
- ❏ Practice 14   Develop a Strategic Plan

III. Continue the Process

- ❏ Practice 15   Develop an Action Plan
- ❏ Practice 16   Implement the Plan
- ❏ Practice 17   Review, Revise or Update the Plan

Recommended Practices

Strategic planning involves multiple steps. Since organizations engage in strategic planning for different reasons and at various times in their organizational history, some steps may apply and others may not.

The director actively leads development of the planning process needed to prepare, create, and implement a strategic plan. The overview that follows provides a framework for the process. You may use these practices to begin strategic planning, to reaffirm earlier planning outcomes, or to guide you through the next phase.

There are also many excellent resources available on strategic planning including ANCA members, consultants, books, training opportunities, and internet sites. **See References, p. 62 and Contacts, p. 73.**

Practices 1- 7 emphasize steps needed to prepare for strategic planning. Practices 8-14 describe steps to create the plan. Practices 15-17 deal with implementation and follow-up.

I.   Prepare for Planning

Practice 1   **Assess if Organization is Ready**

The first step in strategic planning is knowing when -- or if -- to plan. There are many reasons to engage in strategic planning but timing and organizational readiness are very important. Consider the seven critical factors from John M. Bryson and Farnum K. Alston before proceeding.

- Does the process have strong sponsors?
- Does the process have strong champions?
- Are resources available?
- Is the process within the organization mandate?
- Do the benefits outweigh the costs?
- Will the process have real value for the organization?
- Will the process be linked to operational plans and budgets? (Bryson and Alston, p. 26).

Depending on the answers, an organization may decide to proceed, try to change each "no" answer to a "yes," or delay strategic planning until another time.

When assessing readiness, consider resources needed for planning. This will include staff time, board time, and funds (for market research, consultants, etc.). Time will be spent collecting and analyzing environmental information, engaging key stakeholders, gathering historical information, projecting future budgets and cash flow projections, and analyzing options and consequences for organizational and program strategies.

Strategic planning is best delayed if an organization is in crisis (for example, the organization lacks leadership, or a funding shortage threatens cuts to programs or facilities). Concentrate on the short term needs of the organization to resolve the crisis (Laycock, p. 165-167). Lack of skills or resources for strategic planning or lack of commitment by key decision makers for the process are also good reasons to hold off from planning (Bryson, p. 6). Resolve the issues first and then proceed.

See Appendix C, *Are You Ready for Strategic Planning?*, p. 65.

See References, p. 62, for *Creating and Implementing Your Strategic Plan* by Bryson and Alston, and Barry's *Strategic Planning Workbook for Nonprofit Organizations*.

Practice 2

Obtain Leadership Support

The executive director is one of many important people to lead the early stages of strategic planning. Other principal leaders are likely to be board members, donors, constituents, volunteers, or staff with planning experience. Bryson uses the terms "sponsors," "champions," and "facilitators" to describe key leadership roles.

A sponsor:

- Communicates the purpose and importance of strategic planning;
- Commits time, money, energy, and legitimacy needed to make planning possible;
- Fosters action and resulting change;

- Promotes and encourages creative thinking from all sources;
- Welcomes discussion and debate;
- Recognizes the value of outside consultants and is willing to pay for their services, if needed;
- Demonstrates willingness to support the effort;
- Helps keep planning on track (Bryson, p. 214 - 215).

A champion:

- Manages the day to day process of planning;
- Keeps planning on people's agendas;
- Advocates the process;
- Keeps track of progress;
- Pays attention to details (time frame, meeting space, materials) and who is needed to participate for the process to succeed (Bryson, p. 216);
- Makes sure all participants know and understand planning terms and language;
- Models behavior desired in other participants -- "reasoned, diligent, committed, enthusiastic, good spirited pursuit of the common good" (Bryson, p. 215);
- Encourages the planning team through rough spots.

A skilled facilitator:

- Guides the planning process from beginning to end;
- Acts as task master for the group;
- Has well developed group process skills;
- Has excellent interpersonal skills;
- Builds trust among team members;
- Has conflict management skills;
- Has a sense of humor;
- Is knowledgeable and enthusiastic about the strategic planning process;
- Helps groups confront difficulties in the process, manage the tension, and move forward;
- Induces a group to take action;
- Provides emotional support and encouragement throughout the process.

Bring in an outside facilitator to run the strategic planning session. This will allow all planning team members, including yourself, to be fully involved in the discussions, debates and deliberations. **See Appendix D,** *The Role of an External Consultant,* **p. 66.**

Leaders not only provide support for the planning process but bring vital information and critical resources as well. Leaders can assist with other important issues such as providing a space to hold the meetings or make recommendations about who to involve in the planning process (Bryson, p. 47).

Practice 3

Create a Strategic Planning Team

The director will want to be closely involved in creating the strategic planning team. The team is essential because from it, collective leadership for the planning process will emerge.

The planning team oversees the entire strategic planning process. This group will provide ongoing direction and support for strategic planning. The team's challenge is to build a coalition from its membership with shared power, responsibility, and authority to create the strategic plan (Bryson, p. 221).

Select a team leader or rotate leadership. The team leader directs, mentors, and builds relationships among group members.

The team benefits when team leaders:

- Communicate effectively;
- Balance team unity with diversity;
- Define team roles, goals, and norms;
- Establish an atmosphere of trust;
- Foster group creativity and sound decision making;
- Obtain necessary resources;
- Tailor direction and support to team members to fit their competence and commitment;
- Reward achievement and overcome diversity (Bryson, p. 220).

The planning team should:

- Have no more than five to seven individuals;
- Have a combination of "visionaries" (those who envision what the organization can be) and "actionaries" (those who ensure the resources will support the goals and that the tasks are realistic);
- Include members who have formal or informal power and the respect of the organization;
- Include a combination of board, staff, executive director and whoever will write the plan (Support Center, FAQ #5).

The planning team will need to meet early in the process. Retreats are an effective way to conduct planning sessions. **See Appendix E, *How Do I Use Retreats in the Planning Process?*, p. 67.**

Practice 4

Determine Who to Involve

The director, key board members, staff, and a facilitator may all be involved in deciding who serves on the strategic planning team.

This is a critical part of preparing for strategic planning. Key stakeholders may be any number of individuals who are in some way either affected by or can affect the strategic plan. Therefore, a planning team may comprise internal stakeholders, external stakeholders, or both, depending on the key question to be addressed in the strategic planning process.

Internal stakeholders may include governing board members, staff, or volunteers. External stakeholders may be donors, clients, business leaders, community members, or representatives of other agencies and organizations. **See the following page and Appendix F, *Who Should the Planning Process Include?*, p. 69.**

Make Planning an Inclusive Process

A planning process should be designed to include board, staff, and other individuals invested in the success of your organization. An inclusive process

- Helps to build both internal and external enthusiasm and commitment to the organization and its strategies. Individuals take on ownership of the goals and efforts to achieve the stated outcomes.
- Ensures that your information data base reflects the needs and perceptions of internal individuals and external constituents.
- Incorporates a level of objectivity into the process. "Outsiders" can identify jargon or ask critical questions around which "insiders" might make assumptions.
- Develops foundations for future working relationships.
- Develops uniformity of purpose among all stakeholders.
- Establishes a continual information exchange among staff, management, customers, and other key stakeholders.

From Strategic Planning, FAQ #5, *"What are the individual roles in the planning process?"* Copyright © 1994-95, Support Center, San Francisco, CA. All rights reserved. Used with permission. This FAQ is no longer posted on the Internet. For current FAQs on strategic planning, visit CompassPoint Nonprofit Services (formerly Support Center) at www.compasspoint.org.

Practice 5   Design a Strategic Planning Process

A written document summarizing the decision to conduct strategic planning is called a "plan to plan" (Bryson, p. 47-48, from George A. Steiner, *Strategic Planning: What Every Manager Must Know*, 1979). This plan explains the purpose and value of the process, who to involve, anticipated time commitment, steps that will be followed, schedule of meetings, and format and timing of reports.

The "plan to plan" also addresses board and staff education, if needed, staff work load adjustments (Ibid), and the costs and time required to conduct the planning. Be sure to include a description of the group process to be used for brainstorming, discussion, and consensus building.

The director often prepares the "plan to plan." A consultant may also prepare it with input from the director and other planning team members. The consultant will recommend a preferred group process. Be sure you are familiar with the approach and confident of the results to be gained from it.

See Appendix G, *Questions to Prepare for Strategic Planning*, p. 70.

Practice 6 — Identify the Driving or Key Question

The planning team must identify the purpose of the strategic planning session before proceeding with other important elements of the process. A crucial step is to develop a driving or key question (McReynolds, *Adapted Nominal Group Technique*).

The driving question focuses the planning team on one key issue at a time. The question should be broad enough to generate many responses but not be ambiguous (Bryson, p. 266). Make sure to state the key question in the simplest terms and address single issues. For example, restate the question "What are our strengths and weaknesses?" as two separate questions, one focusing on strengths and the other on weaknesses (McReynolds, *Adapted Nominal Group Technique.*).

Use a group process to identify the key question. **See General Appendix, Appendix F, *Adapted Nominal Group Technique,* p. 313.**

Practice 7 — Identify Information Needs

Planning team members also must gather background information to aid discussion during the assessment phase. Select information based on the key question to be addressed during strategic planning session. Assemble what you will need to make well-informed decisions but not so much information that the planning team is overwhelmed (Barry, p. 37).

Consider information gathering techniques such as focus group discussions, interviews with stakeholders, demographic studies, or market studies. Also include information on funding sources and budgets. **See *Conducting Market Research* on the following page.**

Compile all organizational mandates (articles of incorporation, by-laws, laws and ordinances that affect property or programs, or binding agreements). Clarify what is required and allowed.

Conducting Market Research

There are 15 nature centers in the Philadelphia area. LaSalle University, one of the higher education institutions in the region, sought a grant from a major foundation to conduct market research for 11 of the 15 centers. (The other centers opted out.) The university utilized their students who were learning about markets, business, and nonprofit management to do the work, conduct the interviews, and consolidate the data.

Staff from the LaSalle Nonprofit Management Development Center (NMDC) presented workshops on how to conduct market research at the beginning of the project. After the data was collected, the NMDC staff, with input from staff and board, put together market plans for each facility.

This win-win situation provided an educational experience for students, strategic data on some very broad questions for the participating nature centers, and a wonderful partnership project for the funder.

Robert Mercer, Silver Lake Nature Center, Bristol, PA

II.   Create the Plan

Practice 8   Review, Revise, or Create a Mission Statement

An important step in the planning process is to review or create a mission statement. If one exists, review it to make sure it reflects the purpose, primary service and primary audience the organization serves. If the mission statement accurately reflects the organization's purpose, the strategic planning team would simply reaffirm the mission and move on to creating a vision statement (McReynolds, 1996).

If the mission statement no longer adequately reflects the purpose of the organization, revise the mission. Use a group process to establish the primary components of the statement but select one person to draft the statement. The team reviews, modifies and approves it when they reach consensus (McReynolds, Ibid.).

If you do not have a mission statement, create one. The mission should clarify the organization's purpose (Bryson, p. 67). It should be clearly stated, to the point and easy to remember. The mission statement is essential to the strategic planning process and to the long term success of any organization.

Developing A Mission Statement

Examine your answers to these questions and use to draft a mission statement.

1.   Who are we? What is our purpose? What business are we in?
2.   In general, what are the basic social and political needs we exist to fill? Or: What are the basic social or political problems we exist to address?
3.   In general, what do we want to do to recognize or anticipate and respond to these needs or problems?
4.   How should we respond to our key stakeholders?
5.   What is our philosophy and what are our core values?
6.   What makes us distinct or unique?
7.   What is our organization's current mission?
8.   Is our current mission dated, and if so, how?
9.   What changes in the mission would I propose?

From Bryson and Alston, *Creating and Implementing Your Strategic Plan*, p. 51-54. Used with permission.

Dodge Nature Center, West St. Paul, MN
Revised mission statement adopted January 1996.

New Version: The mission of the Dodge Nature Center is to provide a place where the members of our community can experience, study, and enjoy nature, and in so doing be inspired to become responsible stewards of our environment.

Old Version: The mission of the Dodge Nature Center is to make people aware of the natural environment and their interrelationship with it through the development and maintenance of a nature preserve and the development and promotion of related quality educational programs. Through such example and education, the Dodge Nature Center strives to instill the values, skill, and knowledge which will not only inspire those with whom it has contact to love and respect nature and wildlife, but also enable them to become responsible and caring stewards of our natural resources.

Practice 9

Develop a Values Statement

A statement of the organization's core values describes "the principles by which the program wishes to be guided" (Bryson, p. 160). Values such as respect, trust, and teamwork are often emphasized in these statements in addition to a code of behavior for the organization. Values statements can often be instrumental in identifying issues to be addressed in the planning process. **See Aullwood Audubon Center and Farm, p. 51.**

Practice 10   **Establish an Organizational Vision of the Future**

A vision represents what an organization would like to become or achieve in the future and usually represents the desired state over the next five to 10 years.

A vision statement may also include the desired culture of an organization, including its values, beliefs and philosophies to guide how the organization functions (McReynolds, 1996).

Develop the vision through an effective group process by reaching consensus on what the desired future state would be. The vision should be brief, inspiring, clarify the organization's purpose and direction, be future oriented, reflect high ideals and ambitions, reflect the unique qualities of the organization, and capture the desirable features of its history, culture and values (Bryson, p. 157).

As you did when creating a mission statement, ask one person to draft the vision statement. Distribute it for review and approval before the planning team adopts the final version. Then make it available to all staff, organization members and other stakeholders.

The benefits to stakeholders from developing a vision of success include the following:

- Creating clear expectations;
- Having a unified vision that includes all stakeholders;
- Enhancing motivation and a desire to achieve the vision;
- Empowering employees and members to lead and manage themselves, creating leadership at all levels of the organization (Adapted from Bryson, p. 157-159).

See Appendix H, *Perceptions of Ideal Futures: An Exercise in Forming Vision,* **p. 71.**

Real Leaders

Vision

An interview with Mike Riska, Executive Director
Delaware Nature Society, Hockessin, DE
by Corky McReynolds, Ph.D.
Director, Treehaven Education and Conference Center, Tomahawk, WI

Editor's Note: This interview is from a series conducted with executive directors about their experiences for Director's Guide to Best Practices.

CM: What is vision?

MR: I believe it is a clear idea where you want to go and focusing on that vision to get there.

CM: Literature describes "vision" as an important aspect of leadership, and its importance to an organization, but how is it developed at Delaware Nature Society?

MR: Vision is developed through our planning process. It starts with a full staff, full board and committees. A lot of good minds working together.

CM: What is your role in the visioning process?

MR: As I get more experience I get more confident to get the best ideas from everyone and to make the decision from those ideas. I have a sense of our vision but my role is to get everyone's best ideas.

CM: What is the vision of Delaware Nature Society?

MR: In our five year plan, we are looking beyond our nature center. We are looking at our two other preserves and new property as a full farm. Although our endowment has grown to provide one and a half positions, it needs to continue to grow. We are sticking to our main objective of providing environmental education and land management.

CM: What advice do you have for new nature center directors?

MR: I've always wanted to be in the leadership role and I think the director should know what should happen and how to make it happen - not to put it off. I can't keep saying the staff and board should be doing that - I need to be the leader. A nature center needs a strategic plan and involving people is essential.

Aullwood Audubon Center and Farm, Dayton, OH
Vision, Mission, Beliefs and Values Statements

Aullwood Audubon Center and Farm
Aullwood provides appreciation, understanding and stewardship for the Earth.

Vision (1/99)

We would like to see Aullwood in the next 5-10 years ...

- Provide leading edge educational opportunities for life-long learning.
- Develop a land management plan with a comprehensive inventory which eliminates invasive non-natives and increases native diversity.
- Maintain and enhance our fiscal integrity.
- Demonstrate model sustainable organize agriculture practices.

Mission (1/95)

Aullwood Audubon Center and Farm, an Audubon Center of the National Audubon Society for environmental education and organic agriculture, provides activities that increase understanding and preservation of the planet by children and adults through education, research and recreation.

Beliefs and Values (1/97)

Aullwood Audubon Center and Farm conducts business according to our beliefs in:
Education, Stewardship, Scientific Study, People

We value and believe in ...

- The inquiring minds of children and their innate desire to learn.
- Natural history learning through hands-on and field experiences.
- The idea that everyone is a teacher and everyone is a learner.
- Enhancing lives by developing a sense of wonder and providing close contact with nature.
- Empowering experiences which foster appreciation, understanding and stewardship of the Earth.
- Environmental education promoting lifelong behaviors which protect the natural environment.
- Teaching stewardship by example.
- Respecting and protecting the Earth's diversity.
- The intrinsic value of green space, agricultural land, and wilderness.
- Sound scientific principles underlying quality environmental education.
- The importance of understanding ecological concepts and processes.
- Advancing our mission by maintaining a welcoming and friendly atmosphere.
- Strengthening team work through respect, honesty and open communication.

Practice 11   ## Analyze the Organization

The process of gathering and analyzing information to evaluate the organization in its environment is an important part of the strategic planning process. This process involves assessing the situation within and outside the organization.

Provide team members with worksheets prior to the session, asking them to analyze the organization using the SWOT technique (Strengths, Weaknesses, Opportunities and Threats). Refer to workbooks by Bryson and Alston or Barry for sample worksheets, or create your own. **See References, p. 62.** Send the questions and forms to team members at least one week prior to the session.

When conducting the assessment:

❑   First examine opportunities and threats outside the organization before examining internal strengths and weaknesses (Bryson and Alston, p. 58);

❑   Look at external opportunities and threats in forces and trends (political, economic, social, technological), key resource controllers (clients, donors, members), and competitors and collaborators (Bryson, Figure 2.1, p.24);

❑   Look at internal strengths and weaknesses in resources (people, economic, information, competencies, culture), present strategies (overall, business process) and performance (indicators, results, history) (Bryson, Figure 2.1, p. 24; Bryson and Alston, p. 59-60).

SWOT may be done individually outside of the group session with results and reports submitted to the group. Some sources recommend using SWOT in group settings. Discussion and final analysis is always best in the group (McReynolds, 1996). SWOT can halt strategic planning progress if groups get stuck in "analysis paralysis" (Ibid.). Be sure to use an effective group process to avoid this trap.

The greatest benefit of assessing the organization and its environment is the discussions and insights gained from within the group (Bryson, p. 85) and using the information to identify strategic issues.

Practice 12   **Identify Strategic Issues**

What is discovered during the SWOT analysis is central to the process of identifying, discussing and prioritizing strategic issues. A strategic issue is "a fundamental policy question or challenge affecting an organization's mandates, mission, and values; product or service level and mix; clients, users, or payers; or costs, financing, structure, or management" (Bryson, p. 104).

Issues are items that inhibit the organization from moving toward its vision, or are established to develop a vision (McReynolds, 1996). Identify strategic issues by narrowing down the issues to be addressed.

An exciting and sometimes difficult part of strategic planning is identifying the issues. Conflicts may arise over issues and how they will be resolved. An effective group facilitation process is essential to develop, discuss and determine the priorities.

Strategic issues fall into three categories:

1.   Current issues that require immediate action;
2.   Issues on the horizon that are likely to require action in the near future;
3.   Issues for which it is unclear whether any action will be required now or in the future, but that need to be monitored (Bryson and Alston, p. 63).

To begin the process of identifying strategic issues:

❏   Review the mandates, mission, and results of SWOT analysis.
❏   Identify issues by asking team members to respond individually to the following questions:
  1.   What is the issue? Phrase each issue as a question the organization can do something about and that has more than one answer.
  2.   What makes it a strategic issue (mandates, mission, external opportunities and threats, internal strengths and weaknesses)?
  3.   What are the consequences of not addressing this issue?
  4.   What are our goals to address this issue?

❐   Create a master list of major issues identified.

❐   Using a group process, team members select those issues from the master list that are the highest priorities the organization faces.

❐   Brainstorm goals for each issue keeping in mind that strategic issues involve conflict over what the "right" approaches will be.

❐   Produce a list of strategic issues (Bryson, p. 114, p. 121-122; Bryson and Alston, p. 65-67).

Practice 13

Develop, Evaluate and Modify Strategies for Each Issue

A key component of the planning process is to develop strategies for each issue identified. Here again, use a small group facilitation process (McReynolds, 1996).

The planning team responds to questions in writing and develops creative strategies to achieve goals for each issue. Each question does not need to be addressed by every team member but each question should be addressed by the planning team as a whole (Bryson and Alston, p. 79-80).

A.   Sample Strategy Questions

1.   What are the practical alternatives, dreams, or visions we might pursue to address this issue and achieve our goal?

2.   What are the barriers to realizing these alternatives, dreams, or visions?

3.   What major initiatives might we pursue to achieve these alternatives, dreams, or visions directly, or else indirectly through overcoming the barriers?

4.   What are the key actions (with existing resources of people and dollars) that must be taken this year to implement the major initiatives?

5.   What specific steps must be taken within the next six months to implement the major initiatives, and who is responsible for taking them? (Bryson and Alston, p. 79-80).

Write a summary statement for each strategy that includes the purpose of the strategy, key elements of it, how the issue is addressed, how goals will be achieved, what is required to implement the strategy, and how existing programs will be meshed with new goals and strategies (Bryson and Alston, p. 81).

Additional information on strategy development is shown below. The MacMillan Matrix is another alternative technique for formulating organizational strategies. **See Appendix I, *The MacMillan Matrix*, p 72.**

How to Develop Strategies

Strategy formulation is a combination of rational, scientific examinations and educated intuitive best guesses. Many individuals are overwhelmed by the idea of developing strategies, but it can be a fun and invigorating process. The process entails

- Examining the organization's critical issues;
- Determining how the organization's strengths and skills can be employed to address the critical issues;
- Analyzing opportunities and strengths and looking for ways to synthesize the two;
- Exploring and choosing the best approaches for the organization.

During this evaluation, ask these key questions: Does the strategy meet/address critical issues? Is this aligned with our mission? Is this approach financially viable?

One effective method of strategy generation is to list critical issues and organizational strengths onto flip charts and then have staff or board members brainstorm possible uses of those strengths or other skills to address the critical issues. Once the brainstorm session is completed, use a round table discussion to investigate and evaluate the possible strategies. Remember to develop a list of alternative strategies to investigate and keep in the contingency planning file.

Adapted from Strategic Planning, FAQ #10, *"What is a strategy and how do we develop one?"* Copyright © 1994-95 Support Center, San Francisco, CA. All rights reserved. Used with permission.

This FAQ is no longer posted on the Internet. See *"What does a strategy look like?"* and other current FAQs on strategic planning at CompassPoint Nonprofit Services (formerly Support Center) at www.compasspoint.org.

B.   Evaluate Strategies

After identifying each issue and the goals to be addressed, evaluate the strategies against the following performance measurement guidelines. Use this information to modify the strategies.

Performance Measures

- Acceptability to decision makers, stakeholders, opinion leaders;
- Acceptability to general public;
- Consistency with mission, values, philosophy, and culture;
- Coordination/integration with other strategies, programs, and activities;
- Client or user impact;
- Relevance to the issue;
- Technical feasibility;
- Staff requirements;
- Cost and financing;
- Flexibility or adaptability;
- Cost-effectiveness;
- Timing;
- Long term impact;
- Facility requirements;
- Risk assessment;
- Other appropriate criteria (Adapted from Bryson and Alston, p. 82).

Practice 14

Develop a Strategic Plan

The next step is to draft the written plan. Select one or two people to write the results of the group's ideas. Often the executive director or someone from the staff, board or a consultant will draft the plan. What is important is that the plan be written and that it reflects the shared vision and ideas of the group.

Decide who will review and comment on the plan, the period of time allowed for review, and the extent of comments to be accepted by reviewers. Make sure key members of the planning committee decide this in advance so reviewers know what is expected of them. Reviewers would include the planning team and possibly full staff and board. Allow two weeks for comment and review.

A strategic plan:

- Varies in length; use 10 pages as a guide;
- Summarizes why the organization exists, what it is trying to accomplish, and how it will go about doing it;
- Is addressed to anyone who wants to know the organization's most important ideas, issues and priorities (board members, staff, volunteers, clients, funders, peers at other organizations, the press, and the public);
- Is concise and orderly (Support Center, FAQ #11);
- Be sure to include:
  1. Budget information for all strategies;
  2. Monitoring and evaluation plans;
  3. Plans for updating the plan (Bryson and Alston, p. 83).
- Submit final document to the full board for approval and adoption. Once adopted, distribute it to key stakeholders, the media, and the public.

Sample Strategic Plan Outline

I.   Introduction by the President of the Board
Cover letter introduces the plan and endorses it; may be combined with Executive Summary

I.   Executive Summary
Summary of the plan (1-2 pages); highlight goals, note process for developing the plan; thank team.

II.   Mission and Vision Statements

III. Organization Profile and History
Brief history (key events, triumphs, changes over time) in 1-2 pages.

IV.   Critical Issues and Strategies
Sometimes omitted in plans, this is useful to share with readers so they understand the process used by the team. Brief outline form or a narrative that covers several pages.

V.   Program Goals and Objectives
Goals and objectives are the plan of action — what the organization intends to do. Serves as a useful guide for operational planning and as a reference for evaluation.

VI.   Management Goals and Objectives (Note: This is not detailed in the recommended practices.)
Management functions are separated from program functions to emphasize the distinction between service goals and organizational development goals.

VII. Appendices

Adapted from Strategic Planning, FAQ # 11, *"What should a strategic plan include?"* Copyright © 1994-95, Support Center, San Francisco, CA. All rights reserved. Used with permission.

This FAQ is no longer posted on the Internet. For current FAQs on strategic planning, visit CompassPoint Nonprofit Services (formerly Support Center) at www.compasspoint.org.

III. Continue the Process

Practice 15   ### Develop an Action Plan

Develop an action plan based on the issues and strategies identified in the strategic plan. An action plan guides those responsible for implementing the strategic plan, provides a format for periodic progress reports, and is based on the strategies contained in the strategic plan (Support Center, FAQ #12).

Action plans include:

- Roles and responsibilities of staff and other team members;
- Objectives with expected results and milestones;
- Specific action steps with relevant details;
- Schedules for progress and completion;
- Resources needs and sources;
- A communication process;
- A review and monitoring process;
- Accountability processes and procedures (Bryson, p. 176).

Use the action plan when developing your annual operating plans. Individual and program goals based on the action plan will bring unity and consistency to your organization.

Practice 16   ### Implement the Plan

The best plan is only as good as the process used to implement it. Make sure the plan is always foremost in the thoughts and actions of everyone involved with the organization.

To do this:

- ❑ Choose a format for the plan that is easy to use, clear and to the point;
- ❑ Lead the staff and board to follow the plan;
- ❑ Make necessary changes to adopt and incorporate the plan into the organization's programs and operations;
- ❑ Tie the strategic plan's contents to any proposed program expansion or changes;

❏   Establish operational goals and objectives that tie in with the plan (all individual and program evaluations refer to the plan). Use it as a management tool for short-term guidance and decision making;

❏   Regularly schedule opportunities (discussions, meetings, reports) to share progress updates on the plan with the board, staff, and your constituency (Support Center, Adapted from FAQ #13).

Practice 17	## Review, Revise or Update the Plan

The final step in strategic planning leads back to the beginning of the process. Once the plan has been implemented for some time, it is important to look at the process used and the plan itself to evaluate the effectiveness of both. When to do this depends on the organization and the issues addressed.

One option is to look at your strategic direction periodically throughout the year, annually to check on progress, and conduct an overall review every two to three years.

During review, look at successful strategies and those that were not successful. Determine if new strategies are needed or if the current ones should be maintained.

Also look at strengths and weaknesses of your planning process. Look for ways to improve the process and the results during the next round of planning. Seek input on both the process and the effectiveness of the plan from board members, staff, constituency members, and planning team members.

See *Keys to Strategic Planning Success* on the following page for a review of the planning process.

Keys to Strategic Planning Success

Commitment to Quality
- Plan within an understood process using effective tools for participation and decision-making.
- Use outside consultants that are fully capable of educating, as well as facilitating the process.

Commitment to Continuity
- Build and maintain the strategic process as part of the institutional culture.
- Strategic processes are continuous loops of learning, with periodic products.
- Separate board/staff regular business meetings from strategic action meetings and implementation.
- Dedicate at least one meeting per year to reflect and renew the strategic plan.

Commitment to Priority
- Strategic plans create direction and should create focus for action. Keep aligning resources toward the strategic priorities stated within the plan.

Commitment to Time
- Board and staff must realize and accept the extra effort strategies and action will require, while being able to eventually merge regular work plans with strategic initiatives.

Corky McReynolds, Ph. D.
Director, Treehaven Education and Conference Center, Tomahawk, WI

Too Much Planning

Early in my nature center career, almost a quarter century ago, I took seriously expert advice to devote lots of time and energy crafting a long range plan. However, my detailed plans, both professional and personal, were usually torn asunder by unforeseen opportunities.

A few years back, my board had just approved a detailed long range plan when an adjoining farm unexpectedly came up for sale. We tossed the plan aside and successfully raised a pile of money and bought and restored the land. The land purchase put us in a better program, facility, and financial position than if we had adhered closely to our plan. If an organization rigidly follows a detailed plan it risks letting unanticipated wonderful opportunities slip away. Remember what happened to the Soviet Union and its planned economy.

I believe **detailed** long range planning to be a poor use of time. The planning we now do sets a philosophical direction we intend to pursue and general goals. The plan is short, simple and allows much flexibility to seek and seize opportunities.

Rich Patterson, Indian Creek Nature Center, Cedar Rapids, IA

Real Leaders

Strategic Planning Experiences

An interview with Kathleen Brady, Executive Director
Birdsong Nature Center, Thomasville, GA
by Corky McReynolds, Ph.D.
Director, Treehaven Education and Conference Center, Tomahawk, WI

Editor's Note: This interview is from a series conducted with executive directors about their experiences for Director's Guide to Best Practices.

CM: Birdsong Nature Center recently completed a strategic planning process. What were your outcomes?

KB: We achieved consensus among our leadership, a sense of teamwork and an ability to focus our attention toward what we agreed should be our priorities. We also realize it is not over. As we complete tasks, doors open to others, so now we have a need to take the next step, and write out a new set of tasks. The outcome has helped me because it set clear priorities.

CM: Often strategic plans create an incredible wish list of things to accomplish. How has your strategic planning kept things manageable?

KB: The action plans that were developed at the end of our workshop resulted in concise, specific tasks to accomplish by a certain date; therefore, although lots of ideas were generated we developed priorities.

CM: How did your process create ownership toward the outcomes?

KB: The techniques and process that we were led through allowed everyone to say what they needed to say, but then got us to a point to make decisions and priorities. I credit the process.

CM: What advice do you have for a new director?

KB: Get your leadership together and develop a strategic plan as soon as you can. Convince the board of the value to the organization. I wish we could have done this way back in our nature center history. It helps you focus your energy. If funding is an issue, start saving and building it into your budget, then get the best professional outside help. Don't try to do it inside. To me it has been the most valuable thing we have ever done.

References

Barry, Bryan W. *Strategic Planning Workbook for Nonprofit Organizations.* Fieldstone Alliance, Inc., 1997, 2005 . www.fieldstonealliance.com

Bryson, John M. *Strategic Planning for Public and Nonprofit Organizations.* New York, NY: Jossey-Bass Inc., a subsidiary of John Wiley & Sons, Inc., 1995.

Bryson, John M. and Alston, Farnum K. *Creating and Implementing Your Strategic Plan.* New York, NY: Jossey-Bass Inc., a subsidiary of John Wiley & Sons, Inc, 1996.

CompassPoint. References from web site at www.compasspoint.org. Strategic Planning FAQs. Copyright © 2000. All rights reserved. San Francisco: CompassPoint Nonprofit Services.
FAQ # 2: What is strategic planning?
FAQ # 6: What is the difference between strategic planning and operational planning?
FAQ # 7: Is there a difference between strategic planning and long-range planning?

Laycock, D. Kerry. "Strategic Planning and Management by Objectives" in *The Nonprofit Management Handbook,* Tracy Daniel Connors, Editor. New York: John Wiley & Sons, Inc., 1993.

McReynolds, Corky. "Adapted Nominal Group Technique," unpublished monograph.
_____ "The Art of Strategic Planning," unpublished monograph, 1996.

Steiner, George A. *Strategic Planning: What Every Manager Must Know.* New York: The Free Press, a Division of Simon & Schuster, 1979.

Support Center. Now known as CompassPoint Nonprofit Services (www.compasspoint.org). References cited are from the former Support Center's web site and include:
FAQ # 2: What are the key concepts and definitions in strategic planning?
FAQ # 5: What are the individual roles in a planning process?
FAQ # 7: What's in a vision statement?
FAQ #10: What is a strategy and how do we develop one?
FAQ #11: What should a strategic plan include?
FAQ #12: How do you develop an annual operating plan?
FAQ #13: How do we increase our chances of implementing our strategic plan?
FAQ #14: Should I use an external consultant?
FAQ #15: How do I use retreats in the planning process?

Other Resources

Buzan, Tony with Buzan, Barry. *The Mind Map® Book.* New York: Plume, 1996.

Ruskey, Abby and Wilke, Richard. *Promoting Environmental Education.* University of Wisconsin-Stevens Point Foundation Press, Inc., 1994.

Appendix A

What is Strategic Planning?

Strategic planning is a management tool, and like any management tool, it is used for one purpose only -- to help an organization do a better job. Strategic planning can help an organization to focus its vision and priorities in response to a changing environment and to ensure that members of the organization are working toward the same goals. In short, strategic planning is a systematic process through which an organization agrees on -- and builds commitment among key stakeholders to -- priorities which are essential to its mission and responsive to the operating environment.

The particular use for strategic planning is to sharpen organizational focus, so that all organizational resources are optimally utilized in service of the organization's mission. Several key concepts in this definition reinforce the meaning and success of strategic planning.

The process is *strategic* because it involves choosing how best to respond to the circumstances of a dynamic and sometimes hostile environment. All living plants respond to the environment, but as far as we know they do not choose how to respond. Nonprofit organizations have many choices in the face of changing client or customer needs, funding availability, competition, and other factors. Being strategic requires recognizing these choices and committing to one set of responses instead of another.

Strategic planning is *systematic* in that it calls for following a process that is both focused and productive. The process raises a sequence of questions which helps planners examine past experiences, test old assumptions, gather and incorporate new information about the present, and anticipate the environment in which the organization will be working in the future. The process also guides planners in continually looking at how the component programs and strategies fit with the vision, and vice versa.

Strategic planning involves choosing specific *priorities* -- making decisions about ends and means, in both the long term and the short term. Consensus on priorities must be reached at many levels, from the philosophical to the operational. While a strategic plan will stop short of the level of detail in an annual operating plan, it cannot be called a plan if it does not articulate the major goals and the priority methods the organization selects. Long-term goals have implications for short-term action: the two must be congruent with one another for the plan to be valid and useful.

Finally, the process is about building *commitment*. Systematically engaging key stakeholders, including clients and the community, in the process of identifying priorities allows disagreements to be engaged constructively and supports better communication and coordination. The process allows a broad consensus to be built, resulting in enhanced accountability throughout the organization. This commitment ensures that a strategic plan will actively be used for guidance and inspiration, instead of serving as a dust cover for a remote corner shelf.

The strategic planning process can be complex, challenging, and cumbersome at times, but it is always informed by the basic ideas outlined above and one can always return to these basics to make sure one's own strategic planning process is on the right track.

Adapted from Strategic Planning, FAQ #2, *"What is Strategic Planning?"* Copyright © 2000 CompassPoint, San Francisco, CA. All rights reserved. Used with permission.

Appendix B

Strategic Planning Glossary

Action Plan

A plan for the day-to-day operation of a business over the next one to twelve months. It includes a prioritized list of proposed projects as well as plans for all projects that have been funded. Development of an action plan requires no more than two months. The action plan should be reviewed and updated weekly.

Goal

A long-term organizational target or direction of development. It states what the organization wants to accomplish or become over the next several years. Goals provide the basis for decisions about the nature, scope, and relative priorities of all projects and activities. Everything the organization does should help it move toward attainment of one or more goals.

Milestone

A significant date or event during execution of a project — often associated with the end of a phase or subphase.

Mission statement

A statement of organizational purpose.

Objective

A measurable target that must be met on the way to attaining a goal.

Performance measure

A means of objectively assessing the results of programs, products, projects, or services.

Stakeholder

Any person, group, or organization that can place a claim on an organization's attention, resources, or output, or is affected by that output.

Strategic planning

A disciplined effort to produce fundamental decisions and actions that shape and guide what an organization is, what it does, and why it does it.

Strategy

The means by which an organization intends to accomplish a goal or objective. It summarizes a pattern across policies, programs, projects, actions, decisions, and resource allocations.

Values statement

A description of the code of behavior (in relation to employees, other key stakeholders, and society at large) to which an organization adheres or aspires.

Vision statement

A description of what an organization will look like if it succeeds in implementing its strategies and achieves its full potential.

From *Creating and Implementing Your Strategic Plan* (1996) by John M. Bryson and Farnum K. Alston. Adapted by permission of Jossey-Bass Inc., a subsidiary of John Wiley & Sons, Inc., New York, NY.

Appendix C

Are You Ready for Strategic Planning?
Please circle the most appropriate answer.

1. Our mission statement accurately reflects the purpose of our organization.
    TRUE   FALSE

2. Our organization has a clear future oriented direction or vision.
    TRUE   FALSE

3. Our organization has established priorities based on our mission and vision.
    TRUE   FALSE

4. Our organization has identified our strengths and weaknesses.
    TRUE   FALSE

5. Our organization has identified and evaluated issues which might affect our future.
    TRUE   FALSE

6. Our organization has prioritized strategies which will help our organization move forward.
    TRUE   FALSE

7. Our organization has specific action plans (who, when, what) to implement our strategies.
    TRUE   FALSE

8. Leadership in our organization is committed to a fair and open process.
    TRUE   FALSE

9. People in our organization understand the process and techniques of strategic planning.
    TRUE   FALSE

10. Our organization is committed to developing an on-going process rather than just producing "another document."
    TRUE   FALSE

Score number of true responses:
9-10   Send us your plan.
7-8   In the process, can you finish?
5-6   It's a start. Do you have a process?
3-4   Be encouraged and move forward.
0-2   Whoops.

Corky McReynolds, Ph.D. Director, Treehaven Education and Conference Center, Tomahawk, WI
Used with permission.

The Role of an External Consultant

For an organization with little or no experience in planning, an external consultant can enhance the planning process by providing the following services:

- Facilitating of retreats, meetings and the planning process as a whole. The use of a consultant to serve as the "conversation traffic cop" is one method of insuring that good ideas do not get lost in the emotion of the process or personality of the participants. A consultant can work with an organization to minimize planning barriers that impact effectiveness, using his or her experience as a source of tried and true processes.

- Training in planning information and process: It is critical for everyone involved in the planning process to be speaking the same language and using the same planning tools. External consultants can provide that conduit of information flow and education.

- Providing an objective and different perspective in the process: As an outsider to the organization, the consultant can ask questions and challenge existing traditions, assumptions, and routines more objectively than staff and board members. Often planners do not realize that they are using jargon or have made certain assumptions about their constituency. Having an outside consultant participate in the planning process helps ensure that organizations stay true to one of the prerequisites of engaging in the planning process, the willingness to question the status quo.

- The process expert role: The consultant who has facilitated and conducted many strategic planning processes can provide significant information and advice on tools and processes that can best accomplish your process and content goals.

From Support Center Strategic Planning, FAQ # 14, *"Should I use an external consultant?"* Copyright © 1994-95, CompassPoint, San Francisco, CA. All rights reserved. Used with permission.

This FAQ is no longer posted on the Internet. For current FAQs on strategic planning, visit CompassPoint Nonprofit Services (formerly Support Center) at www.compasspoint.org.

Appendix E

How Do I Use Retreats in the Planning Process?

A planning retreat is a meeting typically involving board and staff. It can be one to two days long, sometimes using a facilitator to help structure the process. Retreats are usually held away from the workplace or on weekends to ensure that participants can focus wholly on the issues at hand and are not distracted by the everyday interruptions of the office. Sometimes key stakeholders will be invited to join the retreat in an effort to strengthen the relationship between the stakeholder and the organization or to educate individuals around certain organizational issues.

Part of the value of the planning process is the opportunity for different elements of an organization to work together in defining the organization's future. Retreats can provide the means for achieving this aspect of the planning process.

When a Retreat Should Be Used

An organization can have a retreat at any time during the planning process, but the most common times are either at the beginning or at the end of the process.

Retreats may be organized at the beginning of the process to educate participants on the process or to build enthusiasm and commitment. These types of retreats are opportunities to begin collecting and processing information about the environment. Some organizations have external experts speak on different strategic issues that may be important to keep in mind during the planning process (e.g., changing client needs, potential duplication of services, or opportunities for collaboration, etc.).

Retreats may also be used at the conclusion of the planning process as a means to summarize the analysis and decisions developed during the process and as a communication tool to board and staff. Informing participants of decisions and ideas throughout the process will ensure that they understand and support the plan. The retreat, however, should not be used in place of this routine communication -- it is a time for recognition of commitment and contributions in addition to an opportunity for closure.

How a Retreat Can Be Formatted

Retreats are a combination of small and large group activities and discussions. The small group is used for extensive discussion and consensus building, whereas the large group is for reporting on small group activities, as well as brief discussions and final decision making.

It is important to have a well planned retreat that includes a formal agenda and planned outcomes distributed to retreat participants prior to the retreat. Michael Doyle and David Strauss' book, *How to Make Meetings Work*, provides an excellent reference guide to planning a successful retreat.

Benefits to Having a Retreat

A well planned and managed retreat can accomplish several key success factors that may enhance your planning process. They include:

- **Encouragement of creativity** - many people in group situations stimulate each other to think beyond traditional boundaries.

- **Team building for the organization** - people work together more efficiently once they know each other (e.g., personalities, work styles, methods of communicating, etc.). Retreats provide an opportunity for staff, support staff, and board members to come together and collaborate for the first time.

- **A foundation of common understanding** - for many organizations, this is the opportunity for everyone to hear the same information and messages.

Drawbacks to Having a Retreat

Although using retreats may enhance your planning process, there are several potential drawbacks to having a retreat. They include:

Appendix E continued

- **Consumption of critical resources** - a successful retreat takes a considerable amount of planning. The process also consumes both cash and time resources.

- **Pressure to produce results at the retreat** - often the purpose of a retreat is to identify and discuss issues. Not everyone feels that this is an effective use of time, and the retreat can be viewed as a waste of time and other scarce resources.

- **Generation of work the staff cannot or should not handle** - participants often assume that because it was discussed it should happen.

  Sometimes the group can feel overwhelmed with ideas generated and the planning process as a whole.

When a Retreat is Right for Your Organization
There are a few questions to consider when evaluating whether your organization should plan a retreat during the planning process:

- How knowledgeable is the board about the organization and how much will they be able to contribute in this setting?
- What outcomes are the different parties looking for in the retreat? How realistic is it that all outcomes will be accomplished?
- How willing are the board and staff to commit to the preparation and participation time?

From Support Center FAQ # 15, "How do I use retreats in the planning process?"Copyright © 1994-95, Support Center, 706 Mission Street, 5th Floor, San Francisco, CA USA 94103-3113, 415-541-9000. Used with permission. All Rights Reserved.

For updated FAQs on strategic planning, visit Compass Point Nonprofit Services at www.compasspoint.org.

Appendix F
Who Should the Planning Process Include?

Ideally, all key stakeholders should be involved in the planning process at some level. Stakeholders are individuals who are invested in the success or failure of your organization's mission. Key stakeholders include those persons who can either significantly help or hinder the implementation of your plan.

Key stakeholders may include individuals or groups who you do not traditionally think of including, but are able to contribute valuable perspectives. Examples of key stakeholders may include:

Board of Directors: The role of the full board is one of governance and oversight. As the entity responsible for governing the organization, its focus should remain on the ultimate and overreaching goals and strategies necessary to achieve organizational success. Therefore, the full board should be involved in processing environmental information and the approval of the vision, values and priorities. As the governing body, it should formally vote on adopting the plan as the management framework around which the organization will develop its operating plan(s).

Staff: Nonprofit staff are a critical ingredient to successful planning — they are the link between the visions and the every day activities of an organization. In an inclusive process, the philosophy is to give staff input and, when appropriate, authority when determining the means of the organization. These individuals have the experience and knowledge around critical success factors that should not be ignored. When staff are not an integral part of the planning discussion, they need to be informed of the decisions that have been made. Involving staff will: ensure the realism of the plan; encourage all levels of the organization to take ownership of organizational vision and goals; involve the organization's future leadership in the development of its identity and vision; and unite individual visions into a single collective vision for the organization. You should include current staff (part and full time, salaried, and unpaid).

Clients: In a planning process, it is critical to ask and answer, "How well are we meeting the needs of our customers/clients or members?" Directly involving these constituents (both current and previous clients) in the planning process is one of the best methods for assessing organizational performance and receiving guidance for future client needs and program foci.

Other External Stakeholders: In order for a planning process to be strategic it must address external issues and their potential impact on the organization. Including external stakeholders in the process is one fundamental way of ensuring that these issues will be incorporated into discussions and considered in the organization's future. External stakeholders can educate staff and the board on the perception of the organization in the community, as well as identify areas where services are being duplicated. Involving external key stakeholders in a planning process can establish a solid rapport on which you can develop powerful business relationships.

External key stakeholders include: funders (existing and potential), community leaders, competitors, potential collaborators, other agencies in parallel or related fields, volunteers, etc.

**Adapted from Strategic Planning, FAQ #5, *"What are the individual roles in the planning process?"* Copyright ©
1994-95, Support Center, San Francisco, CA. All rights reserved. Used with permission.**

For current FAQs on strategic planning, visit CompassPoint Nonprofit Services at www.compasspoint.org.

Appendix G

Questions to Prepare for Strategic Planning (SP)

1. What is the desired outcome of a SP process?

2. What are your hopes for a SP process?

3. What are your fears of a SP process?

4. What should the SP process "model"?

5. What should be the SP small group techniques?

6. Who should be involved in the process at what level?

7. Who should serve on the SP steering committee, and what will be its role?

8. What are the parameters (boundaries) of the strategic planning?

9. What information/preparation should be collected before the SP workshop?

10. What commitment can the board make toward the continuation and implementation of the SP results?

11. What should be the key (driving) question to initiate the planning?

© *Corky McReynolds, Ph.D.*
Director, Treehaven Education and Conference Center, Tomahawk, WI
Used with permission.

Appendix H

Perceptions of Ideal Futures: An Exercise in Forming Vision

This is an exercise you may employ to assist your organization in defining its own vision. By using this exercise to develop your organizational vision, you may be better assured that the vision statement that is developed is a shared vision.

At a retreat, or even at a board meeting or staff meeting, take an hour to explore your vision. Breaking into small groups helps increase participation and generate creativity. Agree on a rough time frame, say five to ten years. Ask people to think about the following questions: How do you want your community to be different? What role do you want your organization to play in your community? What will success look like?

Then ask each group to come up with a metaphor for your organization, and to draw a picture of success: "Our organization is like ... a mariachi band — all playing the same music together, or like a train — pulling important cargo and laying the track as we go, or ..." The value of metaphors is that people get to stretch their minds and experiment with different ways of thinking about what success means to them.

Finally, have all the groups share their pictures of success with each other. One person should facilitate the discussion and help the group discuss what they mean and what they hope for. Look for areas of agreement, as well as different ideas that emerge. The goal is to find language and imagery that your organization's members can relate to as their vision for success.

Caution: Do not try to write a vision statement with a group. (Groups are great for many things, but writing is not one of them!) Ask one or two people to try drafting a vision statement based on the group's discussion, bring it back to the group, and revise it until you have something that your members can agree on and that your leaders share with enthusiasm.

From Strategic Planning, FAQ #7, "What's in a vision statement?" Copyright © 1994-95, Support Center, San Francisco, CA. All rights reserved. Used with permission.

For current FAQs on strategic planning, visit CompassPoint Nonprofit Services at www.compasspoint.org.

Appendix I

The MacMillan Matrix

This strategy grid, developed by Dr. Ian MacMillan, is specifically designed to assist nonprofit organizations to formulate organizational strategies. There are three assumptions underlying this approach:

- The need for resources is essentially competitive and all agencies wanting to survive must acknowledge this dynamic.
- Given that resources are scarce, there is not room for direct duplication of services to a single constituency — this is wasteful and inefficient.
- Mediocre or low quality service to a large client population is less preferable to delivering higher quality services to a more focused population.

These assumptions have implications that are difficult and painful for many organizations and individuals. It might mean terminating some programs to improve core services and competencies, giving programs and clients to more efficient, effective agencies, or competing aggressively with those programs that are less effective or efficient.

MacMillan's matrix examines four program dimensions that guide placement on the strategy grid and indicate implied strategies.

Alignment with Mission Statement: services or programs that are not in alignment with the organizational mission, unable to draw on existing organizational skills or knowledge, unable to share resources, and/or unable to coordinate activities across programs should be divested.

Competitive Position: addresses the degree to which the organization has a stronger capability and potential to fund the program and serve the client base than the competitive agencies.

Program Attractiveness: the complexity associated with managing a program. Programs that have low client resistance, a growing client base, easy exit barriers, and stable financial resources are considered simple or "easy to administer." The level of program attractiveness also includes an economic perspective or a review of current and future resource investments.

Alternative Coverage: the number of other organizations attempting to deliver or succeeding in delivering a similar program in the same region to similar constituents.

The MacMillan Matrix provides ten cells in which to place programs that have been reviewed in terms of these four dimensions. Each cell is assigned a strategy that directs the future of the program (s) listed in the cell (e.g., aggressive competition, joint venture, orderly divestment, etc.). One cell of the matrix "Soul of the Agency," requires additional explanation. These are the difficult programs for which the organization is often the clients' "last, best hope." Management must find ways to use the programs in other cells to develop, piggyback, subsidize, leverage, promote, or otherwise support the programs in this category.

From Strategic Planning, FAQ #10, *"What is a strategy and how do we develop one?"* **Copyright © 1994-95 Support Center, San Francisco, CA. All Rights Reserved. Used with permission.**

For current FAQs on strategic planning, visit CompassPoint Nonprofit Services at www.compasspoint.org.

Contacts

CompassPoint Nonprofit Services
706 Mission Street, 5th Floor
San Francisco, CA, 94103-3113
415-541-9000
www.compasspoint.org

CompassPoint's Nonprofit Genie is a source for answers to frequently asked questions (FAQs) about nonprofit management. Visit their web site for free information.
Institute for Conservation Leadership (ICL)
6930 Carroll Avenue, Suite 420
Takoma Park, MD 20912
301-270-2900
301-270-0610 (fax)
icl@icl.org
www.icl.org

ICL offers, programs on executive director development, strategic planning, board development, fundraising, leadership and numerous other programs.

Reviewers

Andy Brown, Battle Creek Nature Center, Prince Frederick, MD
Lynn Corliss, Center for Coastal Ecology, Beaufort, SC
Anne Harper*, New Canaan Nature Center, New Canaan, CT
Peggy Hunt, Pioneers Park Nature Center, Lincoln, NE
Tracy Kay*, Schuylkill Center for Environmental Education, Philadelphia, PA
Greg Lee*, Dodge Nature Center, West St. Paul, MN
Bob Marye*, Louisiana Nature Center, New Orleans, LA
Corky McReynolds, Treehaven Education and Conference Center, Tomahawk, WI
Robert Mercer, Silver Lake Nature Center, Bristol, PA
Judy Miller, Urbana Park District, Anita Purves Nature Center, Urbana, IL
Carl Palmer*, Ogden Nature Center, Ogden, UT
Tim Sandsmark*, Greenway and Nature Center of Pueblo, Pueblo, CO
Christine Turnbull*, The Friends of Hunt Hill Audubon Sanctuary, Inc., Sarona, WI
Robert Venner, DeGraaf Nature Center, Holland, MI
Brian Winslow, Asbury Woods Nature Center, Erie, PA

* Former director

Chapter 3: Boards

Sharing a Common Purpose

An effective board can be a director's greatest resource. Board members bring diverse skills, backgrounds, and experience to help define the organization's mission, vision, and strategic goals. In collaboration with the director and staff, the board's collective wisdom is essential to achieve success.

Whether called a board of directors, board of governors, or board of trustees, boards:

- Establish policies to ensure the organization operates legally, ethically, and effectively;
- Support the executive director who implements policies and manages the organization;
- Develop strategic plans and promote strategic actions;
- Bear financial responsibility for the organization, including fundraising and financial management;
- Serve as community ambassadors;
- Participate in board and committee meetings.

The board is seen as a single entity, although individuals with distinctive opinions, perspectives and preferences constitute its membership. No member may represent his or her opinion as that of the board nor control the work of the organization.

A diverse board with members from a variety of backgrounds and interests ensures broad community representation with the common purpose of achieving the organization's mission.

This chapter begins by discussing different types of governance and provides background information about boards and their responsibilities. Following that are recommended practices to help guide directors toward building a more effective partnership with the board.

Governing Boards

Governing boards vary depending on the type of organization the board represents. The section applies to governing boards for nonprofit organizations, educational institutions and public institutions, and also includes public/private partnerships.

A.   Nonprofit Organizations

Thomas Wolf in *Managing a Nonprofit Organization* identifies five characteristics of nonprofit organizations:

- Must have a public service mission;
- Be organized as a nonprofit or charitable corporation;
- Have a governing structure that precludes self-interest and private financial gain;
- Must be exempt from paying federal taxes;
- Must possess the special legal status that stipulates gifts made to them are tax deductible (Wolf, p. 6).

Charitable organizations under the Internal Revenue Service (IRS) code 501(c)(3) must prove and maintain their status as educational, scientific, artistic, cultural, religious or other "public charity." Foundations (non-operating or operating) also may receive this status.

In 2006, there were 1.4 million nonprofit organizations in the United States with new organizations forming each year. A nonprofit organization does not distribute profits to individuals or shareholders as a for-profit corporation would. A nonprofit organization's revenues may exceed expenses, however, but these "profits" may not be distributed to "owners" of the organization. The owners are the nonprofit board members or its employees.

Organizations incorporated as private, nonprofit corporations may qualify for tax exempt and tax deductible status under the IRS code. Organizations with tax-exempt status do not pay federal income tax. State tax exemption laws vary.

Financial contributors to tax deductible 501(c)(3) nonprofit organizations can take a charitable deduction on their federal income tax returns as allowed by current laws. **See Fundraising and Development Chapter, p. 247-248.**

Bylaws serve as a nonprofit organization's "operating constitution" and detail specific procedures affecting the board members. The bylaws establish fundamental rules such as the size of the board's membership, number of officers, number and size of committees, length of tenure, meeting schedule, and other details to ensure the organization runs smoothly (Wolf, p. 31).

B.   Educational Institutions

Colleges, universities, and school districts have governing boards as well. Boards at educational institutions are structured and govern in a similar manner to private nonprofit organizations. Some may also be governed by state laws and statutes. The board of trustees, board of regents, or school board bears responsibility for policy development, planning, and fiscal authority as well as working with the institution's administrator.

Some school or university programs may have a separate board of directors that serves only for that particular program of the larger institution. Directors of these programs may be accountable and report to a board of directors and to administrators within the institution who report to its governing board.

C.   Public Institutions

Municipal, county, state/province, federal government, and special government districts also operate programs that may have governing boards.

Elected boards of commissioners govern public entities and serve for specified terms of office. Appointed or elected citizen advisory committees represent the interests and concerns of the community to the board. Commissioners make broad policy decisions. Advisory committees represent and meet community needs through programs, services, and facilities.

Government run programs may have multiple layers of authority between the director and the governing board. This model is typical in agency programs and other large organizations with traditional hierarchical lines of authority.

Anita Purves Nature Center   Urbana, IL

The Anita Purves Nature Center is part of the Urbana Park District, a separate unit of local government operating since 1907 under the Illinois state statutes. The park district is governed by a five member Board of Commissioners elected to six year terms in biennial public elections. A 15 member Citizen Advisory Committee also serves the park district and is appointed for three year terms by the board. Members of the advisory committee represent a wide variety of interests from all areas of Urbana.

The Urbana Park District Director reports to the board who sets policy for the district. The nature center manager — as the head of one of many park district programs — reports to the recreation division superintendent who reports to the park director. Nature center policy issues go through the director and advisory committee then on to the board for approval. Administrative issues are handled at the staff level or through the advisory committee. The nature center does not have a separate board.

D.   Public/Private Partnerships

Some organizations are created as public/private partnerships. These groups may form or evolve from associations among multiple agencies, organizations, and educational institutions united for a shared purpose. Public/private partnerships occur more frequently when the mission and common or shared resources including land, buildings, staff, programs, or funding make a joint effort more effective than individual efforts.

A "Friends" organization is a good example of a public/private partnership. Many government-run programs create a separate nonprofit organization to generate community interest and support, solicit and accept charitable contributions, and provide other important governing roles. The Friends organization works on behalf of the founding organization and may be named after the center (such as "The Friends of Silver Lake Nature Center"). **See the following page.**

Value of a "Friends" Organization

Robert Mercer, Director, Silver Lake Nature Center, Bristol, PA
Bucks County Department of Parks and Recreation

The concept of a Friends organization is far from new. Many governmental agencies have developed Friends groups to provide an avenue for citizen support over and above revenues provided by the tax roles.

In Buck County, Pennsylvania, there are three county owned and operated nature centers, one state wildflower preserve and one private nonprofit nature center. Each of the three county centers initiated a Friends organization in the early 1970s.

At that time, the Friends organization was a mechanism to permit the purchase of educational supplies without going through the government purchase process. The Friends organizations gave the local community a way to show their support and resulted in a mailing list of people interested in the centers' programming. As the centers grew, the directors focused on the Friends as the source for growth. Even though they were supportive, a governmental entity pressured to keep taxes low is not in a position to generate substantial increases in operations.

The Friends organization for each county nature center agreed to supplement the programs. To generate the necessary revenues, the Friends instituted program and service fees. These fees, plus fund raising, enable the Friends to fund staff positions as well as materials. Excess funds accumulate instead of being absorbed by the government.

In 1997, each of the three centers received about 50 percent of their approximately $300,000 annual operating income through the revenues generated by the Friends organization. The nonprofit status of these organizations enables them to work closely with funding sources ordinarily not available to a government run nature center. Each of the facilities has or is working on a major capital project which the Friends are helping fund. The respective Friends organizations have solicited grants for capital projects and developed foundation and business support for programs and operations.

The existence of a Friends organization is not without drawbacks, however. The major issue is control over decisions that affect the organization. The Friends organization cannot hire or fire the facility director yet is asked to provide substantial financial support. As the nature center grows, the Friends assume more financial responsibility of the day-to-day operations. This can create conflict when decisions are not in concert with the agency's policies.

The other primary issue is liability. What happens if a staff member funded by "the other side" makes a decision or performs an action which creates a libelous situation? These concerns are best dealt with by having a cohesive plan and mutual understanding. Despite the problems, a well-managed Friends organization can greatly enhance the operations of a governmental agency.

For further information on the Bucks County nature centers, contact:

Silver Lake Nature Center, (215) 785-1177, Robert Mercer, Director
Churchville Nature Center, (215) 357-4005, Chris Stieber, Director
Peace Valley Nature Center, (215) 345-7860, Craig Olsen, Director

Identifying Your Board's Life Cycle

Many directors are challenged and sometimes frustrated by their boards, especially if members become unfocused or unclear of their roles. One reason may be that the board is evolving during its "life cycle" and members' roles and responsibilities are changing (Mathiasen, 1995, p. 5-18). Many changes in board functions are natural and predictable consequences of organizational growth (Mathiasen, 1995, p. 2).

In *Board Passages: Three Key Stages in a Nonprofit Board's Life Cycle*, Karl Mathiasen, III identifies three stages a board goes through as boards evolve from a volunteer "organizing" board to a volunteer "governing" board to an "institutional" fundraising board.

Understanding your board's life cycle may help clarify how it operates and help you determine how better to involve and engage the board to advance the mission.

Every director has a preferred management style. As the organization travels through its life cycle, it needs varying management styles. Each transition can lead to a change in director. Your management style is always needed somewhere, but there are times when you may need to change your style for the good of the organization or move to a place where your style is desired.

Be sure to read Appendix A, *Board Passages,* p. 105, adapted from Mathiasen. See also Appendix B, *Organizational Life Cycles of Boards,* p. 107.

Board Responsibilities

The following section covers information about boards typically found in nonprofit organizations. You may also refer to this section for working with "Friends" groups, advisory committees, or other groups created to benefit or cooperate with your organization. **See Appendix C, *Board of Directors Policy and Procedures Manual,* p. 108, from the Teton Science School.**

Board members serve important leadership roles for the organization. There are six primary areas of responsibility for the board (Wolf, p. 29-30).

A.   Determine the Organization's Mission and Set Operating Policies

As seen in the strategic planning process, developing the mission is a crucial part of leading a successful organization. The board not only helps define the mission, but makes certain the programs and activities of the organization fulfill the mission.

Boards also develop policies to ensure the organization operates within legal and ethical standards and for maximum effectiveness. The director and staff propose policy actions or revisions, draft policy statements for the board, and provide background information to aid the board's review, discussion, and policy adoption.

Policy decisions should be:

* Based on the mission;
* Based on existing governing documents of the organization;
* Made after thoroughly researching the issue;
* Made after consulting those who will be affected by the policy (Burgess, p. 199).

Board approval is generally required for policy decisions such as:

* Change of mission;
* Change of organization name;
* Strategic plan adoption;
* Annual operating budget;
* Fee increases;
* Fundraising campaigns;
* Major program changes;
* Investment guidelines and strategies;
* Property purchase or sale;
* Risk management.

Recommend that the board develop and adopt a policy on organizational values either as part of the strategic planning process or as a separate committee activity by board and staff. The values statement addresses ethical standards for board members, staff, and volunteers who represent the organization and act on its behalf. Include standards for behavior to maintain the public confidence and trust, and to protect the organization from unethical or illegal acts. **See Appendix D,** *Board of Trustees Code of Ethics,* **p. 114 and Strategic Planning Chapter.**

Also develop and adopt a separate policy statement regarding real or perceived conflicts of interest by board members, staff, and volunteers. Increasing awareness of potential conflicts will help prevent them before they occur. A conflict of interest can occur when:

1.   A board or staff member makes a decision that personally benefits the individual and not the common good of the whole organization;

2.   The organization conducts business or a transaction that is financially beneficial to a board member, staff member, or the family of either. Discuss these issues with your legal counsel before drafting and finalizing these policies. **See Appendix E,** *Conflict Of Interest Policy for Board Members,* **p. 115.**

B.   Establish Annual Goals and Engage in Strategic Planning

The board is actively involved in the strategic planning process to create a desired future and to develop strategies to achieve success.

The board:

- Initiates and oversees the process;
- Creates a planning committee whose members participate and report to the board;
- Reviews draft plans;
- Votes to approve and adopt the final strategic plan. **See Strategic Planning Chapter.**

C.   Establish Fiscal Policy

As legal representatives, board members are responsible for protecting the organization's assets. An organization's money, people, property, good will, and integrity are all considered assets (Burgess, p. 211). If the board fails to protect these assets, the board and its members may be held liable.

The board is responsible for overseeing the financial stability of the organization and often appoints a finance committee to handle this duty. However, all board members are obliged to understand fund accounting, review financial statements, and question actions that will incur a financial obligation or risk to the organization.

This includes approving budgets, capital expenditures, salary and benefits packages, program costs, loans, investments, insurance and risk management decisions (Burgess, p. 202).

Risk management issues including liability insurance may not need to be addressed by all boards. This depends on the type of organization (public, private, educational, or public/private partnership) and who is responsible for these issues within the organization. If risk management is a concern to your organization, an excellent resource may be found in *The Nonprofit Board's Role in Risk Management: More Than Buying Insurance* by Charles Tremper and George Babcock. **See References, p. 103.**

Contact BoardSource (formerly National Center for Nonprofit Boards) for up-to-date publications on risk management and other board topics. **See Contacts, p. 132.**

The Board's Role in Risk Management

Property losses: May destroy organization's ability to operate; limited to value of organization's assets.

Liability risks: May result in damage well beyond organization's resources and affect individuals associated with the organization (board members, staff, volunteers).

Goals of Risk Management

1. Ensure safe environment for employees, volunteers, and service recipients.
2. Reduce anxiety and fear of liability of employees and volunteers.
3. Conserve the organization's assets so it can pursue its mission.
4. Ensure compliance with legal requirements.
5. Ensure that an individual harmed by the organization's activities receives adequate compensation.

Risk Management Process

1. Identify risks: Look at what the organization does and what property it controls: both could cause a loss; property could be lost by a claim. Examine claims history and easily overlooked risks.
2. Analyze risks: What makes it risky? Can you afford the risk? Can you afford the loss?
3. Select techniques to control the risks
   a. Avoidance: eliminates the source of risk; **does not mean avoiding the risk by inaction**.
   b. Loss control: decreases frequency and severity of risks. Routinely look for potential risks and do something about it (remove it, post a warning, keep people away, provide staff training).
   c. Separation: to reduce loss, protect valuable files, documents in safe deposit box or by storing in separate location.
   d. Combination: for large organizations or groups; seek group insurance or risk pooling; the greater variety of risks, the less likely all will occur at once.
   e. Retention: some losses are small enough for an organization to bear and may help reduce insurance costs.
   f. Transfer: another organization agrees to bear the risk; done through insurance.
4. Implement selected risk management techniques: board must ensure risk management techniques are incorporated by staff and volunteers into organization operations.
5. Monitor and modify risk management program: stay current on laws which affect risk management policies and update.

Insurance

1. Insurance may be preferred if risks can't be eliminated or reduced. Board may recruit member with insurance specialty. Designate a risk management committee. Seek insurance companies with nonprofit organization experience. Make certain someone reads the policies.
2. Directors and officers (D&O) insurance provides protection for board members but coverage exclusions limit its use for risk management. Consult insurance professionals.
3. Consider group plans for cost effectiveness.

Adapted from *The Nonprofit Board's Role in Risk Management: More than Buying Insurance*, by Charles Tremper and George Babcock; a publication of the National Center for Nonprofit Boards (NCNB). Copyright © 1990 by NCNB. Used by permission. Contact BoardSource (formerly NCNB). See Contacts, p. 132.

D. Provide Financial Resources

The board is responsible for fundraising to ensure the financial stability of the organization. The ideal board/staff fundraising relationship includes:

- A board development committee who leads, inspires and motivates the board to raise funds;
- The rest of the board who give personally at the level they can afford and who participate in the fundraising efforts planned and developed for the board;
- A director who works closely with the board to develop fundraising strategies, coordinate staff and board donor research, provide information, develop materials, arrange meetings, schedule appointments;
- A development director, who conducts overall fundraising planning and works closely to facilitate the board's efforts. **See Fundraising and Development Chapter.**

E. Select, Evaluate, and Terminate the Executive Director

In nonprofit and other organizations, the board recruits, selects, hires, and has authority to terminate the executive director. The board is obligated to provide the director its whole-hearted support and avoid interfering in day-to-day operations (Burgess, p. 201).

The board also assesses the effectiveness of the director's performance. Directors benefit from assessment by having an opportunity to jointly evaluate strengths, identify weaknesses, and openly discuss the director's progress toward achieving the organization's goals (Nason, p. 3).

Just as directors evaluate and support the staff, so should the board provide this level of feedback and assessment for the director. **See Other Resources, p. 104, for** *Assessment of the Chief Executive: A Tool for Governing Boards and Chief Executives of Nonprofit Organizations* **by Jane Pierson and Joshua Mintz.**

F. Develop and Maintain a Communication Link with the Community

The board's community relations role is multi-faceted. Board members provide the organization access to a broad segment of community members and leaders. As a voice for their interests, concerns, and opinions, the board helps the organization understand community needs.

Board members have numerous informal opportunities to represent the organization. With friends, colleagues, or associates, board members may generate positive relations for the institution.

Often board members are asked to represent the organization at conferences or other events. Knowledge of the organization and its issues is extremely important for communicating a unified message.

Board members are essential partners for building community support for strategic planning, fundraising, and other organizational initiatives. They also play a crucial role in defusing potential misunderstandings and conflicts.

Board Tips: Create an Associate Board Membership

Consider developing associate board memberships to attract young professionals and other community members to your organization. The board of directors may offer associate members opportunities to participate in board meetings, committees, and activities which enhance organizational knowledge, interest, and experience. Associate members may be involved without committing to the more demanding responsibilities of regular board membership. This type of membership attracts people with growing careers, busy families, or those who lack board or nonprofit experience.

Associate members may attend and actively participate in all board meetings, express their views and opinions, and serve on committees. Other conditions for an associate board membership include:

- Serving a 1 year term;
- Voluntary attendance at board meetings;
- Involvement on board committees as much or as little as desired;
- No voting eligibility.

The board may assess an associate member's potential as a future board member during the year at meetings and board functions. As a result, associate members frequently are nominated to full board membership.

For more information, contact Mike Riska, Executive Director, Delaware Nature Society, Hockessin, DE

Checklist
The Board Member's Bill of Rights
© Kelly Kleiman

Reprinted from Board Member November/December 1997, Volume 6, Number 10.
A publication of the National Center for Nonprofit Boards (NCNB). Used by permission.

Board members have rights, beyond those of being volunteers, that must be upheld by the board as well as observed by staff.

☐ **The right to understand the role of a board member.** A board member's role is to represent the community in the work of the organization, and to ensure conformity to mission and the availability of resources necessary to continue doing that work and fulfilling that mission.

☐ **The right to be informed about the work of the group.** Board members begin as outsiders but should quickly become insiders; the best way to do that is for staff to share inside information. Ask for regular reports on activities, emphasizing how the organization is serving its constituents.

☐ **The right to be heard.** A silent board is an unhappy board. Board members must welcome each other's opinions and feel that their opinions are welcomed by the staff.

☐ **The right to participate in the work of the group.** Board members who are given nothing to do are more likely to quit than those who have too much to do. Create standing committees, or *ad hoc* task forces.

☐ **The right to staff support.** The staff should spell out specific expectations, write schedules for project completion, recruit other volunteers, and follow up.

☐ **The right to try something different.** Some individuals serve on boards to explore other interests and learn new skills. Don't automatically put the broker on the finance committee. Offer bankers the chance to talk about education or marketing people the chance to think about real estate.

☐ **The right to equal treatment.** All board members should be held to the same standard. Everyone can afford to contribute. Time is not money; every board member should give both.

☐ **The right to relief.** Board terms are the only nonlethal way to get rid of deadwood. Term limits allow for a natural way to bring new blood onto the board.

☐ **The right to be protected from liability.** Directors' and officers' liability insurance is a must. Special care and skill are required to ensure proper handling of finances and taxes.

☐ **The right to know where we've been, where we're going, what we're trying to do, and for whom.** Create a culture and maintain esprit de corps by frequently reiterating mission. Conduct planning sessions every few years. Re-evaluate. Change is not a tragedy; it's what keeps groups alive.

Kelly Kleiman, principal, NFP Consulting, works with nonprofit organizations, specializing in marketing, strategic planning, and fund-raising. See BoardSource, p. 132, for updated information on boards.

Checklist of Recommended Practices

I.   Enhance Board Relations

☐   Practice 1   Develop Skills for Working with the Board
☐   Practice 2   Build a Partnership
☐   Practice 3   Cultivate a Close Working Relationship with the Board Chairperson

II.   Facilitate Board Leadership

☐   Practice 4   Involve and Engage Board Members in Organizational Leadership
☐   Practice 5   Advise the Board on Creating Effective Board Committees
☐   Practice 6   Serve an Active Role on Major Board Committees
☐   Practice 7   Develop the Board's Fundraising Role

III.   Develop Board Effectiveness

☐   Practice 8   Plan and Facilitate Effective Board Meetings
☐   Practice 9   Conduct New Member Orientation with Key Board Leaders and Staff
☐   Practice 10   Facilitate and Encourage Positive Board/Staff Relations
☐   Practice 11   Provide Opportunities for Board Education and Development
☐   Practice 12   Encourage and Support the Board's Self-evaluation Process

Recommended Practices

I.   Enhance Board Relations

Practice 1   **Develop Skills for Working with the Board**

As the organization's leader, the director energizes the board and keeps members focused on the mission, their responsibilities, and duties. Through leadership, the director helps board members succeed in their legal, organizational, and community roles (Herman and Heimovics, p. 54, 56).

The relationship between an executive director and the board may not always be smooth. Poor communication, lack of leadership, or uncertainty about roles can strain a director's ability to work effectively with the board and lead to a breakdown in confidence and trust. Take the following actions:

❑   Learn how boards operate and function; attend seminars, workshops, and training opportunities. Invite the board chairperson or other members to attend with you; have your organization pick up the tab.

❑   Develop clear, written expectations for all board members. Prepare job descriptions for chairperson and executive committee members. **See Appendix F, *Position Description, Member of the Board of Trustees,* p. 116, and Appendix G, *Board Member Responsibilities,* p. 117.**

❑   Establish clear authority and responsibility for staff supervision and organization administration. Board involvement in the director's duties undermine and damage relationships. Assert your leadership role. **See Leadership and Staff Chapters.**

❑   Talk and meet often with the board chairperson to cultivate and develop a strong relationship.

❑   Provide the board information, expertise and knowledge of issues to aid their discussions. Keep written information to the minimum they need to know to function and govern (Mathiasen, 1982).

❑   Inform board members of significant organizational, program and staff issues before they hear about it elsewhere. Boards dislike surprises.

Read Appendix H, *No Board of Directors is Like Any Other*, p. 118.

Practice 2

Build a Partnership

The director and board have a relationship of dual leadership that, at its best, complements each other's unique qualities and results in shared responsibility for the organization (Houle, p. 86). To build an effective partnership, the director and board must recognize the differences in their roles. Some are listed below.

1.   **Planning**: The *director* develops and implements annual plans. The *board, director and staff* jointly develop strategic plans.
2.   **Organizing**: The *director* organizes and manages operations, including positions needed, and keeps the board informed. The *board* focuses on broad issues, not the day-to-day.
3.   **Staffing**: The *director* hires, evaluates, and fires staff. The *board* hires, evaluates, and may fire the director only.
4.   **Directing and Leading**: The *director* directs, motivates, and supports staff through his or her leadership. The *board* leads through the director, not the staff.
5.   **Controlling**: The *director* is responsible for developing and managing the budget. The *board* approves it (Struck, p. 19-20).

Practice 3

Cultivate a Close Working Relationship with the Board Chairperson

While the director must develop and sustain a positive and successful relationship with the entire board, the relationship between the director and board chairperson is pivotal to advancing organizational goals.

The organization is best served when the two most important people in it — the director and the board chairperson — are equally strong (Mathiasen, 1982).

In addition, when these two leaders work well together, potential problems between staff and board may be avoided (Wolf, p. 41-42). The director and chairperson jointly develop the board meeting agenda. Send it well in advance (at least one week) to be sure members have time to carefully review it along with the minutes from the previous meeting and any other materials.

Tips for building a relationship with the board chairperson include:

❏ Communicate frequently, preferably in person;
❏ Consider meeting once a week for a walk, for breakfast or lunch to discuss organization business;
❏ Be open, listen well, and have candid discussions;
❏ Plan, coordinate, and prepare for board and committee meetings;
❏ Submit reports and written information with adequate time for review and discussion.

II.   Facilitate Board Leadership

Practice 4

Involve and Engage Board Members in Organizational Leadership

While each board varies in its style and method of involvement, in general the board's primary responsibilities include policy development, financial oversight, strategic planning, and fundraising. The director is responsible for working with the chairperson to involve and engage board members to work on behalf of the organization.

Involving board members on committees is an excellent way to create ownership for the organization and for them to become involved.

Another way to engage the board is to hold a retreat. Retreats are generally held for one or two days, held away from the usual place of business, and frequently held on weekends. Retreats often coincide with strategic planning or other planning sessions.

The value of a retreat is to bring all board members together, sometimes with staff, to focus on a particular agenda for an extended period of time. Most retreats include ample informal time for socializing and relationship building. **See Strategic Planning Chapter, Appendix E,** *"How Do I Use Retreats in the Planning Process?,"* **p. 67.**

If a retreat is cost prohibitive or members are unable or unwilling to attend, consider other ways of bringing board members together such as a dinner or luncheon. Board members are volunteers; holding an occasional event in their honor is a way to express gratitude, acknowledge their service, and build relationships.

Practice 5

Advise the Board on Creating Effective Board Committees

A well established approach to involve board members is through committees. Some committees may be established in the bylaws (standing committees) and others formed to address specific issues and then disbanded (ad hoc committees).

Key standing committees should complement and parallel the board's responsibilities for making policies, assuring fiscal accountability, developing adequate funding sources, and overseeing the organization (Hirzy, p. 7).

Ad hoc committees are formed for a specific purpose and for a limited time. Examples include an executive search committee formed to find and select candidates for the executive director position, or an event committee created to plan and host a one-time event.

Benefits to forming committees include:

- Informed and involved board members;
- Efficient board meetings (committees make recommendations to the full board for approval);
- Work distributed evenly among board members;
- Full use of the board's talents and knowledge;
- Greater board member satisfaction (Hirzy, p. 1).

Problems occur when:
- Multiple committees have overlapping functions;
- Committees lack a clearly defined purpose;
- A committee is created just to give board members something to do;
- Committees continue that no longer have a clear purpose;
- Too many committees require excessive time commitments from board members and the director.

To prevent these problems:
- ❏ Develop a statement that clearly defines each committee's responsibilities;
- ❏ Clearly define each committee's relationship and responsibility to the full board;
- ❏ Clearly define the committee's role in relation to the staff;
- ❏ Keep a list of all committees and members;
- ❏ Review committee structure and responsibilities annually;
- ❏ Recommend the board disband inactive committees.

Practice 6

Serve an Active Role on Major Board Committees

Organizations vary with the number, size and responsibilities of committees, but if committees exist, the director usually serves on each of them. The director regularly takes an active role with key standing committees (executive, development, finance, nominating) and on other major board committees.

Committees are best created when the board's responsibilities have become so complex that it can no longer operate efficiently as a single entity (Hirzy, p. 2). Special projects or initiatives also are good reasons to create a committee (strategic planning, capital campaign, endowment fund drive, etc.). **See Appendix I, Board Committees, p. 123, and Appendix J, Tips for Successful Committees, p. 124. See also Appendix C, Board of Directors Policy and Procedures Manual, p. 108.**

If key staff positions are part of the organization (development director, chief financial officer, human resource director, education director, etc.), the director usually also appoints that staff person to serve on the appropriate committee.

BoardSource (formerly National Center for Nonprofit Boards) produces numerous publications related to board governance and has an excellent series on committees. **See References, p. 103 and Contacts, p. 132.**

The Nominating Committee

The board's nominating and selection process for new board members benefits greatly from the director's active participation and leadership. The director may influence the board's selection process by providing important community and organizational knowledge.

A director helps the board:

- Determine organizational needs;
- Assess current skills on the board;
- Determine needed skills.

The director also aids the board by :

- Recommending candidates;
- Counseling and advising the nominating committee;
- Finding and recruiting outstanding candidates.

Before recruiting new members, look at skills, experience, length of terms and other criteria for current board members to assess the board's strengths and weaknesses. Identify new skills or knowledge needed on the board. Analyze the make-up of current members and prospects using the same criteria.

See Appendix K, *Board Member Recruiting Matrix*, p. 125.

Practice 7   Develop the Board's Fundraising Role

Fundraising is a primary responsibility of most boards yet directors frequently are frustrated over the lack of response by board members — both in failing to give personally and being unwilling to ask others to give. One clear reason is the members may not have been recruited with fundraising in mind. They may be expected to raise money but not have contacts, experience, or the confidence to do it successfully.

To address this problem, do these three things:

1. Make sure the board chairperson informs board members they are expected to financially support the organization and to help raise money from others;
2. Help existing board members develop their fundraising skills. Ask experienced board members to mentor others less experienced. Provide opportunities for board development and include a session on fundraising;
3. When recruiting new board members, seek people with fundraising experience and contacts. **See Fundraising and Development Chapter**.

III. Develop Board Effectiveness

Practice 8   **Plan and Facilitate Effective Board Meetings**

Effective meetings inspire board members' commitment and involvement. As volunteers, they take time away from other life responsibilities and interests to benefit your organization. Well planned and organized meetings are more rewarding for everyone.

Develop a calendar or schedule of meetings a year in advance so board members can plan to attend. The chairperson and director share joint responsibility for developing each meeting's agenda and preparing financial, policy or other relevant reports for the meeting (Mueller, p. 5). Committee reports should also be mailed in advance. Send this information at least one week or more before the meeting. Board members are expected to read and review it.

Enabling the board to come to closure on as many agenda items as possible requires the experience and skill of the executive director and key board members (Ibid.). All too often, board discussions go on too long, the chairperson fails to keep the meeting and agenda moving, or discussion is allowed to wander without closure. It is no surprise if meeting attendance begins to decline.

See Appendix L, *Checklist for Conducting More Effective Board Meetings*, p. 126, Appendix M, *The Action Agenda*, p. 127 and Appendix N, *Agenda, Board of Directors Meeting*, p. 129.

Tips for Better Board Meetings

❏   Send all materials to board members well in advance of the meeting (minimum one week, preferably more). Include the agenda (developed jointly by you and the board chairperson), minutes from the last meeting, committee reports, and support materials for consent and regular agenda items.

❏   Call board members to encourage attendance and determine if you will have a quorum at the meeting. Have a staff assistant call to remind members of the date, time and place and to confirm their attendance. You may wish to personally call some members as well.

❏   Work with the board chairperson to begin and end meetings on time. Keep meeting time reasonable; the shorter the better, with two hours as a maximum (Mueller, p. 8).

❏   Take attendance at all meetings. Develop a list with each board member's name on it and board meeting dates listed across the top. Check off names of those attending. This is a visible reminder to those who do and do not attend.

❏   Consider adding a consent agenda for routine items on the agenda. This will limit discussion and save time during meetings. Include background information on consent agenda items in the mailed board packet. At the meeting, the board chairperson requests a motion and a second to approve everything on the consent agenda. Once approved, the chairperson moves on to the next item on the agenda.

       If a member wishes to discuss an item on the consent agenda, she or he would ask that the item be removed from the consent agenda and placed on the regular agenda. This takes place before the full agenda is approved at the start of the meeting.

❏   Recommend an action item agenda to the board. **See Appendix M, The Action Agenda, p. 127.**

❏   Be sure the board chairperson and members know the proper procedures for making a motion, seconding a motion, amending the motion, and for discussion. The order is: make a motion, discuss it, and then vote.

Practice 9   Conduct New Member Orientation with Key Board Leaders and Staff

Orientation is essential to familiarize new board members with the organization, their roles on the board, and to introduce them to other board members. It also shortens the period of time members often require to learn the procedures, culture and politics of the organization (Gelatt, p. 186).

Whether you hold group orientations or one-on-one meetings, getting to know board members early on helps build the foundation for long term relationships. It also allows you to discover any "hidden agendas" board members may have that were not revealed in the recruiting process.

Orientations are generally a joint effort of the board, director and key staff. Some centers invite the full board and use the orientation as a time for team building, providing updates and holding an organizational review.

Conduct the orientation in a relaxed, open atmosphere. Encourage questions by new board members and ensure they feel comfortable making observations or raising issues about the organization.

Be sure the board chairperson welcomes each new member and addresses:

- Attendance policy for meetings;
- Committee responsibilities;
- Board, director, and staff roles and relationships.

Provide board members basic information about the organization and their responsibilities. Create a board handbook for easy reference from this list.

Board Duties and Information

- Calendar of board meetings;
- List of board members, officers, committee members;
- Charter or articles of incorporation;
- Bylaws;
- Board policies;
- Minutes (from past year);
- Annual report and financial statement.

Organization Information

- Brief history of organization;
- Fact sheet with site, facility, and program statistics;
- Mission statement;

- Vision statement;
- Values statement;
- Strategic plan;
- Annual plan and budget;
- Organizational chart;
- Staff list with key addresses and phone numbers;
- Recent newsletters, brochures, and news clips;
- Fundraising case statement;
- Funding sources.

In addition, the director:

- Gives an overview of current programs and activities;
- Introduces staff and volunteers;
- Conducts tour of buildings, grounds, and facilities.

Practice 10

Facilitate and Encourage Positive Board/Staff Relations

The director and chairperson set the tone for board/staff relations by how well they work together (Wolf, p. 41-42). The executive director is responsible for leading, managing, and overseeing the organization, its programs, and staff. The chairperson leads the board, is responsible for making sure its members understand their roles, and sees that members do not interfere with the director's ability to do his or her job.

Tension between the board and staff is common and can have both positive and negative effects. The board's influence on the director and staff to perform at higher levels is a benefit of board involvement. When tension exists over programs, personalities, and priorities, relationships and morale are easily damaged. Lack of understanding or lack of respect for each other's roles may contribute to these conflicts.

Some examples include:

- A staff member complains to a board member over a personnel issue without first discussing it with the director;
- A board member directs staff to plan a fund raiser without

consulting the director;

- The director agrees in the middle of the fiscal year to take on a board member's pet project not included in the annual plan and requiring extensive staff time.

These "boundary issues" occur most often in organizations undergoing transition from an active, hands-on volunteer board to a policy-making board.

The director is the center of communication between board and staff although she or he certainly is not the only person who interacts with both. Staff may serve on board committees and attend board meetings. Board members may volunteer in other capacities with the organization and work closely with staff. Some board members and staff may have friendships that preceded the organization but they must be able to set these relationships aside.

Communication between staff and board should be open, frequent and the relationship built on mutual trust and respect (Gelatt, p. xv). But all directors are advised to be certain their authority is clear and is not undermined by staff and board member interactions.

To facilitate positive interactions between the board and staff, encourage staff to attend board meetings. Ask staff to give brief presentations to inform or update the board on issues or programs. Board members will get to know staff better and gain a deeper understanding of programs.

Staff benefit from preparing and delivering well-planned presentations, interacting with board members professionally, and addressing questions the board may have. Make sure staff members are well prepared and their attendance is planned and purposeful.

Practice 11

Provide Opportunities for Board Education and Development

The director encourages board members to expand their knowledge of the organization and their roles. Even though most boards are reluctant to routinely attend more meetings, plan focused sessions to increase their skills and build knowledge and commitment to the organization. Include costs for board development in the annual budget.

Host special topic seminars conducted by a consultant for the board at a retreat or special meeting. Consider asking board members to attend a session sponsored by another organization or institution in your area. This offers the board member an opportunity to network with others on behalf of the organization. The board member can provide a brief summary and share what was learned with the full board at the next meeting.

Local colleges, universities, foundations, community groups, agencies, organizations, and businesses sponsor sessions on a variety of topics of interest to boards. BoardSource (formerly the National Center for Nonprofit Boards) offers excellent resources for board members. **See Contacts, p. 132**.

Consider offering sessions on the following:

- Developing board leadership skills;
- Strategic planning overview;
- Nominating committee responsibilities;
- Fundraising (major donors solicitation; capital campaigns; planned giving);
- Board's role in risk management;
- Board's role in financial management.

Create a board member reference section in your library. **See References, p. 103, Other Resources, p. 104 and Contacts, p. 132.**

Practice 12	**Encourage and Support the Board's Self-evaluation Process**

Boards benefit from periodic assessment to determine how well they are achieving the organization's mission (Houle, p. 156). Encourage and support on-going assessment and assist the board to conduct a more thorough review periodically. A board retreat may be used for a detailed assessment of their efforts.

Develop the ability to assess the board as a whole while at work, such as during a board meeting or retreat. This means "being aware of how the board as a group does its work in accomplishing its goals, and understanding the needs and wants of individual board members as they define their role on the board" (Herman and Heimovics, p. 93).

Note the following:

- Individual board members' interests and needs;
- How various board members depend on each other;
- How changes in one individual's behavior affect others;
- How the actions of certain board members add to or detract from the board's overall effectiveness;
- Board members understanding the mission;
- Board members understanding their roles (Herman and Heimovics, p. 93).

An excellent assessment guide developed by LaSalle University's Nonprofit Management Development Center is *The Board's Role in Monitoring Its Own Functioning and Activities: Areas for a Governing Board to Discuss*. A series of probing questions on the board's roles, responsibilities, and effectiveness may be used to guide the board's self-assessment. **See Appendix O, *The Board's Role in Monitoring Its Own Functioning and Activities*, p. 130.**

References

Burgess, Barbara A. "The Board of Directors," *The Nonprofit Management Handbook: Operating Policies and Procedures,* Tracy D. Connors, Editor. New York: John Wiley & Sons, Inc., 1993.

Gelatt, James P. *Managing Nonprofit Organizations in the 21st Century.* The American Council on Education and The Oryx Press, 1992. Reproduced with permission of Greenwood Publishing Group, Inc., Westport, CT.

Herman, Robert D. and Heimovics, Richard D. *Executive Leadership in Nonprofit Organizations.* New York: Jossey-Bass Inc., a subsidiary of John Wiley & Sons, Inc., 1991.

Hirzy, Ellen Cochran. *Nonprofit Board Committees: How to Make them Work.* Washington, DC: National Center for Nonprofit Boards, 1993.

Houle, Cyril O. *Governing Boards.* New York: Jossey-Bass Inc., a subsidiary of John Wiley & Sons, Inc., and Washington, DC: National Center for Nonprofit Boards, 1989.

Kleiman, Kelly. "The Board Member's Bill of Rights," *Board Member.* Volume 6, Number 10. Washington, DC: National Center for Nonprofit Boards, 1997.

Mathiasen III, Karl. *Board Passages: Three Key Stages in a Nonprofit Board's Life Cycle.* Washington, DC: National Center for Nonprofit Boards, 1995.

_____ *No Board of Directors is Like Any Other: Some Maxims About Boards.* Unpublished monograph. Washington, D.C.: Management Assistance Group, 1982.

Mueller, Robert K. *Smarter Board Meetings.* Washington, DC: National Center for Nonprofit Boards, 1992.

Nason, John W. *Board Assessment of the Chief Executive: A Responsibility Essential to Good Governance.* Washington, DC: National Center for Nonprofit Boards, 1990.

Struck, Darla, Editor. *Board Member Manual.* Frederick, MD: Aspen Publishers, 1997. www.aspenpublishers.com

Tremper, Charles and Babcock, George. *The Nonprofit Board's Role in Risk Management: More Than Buying Insurance.* Washington, DC: National Center for Nonprofit Boards, 1990.

Winters, Owen D., and Simmons, Bora, Touvell, Richard, Weilbacher, Michael and Widmar, Ron, Editors. *Directory of Natural Science Centers.* Roswell, GA: Natural Science for Youth Foundation, 1990.

Wolf, Thomas. *Managing a Nonprofit Organization* © 1984, 1990 by Prentice-Hall, Inc. New York: Simon and Schuster Adult Publishing Group, 1990.

Other Resources

Andringa, Robert C. *The Executive Committee: Making it Work for Your Organization.* Washington, DC: National Center for Nonprofit Boards, 1994.

Carver, John and Carver, Miriam Mayhew. *Basic Principles of Policy Governance.* New York: Jossey-Bass Inc., a subsidiary of John Wiley & Sons, Inc., 1996.

Hirzy, Ellen Cochran. *The Nominating Committee: Laying a Foundation for Your Organization's Future.* Washington, DC: National Center for Nonprofit Boards, 1994.

Holmgren, Norah. *The Finance Committee: The Fiscal Conscience of the Nonprofit Board.* Washington, DC: National Center for Nonprofit Boards, 1995.

Johnson, Sandra L. *The Audit Committee: A Key to Financial Accountability in Nonprofit Organizations.* Washington, DC: National Center for Nonprofit Boards, 1993.

Kanuft, E.B., Berger, Renee A., and Gray, Sandra T. *Profiles of Excellence.* New York: Jossey-Bass Inc., a subsidiary of John Wiley & Sons, Inc., 1991.

Mathiasen III, Karl. "Board Membering: What Kinds of People Make Good Board Members? What Kinds of People are Needed to Make up a Good Board of Directors?" Unpublished monograph. Washington, D.C.: Management Assistance Group, 1986.

_____ "The Board of Directors IS a Problem: Exploring the Concept of Following and Leading Boards." Unpublished monograph. Washington, D.C.: Management Assistance Group, 1983.

Mathiasen III, Karl, with Franco, Nancy and Gross, Susan. "Passages: Organizational Life Cycles." Washington, DC: Management Assistance Group, 1982.

O'Connell, Brian. *The Board Member's Book.* New York: The Foundation Center, 1985.

O'Connor, Judith O. *The Planning Committee: Shaping Your Organization's Future.* Washington, DC: National Center for Nonprofit Boards, 1997.

Park, Jr., Dabney G. *Strategic Planning and the Nonprofit Board.* Washington, DC: National Center for Nonprofit Boards, 1990.

Pierson, Jane and Mintz, Joshua. *Assessment of the Chief Executive: A Tool for Governing Boards and Chief Executives of Nonprofit Organizations.* Washington, DC: National Center for Nonprofit Boards, 1999.

Smith, Bucklin & Associates. *The Complete Guide to Nonprofit Management.* New York: John Wiley & Sons, Inc., 1994.

Tempel, Eugene R. *The Development Committee: Fundraising Begins with the Board.* Washington, DC: National Center for Nonprofit Boards, 1996.

Appendix A

Board Passages

Adapted from Board Passages: Three Key Stages in a Nonprofit Board's Life Cycle, by Karl Mathiasen; a publication of the National Center for Nonprofit Boards (NCNB). Copyright © 1990 by NCNB. Used with permission.

Stage One: **An Organizing Board of Volunteers**

1.   **Boards that Follow the Leader:** the volunteer leader selects a supportive board; tend to be homogeneous, informal; board members have strong commitment to the organization's purpose, and the leader's vision but are relatively passive in their involvement; leader typically takes on most of the work; don't usually fund raise and may not develop strong ownership of the organization as a result.

2.   **Boards that Lead or Control the Organization:** formed by volunteers who work together on a mutually agreed project; very committed to the organization; generally small, homogeneous at first, willing to do tasks needed to get the organization running; play a major role in fund raising and develop a strong sense of ownership. Generally wait to hire staff because they:

1)   Fear a hired staff person may take over tasks they enjoy;
2)   Are reluctant to share the power and authority they hold;
3)   May find some board members wish to be the staff leader and be paid for their services, causing the board to hold off hiring so as not to divide the board. When staff is finally hired, the board may be ambivalent about the staff's role, wanting to maintain control but needing the staff person's help. Board members often serve staff and board functions, both working for and supervising the executive which creates difficulty for the staff. Board fails to trust staff, adding to the difficulty and frustration; this may not change until founding members leave the board.

Transition to Volunteer Governing Board: often occurs during crisis, either financial or a struggle between staff and board leadership; struggles over roles of staff and board members, increasing demands for both staff and board to do more, leads to tension, frustration and exasperation with each other. Transition often results in board members leaving, new board members joining, and a period of continued strain and intensity. Eventually, board sees the need for change and to act "more like a board," and develop shared leadership between staff and board. Results in clearer definition of board and staff roles.

Middle Stage: **The Volunteer Governing Board**
Shifts from performing operational, staff-like tasks or relative inactivity and cheerleading to the gradual assumption of governance and responsibility for the organization's well-being and longevity. Board accepts responsibility for planning and executing the organization's work, for financial oversight, and organizational integrity.

More balanced relationship between staff and board, sharing of power and authority; board chair and executive are principal leaders and assume responsibility for seeing that the work gets done. Board becomes more diverse, committees and task forces become more important, and board does less as a committee of the whole. Board accepts responsibility for organizational accountability and for raising funds. Board may become larger over time to carry out the added responsibilities for finance, policy-setting, and development. Personnel policies, job descriptions, and a personnel manual may be developed through committees. Nominating committee becomes very important and influential. Development committee becomes very important for raising funds, developing policies, strategies, and schedules for board participation in fund raising.

Appendix A continued

Director finds governing boards take more time to staff and support committees, for board orientations and regular meetings, often without immediate results. May take three years to produce a strong, new dynamic between board and staff.

Transition to the Institutional Board: as the board and organization grows, the demands increase. More need for increased fund raising by board and support by professional staff. Board must increase in size to spread the responsibility for this among more members. Results in board expansion and increased delegation to more independent committees; shift is less painful and traumatic than shift from organizing board to governing board.

Mature Stage: **The Institutional and Fund-Raising Board**

Characterized by usually diverse, large (30-60+ members) board, with capacity to give or with access to funders and donors. More prestigious, accepts fund raising role and delegates governance to executive or a management committee of the board. Large size limits boards ability to govern; more work in committees and more authority granted to executive committee. Executive committee meets regularly between board meetings to review organizational activities, finances, make necessary management decisions; keeps full board informed. Board trusts staff and assumes they will follow approved plans and operate organization responsibly.

Notes

- A modified transition from organizing through governing to institutional board may occur without the board assuming all the attributes of a working, volunteer governing board. Would require: 1) board and its members be willing to grant more power and authority to staff and give up day-to-day operational tasks; 2) board would probably continue to concentrate on fund raising as its principal task; 3) a smaller group (executive or management committee) would be delegated governance and financial and operational oversight.

- Not all boards go through this transition especially advocacy and public interest organizations.

- Not all boards want or choose to become "institutional" boards because they dislike the "bureaucratic" sound of the name which implies a "sluggish, hierarchical, unresponsive and inflexible board." Organizations that stay around tend to develop larger boards which act as an "institutional" board, like it or not.

Conclusions

- Change is necessary: boards do and must change as an organization grows. Expectations of boards "can then be sharpened and become more realistic," which requires time and effort.

- Board roles at varying stages in the organization's life are constantly evolving and changing as the organization grows.

- Large boards make it difficult for a leader to develop and maintain relationships with all board members and to ensure they feel — and are — useful, vital and involved in the organization.

- Changing board membership is the key to its health. Orderly rotation of board members as specified in the by-laws may result in both losses and gains to the organization as members cycle on and off. But change renews and revitalizes the board, keeping it current. Also, this is the only way to deal with inactive members or those who block reforms necessary for organizational growth.

Contact BoardSource (formerly NCNB) for more information. See p. 132.

Appendix B

Organizational Life Cycles of Boards

Phase of Creativity	Phase of Direction	Phase of Delegation	Phase of Consolidation
One big family working for the cause; everybody pitch in to help with everything.	Operations procedures are written and standardized; job description, personnel policies; jack of all trades disappears.	Expansion into new projects, areas; staff makes decisions; heightened motivation at lower levels.	More formal and time consuming planning; provide greater coherence, consolidation and organization.
Management Focus: Commitment to cause	Management Focus: Efficient operations	Management Focus: Expansion of market	Management Focus: Consolidate organization
Organizational Structure: Informal/family	Organizational Structure: Centralized	Organizational Structure: Decentralize/geography	Organizational Structure: Team approach
Top Management Style: Individual/entrepreneur	Top Management Style: Directive	Top Management Style: Delegate	Top Management Style: Watchdog
Rewards: Mission/meaning	Rewards: Salary/merit increases	Rewards: Mission, project bonuses	Rewards: Mission, money
Control System: Tangible results	Control System: Standards	Control System: Reports/profit center	Control System: Plans, reports
Communication: Frequent and informal	Communication: Formal/impersonal	Communication: Decentralized	Communication: Frequent staff reporting
Board: Following or Leading Volunteer (Hands-on)	Board: Volunteer Governing (Policy)	Board: Volunteer Governing to Institutional	Board: Institutional (Policy and Fund raising)
No. of employees increases; informal communications inadequate; charters and cause now insufficient to keep organization running; burdened with management responsibility and demand more structure; fears of impending bureaucracy; longing for the good old days; time to let go of your baby.	Hierarchy; lower staff not share ownership; procedures rigid; stifle initiative; demands for greater autonomy and staff participation in decisions.	Projectitis/fiefdoms rampant; top management losing control; coordination breaks down; focus on individual projects; calls for renewed sense of overall direction.	Red tape crisis; proliferation of planning; accountability systems exceed their utility.

From *"Nonprofit Overview: What Every Board Member Needs to Know."* Board of Directors Institute, LaSalle University, Nonprofit Management Development Center. Taken from *"Passages: Organizational Life Cycles,"* adapted for non-profits by Karl Mathiasen, III, Nancy Franco and Susan Gross in 1982. Used with permission. Karl Mathiasen and LaSalle University, Nonprofit Management Development Center, 215-951-1000.

Appendix C

Board of Directors Policy and Procedures Manual
Teton Science School, Kelly, WY

Contents

1. General Guidelines of the Governing Board
2. Board Responsibilities
3. Executive Director Responsibilities
4. Committees Defined
5. Evaluations
6. Officer Job Descriptions
7. Specific Guidelines for the Governing Board

1.   General Guidelines of the Governing Board

The Board has a primary responsibility to its immediate constituents, operating effectively in the interest of those connected with it as students, teachers and parents.

The Board of Directors have in their custody the integrity of the School, its standing and reputation built by the founders and by those who have labored over the years. The Board holds in trust the School's future as well as its present; the collective judgement of the Board will affect it as an institution of service and its future constituents. In short, the Directors are the protectors and the supporters of Teton Science School.

In order for a Board to function well, it requires strong staff, and it is the responsibility of the Executive Director to see that this support is provided. On the other hand, an Executive Director cannot be successful without strong Board support and it is the responsibility of the Board Chairman to see that this support is provided. The Executive Director should welcome the counsel the Board can give him/her. The Board should welcome the direction that the Executive Director can provide. The Board should hold the Executive Director fully responsible for the School's administration and should not attempt to perform any of his/her administrative responsibilities.

The Executive Director should ensure that the Board deals with major matters affecting school policy and not with trivia. The Board of Directors for its part, should seek mainly to establish objectives and policies and to insist upon the selection of competent staff. It is the Board's responsibility (assisted by the Director and staff) to define the Schools's educational objectives and to plan its administrative organization and long-range plans.

Policy Development

Policy development is the Board's most important function. At Board meetings, business decisions or policy statements will be approved after prior study of and recommendation by the relevant committee(s) if appropriate.

The need for policy statements may be recognized by either the Executive Director or Board members. Normally, when such a need arises, the responsibility for preparing the draft policy lies with the Executive Director. He/She prepares the draft and submits it to the board where it is reviewed by the proper committee. An approved draft is then recommended by the committee to the full Board which then votes on it. The resulting approved policy statement thereafter guides future actions of the Board and Executive Director. Policy statement revisions follow the same course.

Appendix C continued

2. Board Responsibilities

Understanding and acceptance of the basic division of responsibilities between Board and Executive Director is critical to ensuring an effective working relationship. The Board will limit itself to Board considerations of purpose and policy. The Executive Director is the operating head of the School. It is his/her assignment alone to run the School. Moreover, the Executive Director suggests policy; the Board establishes policy. The following is a listing of Board responsibilities:

- Support the school financially;
- Hold fiduciary responsibility for assets and funds of the School;
- Establish School policies;
- Elect new Board members as needed;
- Elect new Board officers annually;
- Hire and fire (if necessary) the Executive Director;
- Participate in fund raising events and drives;
- Participate in voluntary School service projects;
- Attend Board meetings;
- Provide counsel and support to School administration and staff as needed;
- Represent the Teton Science School regionally and nationally;
- Recruit students and donors for the School;
- Serve on at least one Board-level School committee.

3. Executive Director's Responsibilities

The Board of Directors shall hire an Executive Director who, subject to the direction and control of the Board and under provisions of the bylaws, shall have the full day-to-day responsibility for the management of the School including, but not limited to the following general areas:

- Assignment of courses of study;
- Employment and removal of staff;
- The promulgation of rules and discipline;
- Determination of standards for admission to the school
- Regular reporting to the Board of Directors and to the Executive Committee;
- Attendance of all Executive Committee meetings and Board meetings in at least an ex-officio capacity (unless the Board requests that he or she be excused);
- Establish and maintain School financial records and procedures;
- Manage the finances of the School.

The Executive Director, subject to the approval of the Board, institutes and carries out activities which are directly related to the principal purposes of the School and which will, in the judgment of the Executive Director, tend to support and enhance these purposes. The Executive Director is a member of all Board committees except when that responsibility is delegated to another staff member.

4. Committees Defined

The standing committees are very important to the smooth running of the Science School. Each Board member is expected to serve on at least one committee. They are: Executive Committee, Finance Committee, Nominating Committee (ad hoc), Development Committee, Facilities Committee, Research/Graduate Education Committee, Events Committee (ad hoc), Strategic Planning Committee (ad hoc), Safety Committee and Personnel Committee. Committees are not limited to Board members and may involve TSS staff and other qualified people when appropriate.

Appendix C continued

Each committee should have a chair, appointed by the Chairman of the Board. Each committee chair should: set agendas and times for meetings in cooperation with the Executive Director and be certain that a record of all important decisions is kept in a file maintained by the Executive Director. Also, committee chairs should regularly report at Board meetings about business handled by the committee since the last Board meeting. Chairs may appoint members to their respective committees. All committees must meet at least once prior to the annual meeting.

Executive Committee

The Executive Committee is composed of the Board offices and past Chairman of the Board with the Executive Director in attendance in an ex-officio capacity. The Executive Committee can conduct business when a quorum (3 members) of the committee are present and by a majority vote. The Board of Directors may act through and delegate all or part of their duties and powers to the Executive Committee. The Executive Committee shall: handle the business and affairs of the corporation in the interim between Board meetings, evaluate the Executive Director and set his/her salary. The Executive Committee will also help in the orientation of new Board members, monitor individual Board performance and make recommendations for removal of Board members who are not performing up to standard.

Finance Committee

The purpose of this committee is to coordinate all activities of the School relating to finances, financial planning and investments, and to help set the annual budget in cooperation with the Executive Director. The committee recommends appropriate programs and courses of action in the financial realm of the Board and has the responsibility for carrying out such programs when approved. Also, the Finance Committee is responsible for overseeing investment and protecting the assets of the School and determining the levels of insurance needed. The staff financial manager serves on this committee in an ex-officio capacity as well as the Executive Director.

Nominating Committee (ad hoc)

The Nominating Committee shall be selected from the General Board by the Executive Committee. The current Board Chairman will always serve on the Nominating Committee. The committee is appointed at a meeting prior to the annual meeting. The Nominating Committee's job is to poll the General Board for a slate of nominees when openings from expired terms on the General Board occur. Prior to the annual meeting, the Chairman of the Nominating Committee Proposes the slate of new Board members to the General Board, then puts each to a vote to determine the outcome by the annual meeting.

Development Committee

The Development Committee implements the fund raising strategies to meet the goals as established by the Board. It also advises the Director of Development regarding timing and processes surrounding the fund raising efforts of the School.

Facilities Committee

The purpose of the committee is to recommend major repairs, renovations and proposed construction to the General Board. This committee is also responsible for long range planning involving buildings and grounds. The committee is appointed by the Board Chairman and makes all recommendations to the Board of Directors after consultation with the Executive Director. Other duties of the Facilities Committee include: oversight of the School's relationship with Grand Teton National Park and Bridger-Teton National Forest, overview of the permits and agreements with GTNP and BTNF and providing counsel on the general subject of utilities and maintenance of the facility.

Appendix C continued

Research/Graduate Education Committee

The Research/Graduate Education Committee meets at least annually in order to review research conducted during the past year and further assists in the formation of research priorities for the coming year. The committee also assists the Director of Education and the Executive Director in assessing graduate program education, direction, and progress.

Events Committee (ad hoc)

The Events Committee is responsible for the planning, implementation and coordination of all School social and fund raising functions at the Board level. Some of the duties of the Events Committee include: planning of and executing the annual auction, the patrons dinner and all special gatherings or events with the exception of staff parties. The Director of Development serves on the Events Committee.

Strategic Planning Committee (ad hoc)

The purpose of the Strategic Planning Committee is to oversee the planning process. It shall meet at least once a year to re-examine the plan in existence and determine what, if any, alterations need to occur. Every three years, the entire plan will be reformulated through a strategic planning process involving staff and Board members.

Safety Committee

The purpose of the Safety Committee is to ensure that the programs and practices of the School determine a safe learning, living and working environment for students, visitors and staff. The committee shall meet at least once per year and report to the full Board as needed.

Personnel Committee

The purpose of the Personnel Committee is to review and recommend changes in salary and benefits for the staff, annually to review the Personnel Policy, review requests for family medical leave and oversee any grievance process.

5.   Evaluations

Executive Director Evaluation

The Executive Director's performance shall be evaluated annually. The evaluation shall be based upon clearly defined expectations based on specific goals and objectives. Job performance must be based upon concrete facts to the extent possible; fairness and specificity are essential. In March, written evaluations by staff, the Executive Committee and selected other directors will be complied by the Chairman and discussed with the Executive Director. Because this task is delicate, difficult and requires considerable give and take, the task of defining job performance standards is delegated to the Board's Executive Committee. The Executive Committee will make its report on the Executive Director's performance to the entire Board which may vote on the acceptability of the Director's performance.

School Evaluation

School evaluation should be on-going in order for the staff and the Board to assess School needs and accomplishments. On a regular basis, department directors will give reports at Board meetings and answer questions on their areas or special projects. Additionally, a School-wide evaluation should occur every five to ten years. Outside consultants will be hired to visit and evaluate the School. This should be done with the full understanding and cooperation of the Executive Director, who will be responsible for providing clearly defined objectives of the process.

Director's Guide to Best Practices

Evaluating the Board

Annual evaluation of the performance of the Board is very healthy. The Board Chairman should choose an instrument for evaluation and conduct a Board self-evaluation. Also, the Executive Director should be asked annually to report to the Chair his perceptions of the Boards's performance, weaknesses and strengths.

6.   Officer's Job Descriptions

Chairman of the Board

The Chairman of the Board is the chief officer of the Board. He/She is largely responsible for the openness, mutual understanding and respect which should exist between Board and Executive Director. He/She is also responsible for the smooth functioning of the Board and its committees and for seeing that School policies are soundly developed, well understood and consistently followed. In addition, he/she must see that the School's long range planning is under control, its annual and capital fund raising are well led (though not generally by the chairman), its relations with its clientele and the community are in good order, that new Board members are wisely selected, that the talents of members are well used and the Directors understand the principles by which they, as individuals, should be guided in their relations with the Executive Director, faculty members, parents, community and the Board itself. It is extremely important that the Executive Director and Chairman work closely together.

The Chairman's duties include: working with the Executive Director, setting agendas for Board meetings and running those meetings, chairing the Executive Committee and setting the tone and level of commitment for all Board members.

Vice Chairman

The Vice Chairman acts as a support and occasional replacement for the Chairman. He/She serves on the Executive Committee and helps set the tone for, and level of commitment, of other Board members. The Vice Chairman may be asked to assume duties delegated to him/her by the Chairman.

Secretary

The Secretary records the minutes for all Board meetings and all Executive Committee meetings. He/She serves as a voting member of the Executive Committee.

Treasurer

Unless otherwise stipulated, the treasurer serves as the head of the Finance Committee. He/She also serves on the Executive Committee. His/Her duties include providing financial leadership for the whole institution.

7.   Specific Guidelines for the Governing Board

New Board Member Orientation

The Nominating Committee, the Chairman of the Board and the Executive Director will responsible for instructing newly elected Board members on the functions and duties of the Board before the new Member's first Board meeting. Each new Board member will receive a Board notebook and it will be the duty of the new Board members to become conversant with he materials given him/her. The Board member will be briefed on the facilities, investment, financial management and fund raising program of the School.

Appendix C continued

Executive Director Preparation for Board Meetings
The Executive Director in consultation with the Board Chairman and the Executive Committee should draw up the agenda for the quarterly Board meetings. When possible, and particularly when a difficult decision is to be made at the Board meeting, the agenda and pertinent materials should be mailed prior to the meeting; this will enable members to make the most thoughtful decisions at the meetings. Each Board member has been provided with a Board notebook, and it is recommended that these notebooks be brought to meetings and updated regularly as materials and minutes are received. Serious decisions should never be made without adequate time for review and careful thought; whenever possible, decision making should follow the following procedure: from the Executive Committee, to relevant committee, to the Board for decision.

Voting Procedure
Any decision concerning the School or Board should follow the procedures as listed in Robert's Rules of Order.

Professionalism
Board members should always represent the School in a professional and positive manner. If there is a problem with the Executive Director, other Board members or a School policy, it must be worked out with the Chairman and/or Executive Director and other Board members; it should not be aired publicly. Internal controversy aired publicly may cause undue harm to the School. Also, if Board members wish to take a stand on controversial community issues, they must do so as individuals; they should not represent the School, or be mistaken as representing the School, unless the Board has endorsed the position by vote.

Visibility
One of the many components of strong School support is visibility. Board members are encouraged to bring visitors to the School and to attend/or lead School classes and functions.

Strategic and Long-Range Planning
Strategic planning for Teton Science School shall consist of the creation of three-year plans with a yearly review of each three-year plan. It should be developed through a strategic planning process involving input from staff and Board members.

Appendix D

Board of Trustees
Code of Ethics
The Wilderness Center, Wilmot, OH

As a Trustee of The Wilderness Center (TWC), I will:

- Do my best to ensure TWC is well-maintained, financially secure, growing and always operating in the best interests of the mission and those we serve.
- Participate actively in board meetings and actions.
- Keep well-informed of developments related to issues which may come before the board.
- Maintain the confidentiality of privileged information.
- Listen carefully to my fellow board members and respect their opinions.
- Respect and support the majority decisions of the board.
- Recognize all authority is vested in the full board only when it meets in legal session.
- Bring to the attention of the board any issues I believe will have an adverse effect on TWC or those we serve.
- Refer complaints to the proper level.
- Recognize my job is to ensure TWC is well-managed, not to manage TWC myself.
- Declare conflicts of interest between my personal life and my position on the board, and abstain from voting and participation in discussion when appropriate.
- Represent all those TWC serves and not a particular geographic area or interest group.
- Always work to learn how to better serve TWC.
- Support the Executive Director and his or her authority with staff members.

As a Trustee of The Wilderness Center, I will not:

- Use TWC for my personal or business advantage or that of my friends or relatives.
- Make unilateral public statements that can be construed as TWC policies or positions.

Signature:_____   Date:_____

Appendix E

Conflict of Interest Policy for Board Members
Teton Science School, Kelly, WY

Board members or Board committee members of Teton Science School shall not use their positions, or the knowledge gained therefrom, in such a manner that a conflict between the interest of the school or any of its affiliates and their personal interest arises.

Each Board member or Board committee member has a duty to place the interest of the Teton Science School foremost in any dealings with the school and has a continuing responsibility to comply with the requirements of this policy.

The conduct of personal business between any Board or committee member and the Teton Science School above $2,000.00 is subject to review by the Finance Committee.

Board or committee may not obtain for themselves, their relatives, or their friends any material benefit from their association with the school. The Executive Director is a qualified exception to this rule.

If a Board member or Board committee member has an interest in a proposed transaction with the school, he or she must make full disclosure of such interest before any discussion or negotiation of such transaction. This would include a significant personal financial interest in the transaction or in any organization involved in the transaction, or holding a position as trustee, director, or officer in any such organization.

Any Board or committee member who is aware of his or her own potential conflict of interest with respect to any matter coming before the Board, Executive Director or a committee may participate in the discussion but shall not vote in connection with the matter.

Appendix F

Position Description
Member of the Board of Trustees
The Wilderness Center, Wilmot, OH

Collective Board Responsibilities

- Determine TWC's mission and purposes.
- Select the Executive Director.
- Support the Executive Director and review his or her performance.
- Ensure effective organizational planning.
- Ensure adequate resources.
- Manage resources effectively.
- Determine and monitor TWC's programs and services.
- Enhance TWC's public image.
- Serve as a court of appeal.
- Assess Board of Trustees performance.

Responsibilities of a Member of the Board of Trustees

- Attend regular and special Board meetings and participate in the proceedings.
- Prepare for Board meetings by reading material distributed prior to the meeting.
- Serve on at least one committee and actively participate in the committee meetings.
- Maintain knowledge of current programs and staff of TWC.
- Make personal financial contributions to TWC.
- Assist in the Center's fundraising efforts.
- Share resources and talents with the organization including expertise, contacts for financial support and contacts for in-kind contributions.
- Serve as an ambassador to the community.
- Be accessible to staff and other Board members as needed.
- Fulfill commitments withing the agreed deadlines.
- Be loyal to the organization.
- Hold in confidence any information given to the Board of Trustees.
- Comply with the Code of Ethics.
- Identify individuals for potential membership on the Board of Trustees and its committees.
- Come to The Wilderness Center regularly.

Appendix G

Board Membership Responsibilities
Teton Science School, Kelly, WY

Meeting Attendance: Board members are encouraged to attend all five annual Board meetings (January, March, May, July, October) and appropriate committee meetings.

Committee Service: Each member of the Board is expected to be a participant on at least one of the TSS Board Committees. These are listed and explained in the TSS Board notebook.

Fundraising and Development: TSS must raise approximately 40% of its annual revenue and additional funds for special and capital projects. One of the functions of the Board is to support this process through committee work on the Development or Auction Committees, assisting in personalizing annual giving letters, personally soliciting for donations, introducing potential donors to TSS programs and mission, or direct contribution according to ability.

Special Events: Board member attendance at the annual Patron's Dinner (June) and the fundraising auction (late August) is strongly encouraged. Your presence helps ensure a successful event. In addition Board members are frequently offered the opportunity to sponsor a special educational or fundraising event.

Public Relations: All Board Members represent the school and can help promote it through speaking frequently of it to community members, potential participants and donors. A supply of School literature will be given to all Members for distribution.

Knowledge of TSS Programs: Board attendance at TSS programs is welcomed. Any Member may sit in on any TSS program at any time. It is appropriate to notify the Executive Director or Director of Education prior to such a visit. The evening speaker series and adult seminars are ideal ways for Board Members to participate in a TSS program.

Appendix H

No Board of Directors is Like Any Other:
Some Maxims About Boards

By Karl Mathiasen, III
Reprinted with permission
Management Assistance Group, 1555 Connecticut Avenue, Third Floor, Washington, DC 20036
202-659-1963

INTRODUCTION

In speaking about boards at seminars and workshops a number of useful generalizations have gradually been developing in my mind and this paper is an attempt to make these generalizations, or maxims, more generally available.

It should be pointed out, however, that the title itself is in some senses contradictory and that the implied contradiction is intentional. First, no board of directors is like any other and my own service on more than twenty-five boards of directors in the nonprofit world has impressed that fact firmly on my mind. But, second, there are some broad dynamics which affect all boards, or nearly all, which can help board and staff members identify the differences among the boards they serve or serve on. This paper lists some of these common dynamics in an effort both to help people become better board members and to help staff understand their boards better. The list continues to expand and any additional maxims which occur to readers would be most gratefully received.

SOME MAXIMS ABOUT BOARDS

It's a funny thing, but boards of directors generally have no memory worth mentioning. Staffs are so preoccupied with their work that they are continually surprised by a board which seems to have irresponsible lapses of memory. Exasperating as it may be for staffs, it is a fact of life that volunteer, very part-time boards of directors do not remember well what happened at the last meeting, much less what they agreed to

do several months ago.

Boards of Directors normally do not read. If a staff's solution to a board's lapse of memory is to provide more and more material, then the agency is in real trouble. The increasing pile of paper will become ever more oppressive to the part-time, volunteer board members and can lead to absences from board meetings. The paper will be put aside to read "sometime," yet that sometime does not occur. In short, a heavy paper flow is one way to incapacitate and to lose board members: "I really haven't read everything and I don't know what's going on so I'd better not go to the board meeting." Some of the hardest work a staff has to do — and this task normally falls to the executive director — is to reduce the information flow to the minimum the board has to know to function and to govern. The board chair can be helpful in assessing the board's needs and also in setting the agenda which will permit the board to concentrate its time and energy on the most critical issues.

Staffs think that their boards "must" know more and do more than they will actually know or do. Staffs are offended by boards that doze and doodle during long reports and endless agendas, but the fact is that boards can only be expected to absorb and digest so much information and to conduct so much business. Committees, board committees, can often delve a lot more deeply into issues, but board members are busy people, they have short attention spans and resent the pressure of endless agendas. Staffs need to ask themselves, "Has our agency ever really suffered, have catastrophes really occurred because an agenda was not completed at one

Appendix H continued

meeting?" If the answer is yes, then the agenda arrangement would seem to be the problem. Avoid agendaitis and put first things first.

There is no right time to bring a new policy or new program to the board. It is always too early or too late. If a staff is considering a new venture and brings it to the board before it has been thought through and developed, the board will look puzzled, often become irritated and will request the chair to ask the staff to bring only those things to the board that it has worked through so as not to waste the board's time. If the staff does that and presents the board with a coherent new policy or activity, one to which the staff has by then become terribly attached, then the board will see itself as a rubber stamp board which is being presented with a *fait accompli*. A good board committee structure can help with preliminary reviews, particularly if there is an opportunity for the staff to bring "docket items" to the committee: these would include new or different issues that don't quite fit within past policies or programs but which have attracted the staff's attention as being important and possibly appropriate issues for the agency.

It is a myth that boards make policies and staffs carry them out. If boards "make policy," they do it very badly unless the staff has been involved in the process from the beginning. Staff should be expected to initiate policy development, present it to the board, listen— really listen — to the board, revise the policies in response to the board or withdraw them and go back to the drawing board. Staffs must take the responsibility for proposing, delving into the board's mind and shepherding the policy-making process to final approval. If the board makes its own policy without staff involvement, the agency inevitably will have two policies: one — the board's — which the board believes the staff is carrying out, and the other — the staff's — which the staff is

actually carrying out.

The two most important people in any nonprofit organization are the executive director or president and the board chair. If one or the other is weak, so probably is the organization. Strong executive directors often hope and conspire with the nominating committee to assure that the board's chair won't be "too" strong. Strong board chairs often hope and try to influence the search committee, to find executive directors who are not going to grab all the power. The agency's best interest will be served, however, if strength on the board seeks countervailing strength on staff so that both the board and staff can feel and be powerful.

By-laws ought to be very general in nature; but they should always include a provision for rotation of board members. By-laws are boring; one certain way to lull a board into a stupor is to engage in the lengthy and annoying process of amending by-laws. To avoid doing this, by-laws ought to be written in very general, lay person terms. Nevertheless, one provision is essential if the agency is to be able to move ahead. Every board needs new blood just as much as it needs the opportunity to dispose of old-timers who have served their time. Regrettably, there is no "nice" way to ask old-timers off the board, and no polite way for them to ask to get off the board without appearing to be unsupportive or in some way disapproving. If by-laws provide for one mandatory year off the board after two terms of three years each, or some such arrangement, then the embarrassments can be avoided. If the board member is really valuable, the member can be re-nominated a year hence. The odds are, however, that simply won't happen. There are few, if any, indispensable board members.

The most important board committee is the Nominating Committee. While it is often appointed at the last minute, just before the annual meeting and instructed to find "some good people," the Nominating Committee should be a permanent committee with year-long responsibilities. These responsibilities include development of a board profile which will graphically display the types of people needed on the board, given the board's purposes and goals over time. The board's needs would be described in terms of age, sex, race, experiences, qualities, skills, educational background, community representation, etc. Current board membership can then be matched with this graph, indicating where the gaps in membership are. The collection of names then begins, with open and frank discussion of each person in terms of the profile and what their references say, not write, about them. Are they people who are willing to commit time and effort to a board, do they have the talent to work well with others in a board situation, and are they interested in the work of this particular agency? The names of all those not nominated ought to be saved and reviewed again next year when the rotation process may well call for people with their talents. Finally, there ought to be a frank discussion with each candidate outlining the board's expectations of this person and eliciting the potential nominee's expectations and interests in serving on the board. If all are in agreement, it may be wise to draw up a contract between the organization and the board members so that mutual expectations are clear to all.

A formal board orientation process is a necessary part of every board member's effective work. The chair and the executive the board member's special skills and interests. New board members should be given board manuals/handbooks which include the articles of incorporation director, separately or together, ought to meet with a new member to explain and clarify the work of the agency, to provide an overview of the organization's history and to find out about and by-laws, the most recent audit and recent financial reports, the minutes of the last several meetings and the most useful and

descriptive program statements available to the organization. At the first board meeting for new board members, all board members, starting with the older members, might be asked to articulate why they decided to serve on this board; what attracts them to the organization and what role do they see themselves playing? While this may seem a bit contrived, it often reveals some surprising values, attachments and interests which can clarify and improve the quality of board meetings and board member participation.

The principle of the last two points is that while a wise, careful selection process and a good orientation program are hard, they are a lot easier than trying to train a bad board so that it can become a good board.

If a board is ineffective and feels itself to be powerless, there are two general reasons for this: a founder leader or a controlling Executive Committee. In the first instance, someone, most often the founder leader, is seen as being so strong, so competent and committed, so much the owner, that he or she will do everything needed to make the organization's work go forward. The board quickly figures out that what it forgets to do or simply doesn't do will be done by the leader. Tasks that the leader hands out are quickly handed back. Unless the leader is willing to risk failure or the dropping of some critical tasks, the board will probably never learn that it must work. If a strong leader can't let anything fail, that strong leader must know that she/he is the root cause of the board's sense of powerlessness.

In the second instance, a strong Executive Committee can quickly become the governing board of an agency. The board members who are not members of the Executive Committee will then know themselves to be a rubber stamp. An Executive Committee ought to restrict itself to acting in true emergencies between board meetings and to the careful preparation of a useful and meaningful agenda for the board meetings.

Appendix H continued

Boards do not raise money unless they raise it for themselves. Often executive directors or agency leaders make the statement that "my board doesn't raise money for my program." Board members, like most of us, do not raise money for something in which they are not invested, to which they are not committed, in which they are not involved and over which they do not have some authority and control. If boards perceive that the program belongs to a strong leader, they will expect that leader to raise the money for that program. Only as a strong leader is willing to relinquish power and authority to a board will the board begin to translate its sense of ownership into a sense of responsibility for finding the resources needed to keep the program going. Even then, the staff must remember that fund-raising is a staff, as well as, a board function. If you are the leader of an organization, paid or unpaid, you may need to spend 50 percent of your time doing fund-raising, both direct fund-raising and supporting the board in that work. The latter involves an enormous amount of time coaxing, guiding and stroking the board so that it feels supported in its fund-raising efforts and feels that it can be successful.

In the nonprofit world, there will always be some tension between the board and the staff. Board members need to remind themselves that this is the way it has been set up. A staff of skilled professional workers, paid or unpaid, must interact with a governing board which is most often volunteer and generalist in nature. The tension will be there. Unless the tension becomes destructive, unrelieved and unbearable, it is probably best to leave things be. In other words, be satisfied if things work reasonably well and remember the old adage, "If it ain't broke, don't fix it."

The behavior of a board will be in part a reflection of how the organization began, who began it and how the initial leader/leaders ran it. Obviously, the impact of a board's beginnings will be more profound and noticeable in an organization's early years; nevertheless, the initial dynamic may linger for years and profoundly affect the way boards operate. If the organization has been founded by one person who remains as chair of the board, then that organization is almost bound to have a strong, leading board from which the staff will take its cues and its sense of direction. If the founder becomes the staff director then the dynamic will be reversed and the board will be a following board. These dynamics will continue surely as long as the founders remain in their roles and perhaps well beyond as boards will often try to replicate old patterns of operation when choosing new leadership.

A note of caution: These dynamics need not flow from some malevolent desire on the part of the founder to retain power or control. Often founders will honestly try to share power. But giving up and sharing power is one of the hardest tasks humans face and, moreover, boards often find great comfort in following a leader and do not want to have the authority or the responsibilities called for in the sharing of leadership.

A board's behavior also reflects where the organization is in terms of its age and growth. At one extreme, an organizing board is usually small, its work is often ambiguous and thus very hard, frustrating in its lack of clarity, frequently very unrewarding, and usually not very prestigious. At the other extreme, a mature agency will have defined board and staff roles, staff leaders will normally be strong, the chair will also be strong, and the board will help raise funds for the organization. There will often be a strong Executive Committee which manages the agency's affairs, and the board is usually quite content as it

Director's Guide to Best Practices

is pleasant and prestigious to serve on a mature board with one's peers.

A board's behavior will often be a reflection of a recent crisis or radical change. The loss of a strong leader, particularly the founder, will dramatically affect how the board works, often causing confusion and distress. A financial crisis will often cause the board to focus almost exclusively on issues of financial control and on financial reports, with substantive issues receiving little useful attention. A change in an agency's funding environment will often panic the agency and fund-raising may become a continuing and alarming focus for a board's work over a considerable period of time.

These last three points simply emphasize the importance of knowing the history of the agency and of the board of that agency. Knowing how the agency was founded, understanding how it has grown and aged, and being aware of recent cataclysmic events will help explain a board's behavior for new board members.

The Board of Directors, its strength, involvement and commitment is probably the most important determinant of whether the organization stays alive.
Often the question arises, "Why bother spending so much time on building a good board of directors?" The simple answer is that a good board will probably make the difference between an agency dying when the strong leader leaves or going on beyond that loss.

No board is like any other. To reiterate, this is the final and most important maxim, yet one easily forgotten by even the most experienced board member. We all want boards to act like and to be like the other boards we have served on, but while all boards have similar characteristics, the dynamic of each board is different. In most instances, the dynamic is appropriate and adequate for that board; one that has emerged naturally from its history. There is not, after all, one single correct relationship between a board and a staff. Although the one question most often asked in seminars about boards of directors is, "What is the appropriate relationship between the board and the staff?", there must be dozens of appropriate responses and relationships.

When this paper is presented to the board and staff of an agency, both board and staff members will recognize the truth and value of most of the maxims, because of their experiences elsewhere, but they will question the applicability of the maxims to "our" agency. While people enjoy reading or hearing about general board behavior, they will often turn and ask, "Why is this material being presented to this board and staff?" Interesting, isn't it?

Appendix I

Board Committees

Executive Committee

The executive committee is composed of board officers and chaired by the board chairperson. It recommends actions for approval to the full board and is empowered to make decisions and take action on behalf of the board between meetings. The executive committee is central to the effective operation of the committee structure, the board, and the entire organization. The executive committee usually evaluates the director's performance and serves as the director's principal support and sounding board. The director works closely and frequently with the executive committee.

Development Committee

The development committee inspires and leads the board toward reaching their annual and long range fund raising goals. They plan, guide, and implement the board's development efforts and work closely with the finance committee. This committee establishes guidelines for board giving. It leads the board but should not assume responsibility for all fund raising to be shared by the full board. The director works with the committee to plan funding needs, set funding targets, identify prospects, and solicit funds. If a development director is on staff, he or she plans overall fund raising and, along with the director, serves on this committee.

Finance Committee

The finance committee oversees the organization's assets and budget, and reviews monthly financial reports. This committee generally is chaired by the board treasurer and includes the director, staff finance director or officer and development director if these positions are part of the staff. The finance committee advises and reviews budgets which are generally developed by staff. Financial reports may be generated either by staff or an accounting firm and are reviewed and reported to the full board by the finance committee. This committee works with other board committees (executive, development, audit, strategic planning, and investment). The committee may handle audits and investments or establish separate committees for this.

Nominating Committee

The nominating committee identifies, recruits and recommends a slate of board nominees to the board or membership for approval. This committee is often the most important and influential because its recommendations ultimately affect the success or failure of the organization. The nominating committee determines a plan for seeking new members, solicits board candidates, meets and interviews them, and recommends candidates for approval. The committee may also be responsible for organizing continuing education programs for the board to enhance their knowledge of governance responsibilities. In some organizations, the nominating committee evaluates individual members and the board as a whole.

The director works closely with this committee to facilitate and contribute to the nominating process, identifying organizational needs, recommending candidates, cultivating prospects, and conducting new member orientation.

From *Nonprofit Board Committees: How To Make Them Work*, by Ellen Cochran Hirzy; a publication of the National Center for Nonprofit Boards (NCNB). Copyright © 1993 by NCNB. Used with permission. Contact BoardSource (formerly NCNB) for new, updated and expanded titles. See Contacts, p. 132.

Appendix J

Tips for Successful Committees

1. Develop written statements of committee responsibilities, guidelines, and annual goals, and review and revise them periodically.

2. Appoint an effective chairperson who clearly understands the organization, the role of the committee, and the importance of conscientious committee leadership.

3. Choose committee members whose experience, skills, and interests support the goals of the committee and complement the abilities of their fellow members.

4. Create written job descriptions for committee members. State expectations clearly. Distribute tasks reasonably among members.

5. Arrive at a clear understanding of the relationships and respective roles of board, committees, chief executive officer, and other staff.

6. Give committee members thorough information to aid in their decision making.

7. Make timely reports to the board on committee actions and recommendations, allowing the opportunity for members to consider the information before discussion.

8. Set terms of service for committee members to ensure new perspectives and to give board members the opportunity to contribute in different areas.

9. Set meeting schedules well in advance, in consultation with members. Make effective use of meeting time by sending materials and an agenda to members well ahead of scheduled meetings and by moving through the agenda in a business-like way.

10. Schedule an orientation for new committee members.

11. Conduct an annual evaluation to assess the committee's accomplishments in relation to its goals.

12. Recognize and express appreciation for the achievements of committee members.

Taken from *Nonprofit Board Committees: How to Make Them Work,* by Ellen Cochran Hirzy; a publication of the National Center for Nonprofit Boards (NCNB). Copyright © 1993 by NCNB. Used by permission. Contact BoardSource (formerly NCNB) for new, updated and expanded titles. See Contacts, p. 132.

Appendix K

Board Member Recruiting Matrix

Use this matrix to recruit new board members for your organization. Incorporate current and desired skills, experience, backgrounds, and other criteria you seek. Analyze current strengths and weaknesses, and anticipate present and future organizational needs.

SKILLS AND EXPERIENCE

MEMBER/ PROSPECT NAME									COMMENTS
FUNDRAISING									
PLANNING									
COMMUNITY CONNECTIONS									
MARKETING PUBLIC RELATIONS									
FINANCE/ ACCOUNTING									
PERSONNEL									
EDUCATION									
LEGAL									
DESIGN/ CONSTRUCTION									
GENDER M/F									
RACE/ETHNICITY/ DISABILITY									
OCCUPATION									
AGE									
QUALITIES									
PERSONAL STYLE									

Appendix L

Checklist
Conducting More Effective Board Meetings

Reprinted from Board Member July/August 1997, Volume 6, Number 7.
A publication of the National Center for Nonprofit Boards (NCNB)* Used with permission.

A nonprofit board's effectiveness depends largely on how its meetings are conducted. Long, rambling "marathons" waste members' time and often accomplish little. Strict, authoritarian-style meetings can leave board members feeling disempowered and manipulated. A board wishing to improve its meetings can do several things before, during, and after every meeting, including:

❑ **Establish a clear purpose.** For each board meeting, specify the purpose in terms of expected outcomes. Example: to review and approve revised fund-raising policies. In examining the purpose, ask whether the board meeting is the right forum. Is the issue more appropriate for committee work?

❑ **Prepare, prepare, prepare.** Develop a prioritized agenda that allows a realistic amount of time to cover the most important issues, and schedule them first. Send detailed information to members in advance to review.

❑ **Appoint a facilitator**, under certain circumstances, to help prepare the agenda and conduct the meeting process - someone other than the board chair/president or executive director. The facilitator remains "issue neutral" and serves the board by encouraging participation, adhering to time parameters, and keeping the board focused.

❑ **Maintain focus during the meeting** by managing time and by deferring side or tangential issues until later. Remind members often of the purpose and make sure that discussions stay focused to accomplish it.

❑ **Include activities to foster fellowship** among board members. Consider designating the first 15 minutes of each meeting as unstructured fellowship time.

❑ **Strive for consensus on decisions.** This does not mean forcing some members to "cave in" or severely compromise their position. It does mean seeking a win/win outcome that is acceptable to every board member.

❑ **Seek completion.** Every decision should be coupled with action steps: who will do what by when. Another aspect of completion is to tie up "loose ends" such as deciding how and when to address side issues that were deferred.

❑ **Critique the board's meeting performance.** This includes acknowledging things that worked and identifying areas for improvement.

Adapted from *First Aid For Meetings* by Charlie Hawkins, available in bookstores or by calling 888-285-4295.
*Contact BoardSource (formerly NCNB) for new, updated and expanded titles. See Contacts, p. 132..

Appendix M

The Action Agenda
by Tim Merriman, Ph.D.

Reprinted from Directions, Volume 4, #1, January/February, 1994
Association of Nature Center Administrators, Dayton, OH

One of the most frustrating experiences of a non-profit executive has to be the common phenomena that can occur in a business meeting of the governance board - wandering without focus. A board president who lacks the meeting management skills to keep a meeting on track will allow it to consume incredible quantities of time on an issue of no importance and leave a critical budget or operational decision to be made in too little time or delayed to a future meeting. The executive usually does not control this process but the organization can be protected from meeting mismanagement by coaching for the use of an approach that mitigates the problem.

The Action Agenda is a valuable tool in meeting management. It is based by design on:

- prioritized agenda items in 3 categories;
- strict time control during the meeting.

Agenda:

Action items - These require definite decisions to be made during the meeting. They should command the most time and should be in order from most important to least important. Encouraging board members to have motions written out in advance can mitigate the time consuming process of framing a new motion during the meeting. The latter would be appropriate in the discussion mode but not during handling of action items. These are those critical decisions that cannot be delayed. It is reasonable to set time limits on comments before voting on action items.

Discussion items - These may involve a motion or decision but might also result in any decision being held over for a future meeting. They should also be in priority order from most to least important. Time should be limited for each discussion item at the beginning.

Information items - These should be very short presentations of information without any discussion.

Encouraging committee reports and staff reports to be presented in writing during this time can cause this to be very fast and efficient.

Time control in this entire process is critical. The chairperson or president must set limits on discussion of even the most controversial issues to insure that a timely decision is made. Asking people to not repeat the points made by others is helpful. If you agree with someone else's comments it is easy to say just that. If the chair is not a good timekeeper, encourage her or him to appoint another member to watch the clock and help pace the meeting.

Setting a finish time for the meeting and sticking to it is also critical in this agenda. The group learns that everyone will leave at the announced time and they all become participants in holding discussion down to salient points. Those items that do not get covered will simply be deferred to the next meeting. That is the reason for written informational reports which can be handed out without explanation.

One important matter when using the Action Agenda is to review agenda item placement at the beginning of the meeting. That can be done by asking, "Do we have a motion for certain for each Action Item?" Or you can ask, "Are any of our discussion items really reports?" Moving agenda items at the beginning can be very time saving, especially if you have a particularly long agenda for the meeting.

Controversial issues can often be held to a specific time allotment by asking that each member hold comments to 2 minutes and then take comments on a round robin basis allowing members to pass on the first go-round if unready to comment. The second round for those who passed will usually ensure that everyone gets input. It also keeps the aggressive members who usually dominate commentary from overwhelming others through repetitious remarks.

Appendix M continued

The Action Agenda can radically reduce meeting time for organizations that meet infrequently. I presided over a national organization for several years that held bi-annual meetings. The meetings often had over 100 agenda items and meetings usually lasted for 22 to 24 hours. That meant that we would fly into a meeting location and stay in the meeting room for the entire weekend and often some of our most important discussions were held when the fatigue factor could affect the quality of decision making. We put in place the Action Agenda and reduced meetings to 6 to 8 hours after a year or so of experimentation with the process. The free time at meeting sites permitted more social interaction and that was very constructive for informal resolution of controversial issues.

Organizational meetings are not the only settings for Action Agendas. The weekly staff meeting can also be made more concise through this process. Having a one hour meeting each week that ends on time is much less frustrating and maintains a high quality communications environment. Hold the meeting even if key members are out of town to allow everyone to continue to communicate about weekly business.

If the person controlling the meeting is really the problem, get someone to suggest the Action Agenda who is perceived by the leader as a peer. Some chairpersons and executives do not take suggestions well unless it comes from a person of equal status in the organization.

Using the Action Agenda layout without the control of time may only serve to frustrate you. Have your time-keeper monitor the next meeting or two you have without time control and see how much time you devote to the issues of substance compared to information items. That often reveals how critical it is to control the meeting up front with the agenda and time constraints.

The Action Agenda does not resolve all meeting problems but with a little practice it will place you on a better track for greater efficiency. Doing first things first is always the right way to do business. The quality of work done in meetings often relates directly to the planning quality in preparing for the meeting. Try the Action Agenda for one year and see the difference. You'll have more time to move that stack of untouched paperwork on your desk into the recycling bin. Good luck!

Appendix N

SAMPLE BOARD AGENDA

(Name of Organization)
Board Meeting Agenda
(Month, Day, Year)
(Location)
(Planned Starting Time to Ending Time)

Activity	Action
1. Minutes from previous meeting	Approval
2. Chief Executive's Report	Discussion
3. Finance Committee's Report	Approve Budget Changes
4. Development Committee's Report	Approve Fundraising Plan
5. Stewardship Committee's Report	Approve Facilities Plan Review Master Plan
6. Board Development Committee	Approve Plans for Retreat Adopt Resolution to Change Bylaws
7. Other Business Old New Announcements	
8. Roundtable Evaluation of Meeting	
9. Review of Actions from Meeting	
10. Adjourn	

Appendix O

The Board's Role in Monitoring Its Own Functioning and Activities: Areas for a Governing Board to Discuss

Reprinted with permission. LaSalle University, Nonprofit Management Development Center, 215-951-1701.

A. **Board Meeting Content**
1. Are board meetings effective? Are we talking about the right things?
2. Does the board make or monitor policies (as opposed to re-doing the committee's or staff's work, or "out-exec"ing the executive director)?
3. Does the board focus much of its attention on long-term, significant policy issues rather than short-term administrative matters? Are overarching organizational issues discussed by the full board?
4. Does the board have too much/too little/enough information?

B. **Board Meeting Processes (procedures and decision-making)**
1. Does the board obtain a quorum regularly at board meetings?
2. Are we satisfied with the way decisions are made? Does the board actively participate in the decision-making process? Is the board's decision-making process an effective and useful one? Is there too much or adequate participation and discussion? How could it be improved?
3. Does the board differentiate between information presented: what is just information presented purely to inform us? What is information presented so that we can provide counsel or advice to the presenter? What is information we need to act upon to assist us in task implementation? What is information presented in order for us to make decisions or policy?
4. Does the board agree to and adhere to Roberts Rules of Order/parliamentary procedure, consensus, or some other agreed-upon decision-making procedure?
5. Are board minutes accurate, helpful and mailed in timely fashion?

C. **Board/Management Volunteer Responsibilities and Boundaries**
1. What has been the historical role of the board? What is the current role of the board?
2. What has been the relation between the staff and the board? How well-understood and appropriate are the boundaries?
3. Is there balanced involvement in day to day functions?
4. Is there sufficient involvement in policy functions? To what extent have board members demonstrated the ability to make policy and govern?
5. Are there clearly defined, written general board responsibilities? Committee job descriptions? Individual board member agreements? Executive director job description?
6. Have the bylaws been reviewed in past 24 months?
7. Does the board have, or has it discussed not having, Directors and Officers Liability insurance?
8. Does the board understand its legal and fiduciary responsibilities?
    a. **Support and Review the Executive Director**
        i. Is there a climate of mutual trust and respect between the board and executive director?
        ii. Does the board give the executive director enough authority and responsibility to lead and manage the organization successfully?
        iii. Does the board evaluate the performance of the executive director annually in an objective manner, based on performance goals delineated in the organization's strategic plan?
    b. **Monitor the Organization's Services; Engage in Strategic Planning**
        i. Does the board have sufficient knowledge of this organization's program and service issues? Does the board know the strengths and weaknesses of each major program?
        ii. Has the board been adequately involved in developing and monitoring a comprehensive organizational plan? Does the board periodically consider adopting new programs, and modifying or discontinuing current programs?

Appendix O continued

        iii.   Does the board have a strategic vision of how the organization should be evolving over the next 3-5 years?

        iv.   Does the board periodically engage in a strategic planning process to consider how the organization should meet new opportunities and challenges?

    c.   **Raise Money**

        i.   What is the board's role in fundraising? Is it effective and adequate?

        ii.   Does the board have a clear policy on each individual's responsibility to raise money?

        iii.   Does each board member contribute financially?

        iv.   Do board members actively ask others in the community to provide financial support to the organization?

    d.   **Ensure Effective Fiscal Management**

        i.   What is the board's role in financial oversight and financial control systems'? Is it effective?

        ii.   Does the board thoroughly discuss the annual operating budget before approving it?

        iii.   Does the board receive and review financial reports on a regular basis that are understandable, accurate and timely?

        iv.   Does the board review historical financial performance vs budgeted performance at meetings? Are variances accounted for?

        v.   Does the board require and review an annual independent audit and consider the auditor's recommendations?

    e.   **Enhance the Organization's Public Image**

        i.   Do board members talk about the organization to key people?

        ii.   Does the board understand who can serve as official spokesperson for the organization?

        iii.   Has the board approved an effective marketing and public relations strategy for the organization?

D.   **Committee Structure and Composition**

    1.   What is the board committee structure? Is it effective? Are there permanent functions for financial oversight, fundraising, strategic planning and evaluation, and board development?

    2.   Are committee meetings scheduled regularly? Is there majority attendance?

    3.   Does each committee submit a written yearly work plan to the full board?

    4.   Is committee work done in committee, and recommendations brought to the board for action?

    5.   Are there sufficient numbers of board members and non-board members serving on committees?

    6.   Are there advisory boards with a clear, separate purpose from the board of directors?

E.   **Board Composition (expertise, affiliations, numbers of members)**

    1.   Does the board contain a sufficient range of expertise and experience to make it an effective governing body? Has the board profile been determined, currently and ideally? How close is the board to representing its ideal?

    2.   Is the board nominating/development function active year round? Does the board regularly identify candidates who offer the characteristics needed to strengthen board composition?

    3.   Does the nominating/board development committee assure timely, comprehensive orientation of new board members (including board member responsibilities, and important program and administrative information)? Is there an accurate, sufficiently comprehensive board manual given to each board member?

    4.   Is the board rotation policy effective?

F.   **Board Self-evaluation**

    1.   How effective is the board as a whole? Does monitoring and feedback happen in a regular, objective fashion, formally and informally?

    2.   How effective is each board member individually? How does monitoring and feedback happen?

G.   **Summary of board initiatives for this year**

Contacts

Aspen Publishers, Inc.
200 Orchard Ridge Drive, Suite 200
Gaithersburg, MD 20878
800-234-1660 (customer service)
800-638-8437 (orders)
800-901-9075 (fax)
www.aspenpub.com

Board of Directors Institute (BODI)
LaSalle University
Nonprofit Management Development Center
1900 W. Olney Avenue
Philadelphia, PA 19141-1199
215-951-1701

Jossey-Bass, Inc., Publishers, a John Wiley Company
350 Sansome Street
San Francisco, CA 94104
800-956-7739
800-605-2665 (fax)
www.josseybass.com

BoardSource*
1828 L Street NW, Suite 900
Washington, DC 20036-5114
202-452-6262
800-883-6262
www.boardsource.org

* Formerly National Center for Nonprofit Boards (NCNB)

Reviewers

Andy Brown, Battle Creek Nature Center, Prince Frederick, MD
Lynn Corliss, Center for Coastal Ecology, Beaufort, SC
Ken Finch*, Fontenelle Forest Association, Bellevue, NE
Peggy Hunt, Pioneers Park Nature Center, Lincoln, NE
Greg Lee*, Dodge Nature Center, West St. Paul, MN
Bob Marye*, Louisiana Nature Center, New Orleans, LA
Robert Mercer, Silver Lake Nature Center, Bristol, PA
Carl Palmer*, Ogden Nature Center, Ogden, UT
Rich Patterson, Indian Creek Nature Center, Cedar Rapids, IA
Tim Sandsmark*, Greenway and Nature Center of Pueblo, Pueblo, CO
Christine Turnbull*, The Friends of Hunt Hill Audubon Sanctuary, Inc., Sarona, WI
Robert Venner, DeGraaf Nature Center, Holland, MI
Pat Welch, Pine Jog Environmental Education Center, West Palm Beach, FL
Brian Winslow, Asbury Woods Nature Center, Erie, PA

* Former director

CHAPTER 4: STAFF

An Organization's Greatest Asset

People are an organization's greatest asset and this is especially true of staff. Staff members plan, conduct, and carry out programs and activities. They represent the organization to its constituents on a daily basis, and provide important services and support to customers, visitors, members, donors, and the general public.

Most organizations operate with paid staff who, in partnership with the director, board members, and volunteers, work to achieve the organization's mission.

Organizational Culture

Each organization is a unique entity with a distinctive organizational culture. This is shaped in part by regional and community differences, the people who utilize the programs and services the organization provides, and the people who work there.

Mission, vision, and values define an organization and attract people to it.

- *Mission* describes the reason the organization exists and attracts people who share a belief in its purpose and goals.
- *Vision* describes what the organization will be if it succeeds in implementing strategies and inspires people who want to be part of that future.
- *Values* describe the way an organization treats people and conducts business, appealing to people's desire to be treated well and to work in a quality environment.

An organization's culture also includes distinctive features or methods of operating that distinguish one organization from another. Urban or rural? Casual or formal? Regular hours or flexible schedule? Teams or hierarchy? People choose the places, people, and causes that resonate with their own beliefs and values.

The culture may be its strength or weakness, attracting some and turning off others. Organizational culture can be changed, but it may not happen quickly or at all, depending on who desires the change. It can be challenging at best, difficult at worst, and met with resistance if changes are made without staff involved in the process. Employees who contribute to defining the culture will be more receptive than those who are simply expected to make changes they may not desire. **See Leadership Chapter, Appendix A, Part III, p. 26.**

Human Diversity

Staff members are as diverse as the organizations that employ them. Professional, educational, cultural, and social differences found in the staff add richness and variety to any organization. It also challenges directors and their staffs to develop, practice and implement increased awareness, acceptance and tolerance for others. **See Practice 11, p. 162-164.**

Each director brings an individual style and approach to working with staff, adding to the human diversity mix. While the best practices in this chapter offer guidelines for directors, staff members are individuals who require and deserve individual treatment.

Staff Turnover

Staff changes occur throughout the work force for a variety of reasons – new opportunities, family responsibilities, change in work hours or conditions, a move, a planned job ending, or dismissal.

Directors who help employees advance their professional and personal goals are better prepared for these changes. View change as positive while acknowledging the loss of a valued employee or the separation from a disgruntled one. Staff continuity lends stability to an organization but it can also lead to stagnation. Cultivate fresh perspectives and new ideas in all employees.

Use the best practices to assess how your organization values employees. Unclear duties and responsibilities, overwork, or a negative environment may lead to discord and staff turnover.

Legal Requirements for Employers

Employers are required by federal and state laws to inform employees about their legal rights. Contact federal and state employment offices for current materials, posters, and other information to display in the work place.

It is your responsibility to stay up-to-date and comply with all federal, state or local laws regarding employment. Have all personnel policies reviewed by an attorney or other professional knowledgeable in employment law before the board authorizes any policy revisions or additions. **See Practice 15, p.168.**

For more information, contact the following:

United States Equal Employment Opportunity Commission (EEOC)

Enforces: Title VII of the Civil Rights Act of 1964, as amended, which prohibits discrimination on the basis of sex including sexual harassment and pregnancy, religion, race, color, and national origin; Age Discrimination in Employment Act (ADEA); Equal Pay Act (EPA); and Title I of the Americans with Disabilities Act (ADA).

EEOC
1801 L Street, NW
Washington, DC 20507
800-669-4000; call will be routed to the nearest city with jurisdiction in your area.
www.eeoc.gov.

United States Department of Labor

Employment Standards Administration
200 Constitution Avenue NW
Washington, DC 20210
www.dol.gov. Visit web site for phone numbers and various department contacts.

State and Local Laws

State and local laws also apply. Check with your state employment office to be sure of current laws that affect your organization.

Staff Leadership

Staff leadership and management covers a wide-range of strategies with many proven techniques, out-of-date approaches still in use, and an array of popular new trends. Keeping up with the many demands inherent in a director's job while incorporating new staff leadership techniques can be challenging, even to the most willing.

Identify the staff leadership approach you use and determine if changes or modifications could enhance your ability to work effectively with staff. A willingness to integrate new ideas and approaches will likely strengthen your relationship with staff members and demonstrate your openness to change.

A Management Continuum

Traditional hierarchies and teams represent two ends of a management continuum that includes many different approaches to working with people. Very few directors find themselves operating exclusively at one or the other end of this spectrum. Most directors will find a certain style or technique works well in one situation but may not work in another. A successful director develops a full complement of management tools and techniques and learns to recognize when to use them.

1.   Hierarchies

Many large organizations use a traditional management approach that practices top-down leadership. This model, the hierarchical pyramid, makes a clear separation between authority and responsibility and places control in the hands of leaders (Block, 1981, p. 14).

Large nonprofit organizations, educational institutions, or government entities probably operate with a high degree of hierarchy, as do many other organizations. This approach provides structure and clear lines of authority.

In a traditional hierarchy, a director most likely reports to a division   or department supervisor who reports to an administrator and up a chain of command to the highest position of authority.

The director supervises staff who report and are accountable to the director as manager.

In smaller organizations, an executive director at the top of the pyramid supervises department directors or managers who in turn supervise others. While there may be significant staff input, the director ultimately bears authority, delegates responsibilities, and assigns duties to staff.

A staffing structure sometimes found in hierarchical organizations is a working group. Working groups thrive where individual, not group, accountability is highly valued (Katzenbach and Smith, p. 89).

Working groups have the following characteristics:

- Members' roles match the formal organizational positions they hold;
- Members get together to share information and make decisions to help individuals accomplish their goals;
- Rely on individual performance and accountability;
- Benefit from having a clear purpose and agreement on how performance will be measured;
- Members usually delegate "real work" to others outside the group;
- Members typically compete with each other;
- Members do not take responsibility for the work of others (Ibid.).

Top down leadership may not always be the best management approach. Many organizations have shifted away from traditional hierarchies to more collaborative and participatory styles of management (Block, p. 14). By incorporating other methods, the pyramid structure may be flattened with responsibility distributed and shared.

2. Teams

Most organizations engage staff in major decisions such as planning, designing, and implementing organizational initiatives and programs. Staff members lead departments or programs and are responsible for the performance and achievement of goals.

Within departments, groups of workers may develop shared goals, be mutually accountable, and view group success as personal success. These staffing arrangements may not be called a "team" but may in fact be operating as one.

TIn *The Wisdom of Teams*, Jon R. Katzenbach and Douglas K. Smith define a team as:

> "... a small number of people with complementary skills who are committed to a common purpose, performance goals, and approach for which they hold themselves mutually accountable (Katzenbach and Smith, p. 45).

Staff is viewed as a collective resource rather than a number of individual contributors. Team members work collaboratively with each other to solve problems, resolve issues, and make major organizational decisions. This approach encourages ownership, involvement, and mutual accountability by staff members. Other benefits may include enhanced performance and commitment as well as increased organizational and personal accountability.

Teams may not always be the best approach to use either. Chief drawbacks to teams are that they:

- Can be time-consuming, not leaving enough time for regular work;
- Appear confused, disorderly, and out of control;
- Create role confusion, and members have difficulty leaving "hats" at the door;
- Are viewed negatively by people who like order and control;
- Require a long time to produce results;
- Require people to change (Harrington-Mackin, 1994, p. 2).

Teams can be part of an organization with traditional reporting structures and may compliment and enhance performance results (Katzenbach and Smith, p. 256). **See Appendix A, *Types of Teams*, p. 189, and Appendix B, *Why Teams Don't Work*, p. 191.**

Form teams when there is a clear purpose and need for what the team can accomplish, not because it's the trendy thing to do. If there are problems with communication, quality of work, and productivity, these issues will not go away by creating teams. The root causes for the problems need to be addressed first (Robbins and Finley, p. 13).

Teams and teamwork are not the same thing. Teamwork is necessary in any organization and is a recommended practice no matter what type of management structure is in place. **See Practice 10.**

There are many resources available on teams and management. **See References, p. 186.**

Common Approaches to Building Team Performance

1. **Establish urgency and direction:** Team members need to believe the team has urgent and worthwhile purposes, and they want to know what the expectations are.

2. **Select team members based on skills and skill potential, not personalities:** Relevant skills include 1) technical and functional, 2) problem solving, and 3) interpersonal.

3. **Pay particular attention to first meetings and actions:** The team leader and those in charge set the tone for how the team will operate; must pay special attention to their own actions.

4. **Set some clear rules of behavior:** Develop rules of conduct including attendance, discussion, confidentiality, analytic approach, end-product orientation, constructive confrontation, and most important, making contributions. Rules promote focus, openness, and trust.

5. **Set and seize upon a few immediate performance-oriented tasks and goals:** Set goals early on that can be assessed and require members to "stretch."

6. **Challenge the group regularly with fresh facts and information:** Causes a potential team to redefine and enrich its understanding of the performance challenge, shape a common purpose, set clearer goals, and improve on common approach.

7. **Spend lots of time together:** Scheduled and unscheduled time both produce personal bonding and creative insights.

8. **Exploit the power of positive feedback, recognition, and reward:** "Giving out gold stars" helps to shape new behaviors critical to team performance.

Checklist of Recommended Practices

I. Create an Environment for Success

☐ Practice 1 Assess Personal Management Style
☐ Practice 2 Create a Shared Vision and Sense of Ownership
☐ Practice 3 Develop Joint Goals and Measurable Objectives
☐ Practice 4 Empower Staff
☐ Practice 5 Create Clear Performance Expectations

II. Build Strong Relationships

☐ Practice 6 Hold Effective Meetings
☐ Practice 7 Create Opportunities for Staff Interaction
☐ Practice 8 Build Trust
☐ Practice 9 Communicate Effectively
☐ Practice 10 Promote and Encourage Teamwork
☐ Practice 11 Support Human Diversity
☐ Practice 12 Support Professional and Personal Development
☐ Practice 13 Recognize Accomplishments and Celebrate Successes
☐ Practice 14 Recognize Problems and Find Solutions

III. Establish Policies and Procedures

☐ Practice 15 Develop Written Personnel Policies
☐ Practice 16 Develop and Implement Standard Personnel Procedures
☐ Practice 17 Keep Detailed Personnel Records

Recommended Practices

There are countless ways to work effectively with people. Within nonprofit and other organizations, approaches differ significantly since directors and staffs are as varied as their systems of governance. Given these variables, use the following recommended practices as a guide and adapt them to fit your needs.

I.   Create an Environment for Success

Leadership is an essential quality of any successful director and includes inspiring, motivating, and supporting staff. The leadership chapter in this handbook identifies practices to develop these abilities. Use it to complement the following practices and enhance your ability to work effectively with staff.

Develop leadership skills among staff members too. As they become more competent and confident in their jobs, they will take on greater decision-making responsibility and ownership for their work and the organization.

Practice 1   **Assess Personal Management Style**

An individual's leadership and management style is shaped by experience, training, and exposure to new ideas. It is also influenced by the organization's style of management. Different approaches produce varying results.

For example, a style which empowers staff and encourages innovation, initiative, and commitment will likely encourage creative thinking and problem solving. It could also produce conflicts over different perspectives and slow progress toward achieving targeted goals while disputes are settled.

On the other hand, a director who attempts to control the staff's actions may be squelching independent thinking, ownership of ideas, and responsibility for outcomes. Clear guidelines for what is acceptable and unacceptable behavior is essential, however. **See Practice 5, p. 152.**

Increased self-knowledge and awareness of your personal management style enhances your effectiveness. To begin:

- ❐ Assess your strengths and weaknesses;
- ❐ Recognize styles and behaviors that are effective;
- ❐ Identify styles and behaviors that are not effective;
- ❐ Be willing to learn new skills;
- ❐ Dedicate time and energy to change.

Consider the following questions to assess your personal management style:

1. Do staff share the organization's vision? Are their goals and objectives measurable and developed jointly with strategic, department, or team goals? Are staff empowered to do their work? Do they know what constitutes success? **See Practices 2-5, p. 146-152.**

2. How are meetings and other staff interactions developed for effectiveness? How do you know if you really trust your staff? If they trust you? **See Practices 6-8, p. 153-157.**

3. Have you created a safe atmosphere for communication? Do you practice open communication? Do you ask for regular feedback? Are you open to suggestions and recommendations? Do you practice listening? **See Practice 9, p. 157-160.**

4. Do you practice teamwork and encourage it from your staff? Do you recognize and support differences among people? Do you support staff development and networking? **See Practices 10-12, p. 161-164.**

5. How do you recognize the work of others? Do you celebrate success? How do you handle conflicts or performance and behavior problems? **See Practices 13-14, p. 165-167.**

6. Have you established policies and procedures for hiring, orientation, evaluation, disciplinary action, grievances, and termination? **See Practices 15-16, p. 168-183.** Do you know what information is important to keep in personnel files? **See Practice 17, p. 184-185.**

7. What are you doing to improve your leadership? **See Leadership Chapter.**

See Appendix C, *Four Management Paradigms,* p. 192, Appendix D, *Assessing Staff Management Skills,* p. 193, and General Appendix, Appendix E, *Core Competencies,* p. 307.

Practice 2

Create a Shared Vision and Sense of Ownership

Create a shared vision, plans, strategies, and goals in collaboration with staff to build mutual goals and mutual reliance (Kouzes and Posner, p.266). **See Strategic Planning Chapter, Practice 10, p. 49.**

Invite representatives from various departments to participate in planning sessions. Encourage different people to bring new ideas and perspectives, add variety to the discussions, and to encourage diverse representation.

Think about how you represent the vision, plans, and goals of the organization. Reinforce the idea that goals are collaborative by using language that is inclusive (Kouzes and Posner, p. 270).

Say "We"

Ask someone to observe your speech at a meeting and count the number of times you say *I* and *we*. On balance, there ought to be more references in first-person plural than first-person singular.

Use this technique when interviewing candidates for positions which require leadership abilities. Those who use *I* more than *we* will make poor leaders, and the organization will suffer from their attempts to claim credit for themselves.

Adapted from Kouzes and Posner, *The Leadership Challenge,* **p. 270. Used with permission.**

The benefits of having a shared vision, plans, and goals is that the process:

- Creates clear expectations;
- Includes all stakeholders;
- Enhances the motivation and desire to achieve the vision;

- Empowers employees and members to lead and manage themselves;
- Creates leadership at all levels of the organization (Adapted from Bryson, p. 157-159).

Leadership is more essential when collaboration is required (Kouzes and Posner, p. 243). Learn to master these essentials of collaboration:

❏ Create a climate of trust;
❏ Facilitate positive interdependence;
❏ Support face-to-face interactions (Ibid.).

Practice 3

Develop Joint Goals and Measurable Objectives

To advance the organization's strategic initiatives, develop shared goals that ensure staff efforts are unified. Jointly developed annual goals link each staff member to the organization's strategic goals as well as to the individual's program, department, and team. **See Strategic Planning Chapter.**

A. Department and Program Goals

Department and program goals should advance strategic initiatives and carry out specific programs and objectives. Use a group process to identify key goals, strategies, actions, and people responsible for achieving the goals. **See General Appendix, Appendix F,** *Adapted Nominal Group Technique,* **p. 313.**

Consider the following:

❏ Engage all department or program staff in a goal planning session prior to creating the annual budget. Hold a special meeting or retreat to gather ideas and discuss priorities for coming year.
❏ Coordinate overlapping department or program goals with other departments and people who are affected by the goals. For example, development's goals should reflect the education department's plans to fund two new positions; human resources' goals should reflect education's goals to recruit and hire two new positions when funded;

❑   Seek board committee input, where applicable;

❑   Share department goals with director and full staff;

❑   Recommend to the board for final approval.

See Appendix E, *Goal Setting Process*, p. 194.

B.   Individual Goals and Objectives

Each staff person develops individual goals and objectives that are integrated with department, program and strategic goals.

Individual objectives guide the employee's direction and establish what the individual must do in the coming year. Objectives may include personal development, training, and shared organization-wide goals such as diversity awareness, organizational outreach, or networking. Develop individual objectives when an employee is first hired, as well as, annually during the performance appraisal process.

Consider using the **SMART** guide when developing objectives. Ask if objectives are:

- **S**pecific - Is it focused?
- **M**easurable - How will you tell if it is accomplished?
- **A**ttainable - Is it a realistic target?
- **R**esource-based - Do you have what you need (funds, time, skills) to do it?
- **T**imely - When will it be done for the greatest value? (The Nature Conservancy, Employee Notebook, p. 2).

Other recommendations include:

❑   Make sure each employee has a copy of the organization, program, or departmental goals;

❑   Provide support and feedback as employees develop objectives. Remind them to:
- Use the **SMART** guidelines;
- Link their objectives with goals and job duties; include personal growth and training;
- Be sure the objectives can be achieved by the employee;

- Limit the number of objectives to 10 or less;
- List objectives in order of priority;
☐ Encourage employees to post objectives where they can see them;
☐ Encourage employees to track progress (weekly, monthly, quarterly) and discuss progress or problems with their supervisor;
☐ Revise or modify objectives, if necessary;
☐ Remind employees to document achievements during annual performance appraisal. **See Practice 16. See Appendix F, *Goals and Objectives*, p. 195.**

C.   Team Goals

Teams develop shared goals and objectives through a similar process although accountability is different. The interdependence of team members make them mutually accountable for the team's goals, not for just accomplishing their individual goals.

In *Keeping the Team Going*, Deborah Harrington-Mackin recommends that teams develop goals:

- Annually to be sure overall goals are in alignment with organizational goals;
- Every four to six months for project-specific goals;
- At every meeting as agenda items are discussed;
- When the team is lost and discussion seems to be going nowhere;
- When the team is polarized and loses sight of the big picture (Harrington-Mackin, 1996, p. 69).

Practice 4

Empower Staff

Leaders who recognize the creative energy, resourcefulness, and initiative in people will encourage participation in decision-making, self-direction, and self-management in work that is both challenging and fulfilling (Covey, 1990, p. 178-180). **See References, p. 186.**

Empowerment means:

- Developing employee competence in their work and confidence in themselves;
- Moving decision making to the level of the organization most affected by the decision;
- Matching decision making with the people who have the knowledge or information necessary to make the decisions;
- Trusting employees to make good decisions (Easton, 1995).

Empowered employees contribute to creating the organization's culture, produce results for the organization, and are responsible "for the quality of their own experience" (Block, 1996, p. 50).

Individuals must decide to exercise their rights, to speak up, take responsibility, and make a commitment. Not everyone wants to assume these roles, especially if they are more accustomed to having fewer choices, fewer responsibilities, and more control exerted over them.

People cannot be empowered to act but must empower themselves (Robbins and Finley, p. 147). By creating an atmosphere where people feel free to take risks, they are more likely to feel empowered. If staff are more accustomed to asking for permission before acting, they may resist efforts to empower them (Ibid.).

In *The Leadership Challenge,* James M. Kouzes and Barry Z. Posner identify four leadership essentials to strengthen others (p. 284-301):

1. **Ensure self-leadership**: leaders who share power with others demonstrate "profound trust in and respect for others' abilities" (p. 287); puts people in charge and control of their own lives, "liberating people to use the power and skills they already have" (p. 288);

2. **Provide choice**: give employees greater latitude and discretion in their jobs, so they are able to take non-routine action, exercise independent judgment, and make decisions without having to check with someone else (p. 291); allows people to be creative and flexible with more broadly defined roles (Ibid).

3. **Develop competence and confidence**: invest in training and development; develop skills and competencies, and share

information and resources; place employees at the center of solving critical problems and contributing to key goals (p.293); create conditions that strengthen employees self-esteem and self-confidence for improved performance (p. 295); leaders coach and demonstrate faith in others by letting them lead (p. 296);

4.   **Foster accountability**: make certain people recognize their interdependence by fostering accountability; expect individual responsibility and hold people accountable; collaboration can build trust and cooperation if a leader sets up conditions that enable all team members to feel ownership (p. 299).

See Appendix G, *Six Conditions of Empowerment,* **p. 196, and Appendix H,** *Empower Employees,* **p. 197, for a quick self-assessment.**

See References, p. 186, for books by Block (*Stewardship***), Covey, Katzenbach and Smith, and Kouzes and Posner.**

Practice 5   ## Create Clear Performance Expectations

The staff needs to know how their performance will be measured. Establish clear performance expectations to enhance responsibility for goals and objectives.

Stephen R. Covey describes "stewardship delegation" as an approach that focuses on results gained rather than the methods used. This establishes clear expectations, commitment, and mutual understanding of what is expected (Covey, 1989, p. 174).

The five elements of stewardship delegation include:

1. **Desired results**: have clear, mutual understanding of what needs to be accomplished; focus on results, not methods;
2. **Guidelines**: parameters within which the individual should operate; should be as few as possible. Point out potential failure paths; tell them what not to do, not what to do;
3. **Resources**: identify human, financial, technical, or organizational resources the person can use to accomplish the desired results;
4. **Accountability**: set up performance standards to evaluate results and times when reporting and evaluation will take place;
5. **Consequences**: specify what will happen, both good and bad, as a result of the evaluation. This could include financial rewards, psychological rewards, change in position, or what consequences may result to the organization (Covey, 1989, p. 174). **See References, p. 186.**

Hold employees accountable for meeting the organization's core values and code of ethics by including these statements as part of their performance expectations.

See Appendix I, *Performance Indicators*, p. 198. See Strategic Planning Chapter, Practice 9. See General Appendix: Appendix B, *Self-Test on Individual Ethics*, p. 302, Appendix C, *Building Opportunities for Ethical Reflection*, p. 304, and Appendix D, *Steps to Take When Faced with an Ethical Challenge*, p. 306.

II.   Build Strong Relationships

The job of directing and managing staff is likely to be both a source of great satisfaction and deep frustration for many directors. The role requires constant attention to the organization's needs, sensitivity to the needs and desires of employees, awareness of employees' behavior, and awareness of your own behavior as well.

Build strong relationships with staff to enhance your leadership ability. For some people, this may come naturally and easily. For others, it requires dedicated effort and hard work.

Practice 6

Hold Effective Meetings

Meetings bring people together to plan, exchange information, discuss, or reflect. Each type of meeting requires different thought processes and ways of interacting. For example, try to schedule planning meetings separate from information meetings and discussions separate from reflective gatherings. This allows participants to focus more completely on the meeting's purpose.

If the staff thinks there are too many meetings keeping them from doing their *real* work, the cause is probably ineffective meetings.

A.   Roles in Meetings

For more effective meetings, establish key roles and responsibilities in advance. The following are examples of meeting roles and typical duties:

- **Leader:** guides and shapes the meeting; approves the agenda; could be the director or not;
- **Facilitator:** runs the meeting; follows the agenda; encourages participation; clarifies comments; resolves conflicts; remains neutral. The facilitator and leader may be the same person or not;
- **Scribe:** keeps track of discussion topics and key points (using a laptop computer, flip charts, dry erase board, audio recordings, or video recordings);
- **Timekeeper:** keeps meeting on schedule by ensuring time limits on agenda items and breaks;

- **Participant:** prepares for each meeting; attends and participates; voices opinions on topics; completes assignments (Adapted from Harrington-Mackin, 1994, p. 14-21).

Encourage staff members to serve different roles at the meetings. This will help each person gain confidence and experience in various roles and enhance shared responsibility and teamwork.

B. Agenda

Agendas are essential and should be prepared and distributed in advance. For meetings of staff located at the same site, create the agenda by posting a blank agenda in a known area accessible to everyone. Ask staff to suggest agenda items, noting the priority, who will lead the discussion, and time needed (Harrington-Mackin, 1996, p. 71). This involves everyone in setting the agenda.

Email is an easy way to create an agenda with multiple people or staff at different locations. Also, use electronic calendars for scheduling meetings in the same way.

Another way to create an agenda is to submit items to the director, meeting leader, or facilitator. This person establishes the priorities and prepares the agenda to be distributed prior to the meeting.

C. Conducting the Meeting

The facilitator makes sure staff assume meeting roles, reviews the agenda, and begins and ends the meeting on time. Keep within the time allotted for discussing each item, giving greatest time to problems and planning items on the agenda. This is often the most difficult part in running an effective meeting.

Each action that results from the discussion items on the agenda must have someone responsible for following through. If action is postponed, note this in the meeting minutes.

Use standard discussion techniques such as brainstorming or other small group facilitation methods to generate full staff participation. **See General Appendix, Appendix F, *Adapted Nominal Group Technique*, p. 313. Also see Boards Chapter, Appendix M, *The Action Agenda*, p. 127.**

At the end of each meeting, all participants should know what was discussed, what actions are required, who will follow through, and what has been delayed or postponed for another meeting. Establish the date and time of the next meeting.

Schedule staff meetings on a given date and time, rather than being spontaneous. This allows people time to plan and prepare, and results in better meeting attendance. The frequency of staff or team meetings varies significantly from weekly, to bi-weekly, to monthly or more depending on the organization, the number of staff, their locations, the issues to be discussed, and the actions to be taken.

In general, keep meetings to no more than two hours (Harrington-Mackin, 1994, p. 37). Retreats and workshops are exceptions.

D.   One-on-One Meetings

Personal interaction builds trust, confidence and focuses attention on the staff person's interests, concerns, needs, hopes, fears, and doubts (Covey, 1990, p. 112). **See References, p. 186.** Meet one-on-one with staff to establish this relationship. **See Practice 9.**

Individual meetings with staff may be planned or spontaneous. An "open-door" policy encourages people to stop by to talk over an idea or issue on an informal basis. This is one important way to build trust, generate interaction, and solve problems.

Engage in impromptu meetings with staff while they are at work. Called MBWA (Management By Walking Around), this lets staff know you are interested in them and their work and are available to talk. Be sure the message you convey is interest, not a lack of trust or confidence.

Schedule one-on-one meetings to concentrate attention on a specific issue, discuss an employee problem, or for focused discussion. Be sure the purpose is clearly articulated and understood by the director and the staff person to make the best use of time and to produce the greatest results. **See Practice 14 and Practice 16.**

| Practice 7 | ### Create Opportunities for Staff Interactions |

Meetings are just one way to bring people together. Create other opportunities for people to get together informally as well as in more structured settings. Consider the following possibilities:

- ❏ Designate an in-office snack or gathering area;
- ❏ Hold a full staff retreat annually;
- ❏ End work early some day for social time;
- ❏ Schedule a working breakfast or lunch;
- ❏ Have lunch for fun without talking about work;
- ❏ Sponsor a training seminar;
- ❏ Take a walk, canoe, or hike with staff;
- ❏ Take field trips to visit other organizations and facilities;
- ❏ Bring breakfast for the staff;
- ❏ Send two or more staff to the same conference;
- ❏ Celebrate an achievement with a party.

| Practice 8 | ### Build Trust |

Trust is *the* central issue in human relationships within and outside the organization and is at the heart of collaboration (Kouzes and Posner, p. 244). Relationships based on trust make creating a shared vision, having open communication, working as a team, and collaborating to achieve ambitious goals and strategies possible. Trust is also the most significant predictor of individuals' satisfaction with their organization (Ibid., p. 247).

Trusting others is an essential element of leadership and without it, directors — and staff — will fail. People who don't trust each other feel vulnerable and often distort or ignore facts, ideas, conclusions, and feelings they believe will make them more vulnerable. When a leader lacks trust in the staff, the staff will lack trust in the leader (Ibid.).

Be the First to Trust

To promote trust throughout the organization, be the first to:

- ❏   Disclose information about yourself and what you believe.
- ❏   Admit mistakes.
- ❏   Acknowledge the need for personal improvement.
- ❏   Ask others feedback – positive and negative.
- ❏   Listen attentively to what others are saying.
- ❏   Invite interested parties to important meetings.
- ❏   Share information that's useful to others.
- ❏   Openly acknowledge the contributions of others.
- ❏   Show that you're willing to change your mind when someone else comes up with a good idea.
- ❏   Avoid talking negatively about others.
- ❏   Say "We can trust them," and mean it.

Source: *The Leadership Challenge*, James M. Kouzes and Barry Z. Posner (2002) , p. 288. Used with permission.

Practice 9

Communicate Effectively

Clear communication is necessary for visions, goals and strategies to be shared, understood and carried out. Consistency in words and actions builds trust, prevents misunderstandings, and is a sign of an effective leader.

> *"Communication that carries integrity always considers timing and context before the delivery of content. So often we know exactly what we want to say, but we do not consider whether it is the right time or the right place in which to deliver the content of our communication. Direct communication — giving voice to what we see without blame or judgment — means we must consider the alignment of appropriate word choice, tone of voice, and body posture."*

Angeles Arrien, *The Four-Fold Way* (p. 83).

Peter Block in *Stewardship* supports "full disclosure" in dealing with people, which includes giving employees complete information and not keeping secrets (Block, 1996, p. 67). Full disclosure also means telling the truth all the time, and openly discussing bad news and difficult issues (Ibid.).

While a director will want to use discretion on which issues (big or small) to bring before staff and board members, sharing knowledge and information is a powerful way to demonstrate trust, confidence, and teamwork.

Communication experts estimate 10 percent of communication is represented by the words people say and 30 percent represented by the sounds (tone of voice). The other 60 percent is communicated through body language (Covey, 1989, p. 241). **See References, p. 186.**

A.   Oral Communication

Effective oral communication skills are essential for executive directors. Oral communication includes not only the content of what is said (giving clear instructions, complementing someone on work done, requesting a report, responding to questions asked and suggestions made) but the tone of voice used when speaking.

1.   Humor

An effective way to build strong relationships is to develop and practice a sense of humor. The ability to be light-hearted under pressure, to laugh at yourself, and introduce humor into a tense situation is a valuable skill.

Not everyone is comfortable telling a joke or funny story. Each person's style is unique and so are people's ideas of what is funny and what isn't. There is always the chance humor could offend, rather than build close relationships. Inappropriate or offensive humor is always damaging to people and should never be practiced.

2.   Questioning Skills

In *Keeping the Team Going*, Deborah Harrington-Mackin says nothing builds relationships more effectively than developing the ability to ask questions, rather than make statements (Harrington-Mackin, 1996, p. 100). Questions demonstrate appreciation and value for the other person's thoughts, feelings, and experience.

Good questions:

- Begin with *who*, *what*, *where*, *when*, and *how*;
- Can't be answered with a *yes* or *no*;
- Help focus on issues and evaluate the situation;
- Encourage people to say what they think and feel;
- Help people explore a situation from a variety of perspectives;
- Make the person feel the questioner is paying attention and wants to know more (Harrington-Mackin, 1996, p. 100).

Questions to avoid include:

- *Yes* and *no* questions: fail to gather more information and limit further conversation;
- *Why* questions: sound judgmental, put people on the defensive, and assume the answer is already known;
- Rapid-fire questions: make a person feel overwhelmed;
- Questions that contain the answer ("You forgot to lock the building again, didn't you?");
- Questions that begin with *can* and *could* when someone is being asked to do something. Use *will* or *would* instead (Adapted from Harrington-Mackin, 1996, p. 100-101).

B.   Listening Skills

To truly understand others, listening is the most important practice of all. Stephen R. Covey in *The Seven Habits of Highly Effective People* emphasizes *empathic* listening. Empathic listening "seeks first to understand" by seeing the world from the other person's point of view (Covey, 1989, p. 240). **See References, p. 186.**

Empathic listening pays attention to the nonverbal body language as much as it does the verbal. Empathic listening means trying to understand not just the content, but the emotion behind what is said (Robbins and Finley, p. 116).

Empathic listening differs from *active* or *reflective listening*. Reflective listening restates to the person what he or she just said. It is effective for encouraging the person to rethink a statement. *Paraphrasing* someone's statement reiterates what was said but in different words. Practicing both requires patience but may help clarify what the person is saying (Harrington-Mackin, 1996, p. 96).

C. Written Communication

Directors need outstanding written communication skills for both internal and external communications. Try the following:

❐ Send a written note or email of praise, encouragement, or support to a staff member; this demonstrates appreciation for his or her work. Keep it short. Attach a post-it on a report or jot a few words on a memo.

❐ Write a formal letter of recognition for exceptional work by an individual, department, or team. These letters become part of the employee's personnel file and can be a source of great pride. **See Practice 17.**

Other written communication includes:

• Goals and objectives, performance appraisals, and other performance agreements. **See Practice 17.**

• Documents that address performance issues or other problems. Clear, direct communication in writing is essential when addressing performance problems. A letter may document a problem, request corrective actions, list terms for improvement, or state conditions for termination. **See Practices 14, 16, and 17.**

D. Body Language

Body language communicates subtle and sometimes very obvious messages. A relaxed posture, leaning toward the speaker in an interested, non threatening manner, direct eye contact, or open relaxed arms and hands may indicate ease and comfort. Angry expressions, lack of eye contact, arms folded over the body, tensed hands, or nervous shifting are usually signs of discomfort.

Learn to pay attention to your own body language for what you may be communicating unknowingly. Since so much of what a person thinks and feels is written in these nonverbal messages, improve skills to "read" and "send" better messages.

Practice 10   **Promote and Encourage Teamwork**

In *The Wisdom of Teams*, Jon R. Katzenbach and Douglas K. Smith define teamwork as "... a set of values that encourages behaviors such as listening and constructively responding to points of view expressed by others, giving others the benefit of the doubt, providing support to those who need it, and recognizing the interest and achievements of others" (Katzenbach and Smith, p. 21).

Any organization, large or small, can and should practice teamwork. Support for teamwork begins with leaders who model and encourage the following behaviors in themselves and others:

☐   Practice listening;
☐   Encourage all ideas;
☐   Encourage creativity;
☐   Practice tolerance;
☐   Share knowledge and power;
☐   Take risks and challenge staff to take risks;
☐   Support staff during success and failure;
☐   Treat failure as a learning experience;
☐   Encourage and expect participation;
☐   Build upon individual strengths and group synergy.

Conduct a Collaboration Audit

Rate the extent to which you agree or disagree that each statement describes the actions of people of your organization. Use the following scale to indicate your level of agreement or disagreement.

Strongly Disagree	Disagree	Neither Disagree nor Agree	Agree	Strongly Agree
1	2	3	4	5

Around here, people ...

_____ 1. Act in a trustworthy and trusting manner
_____ 2. Ask others for help and assistance when needed.
_____ 3. Treat others with dignity and respect.
_____ 4. Talk openly about their feelings.
_____ 5. Listen attentively to the opinions of others.
_____ 6. Express clarity about the group's goals.
_____ 7. Make personal sacrifices to met a larger group goal.
_____ 8. Can rely on each other.
_____ 9. Pitch in to help when others are busy or running behind.
_____ 10. Give credit to others for their contributions.
_____ 11. Interact with each other on a regular basis.
_____ 12. Treat every relationship as if it will last for a lifetime, even if it won't.
_____ 13. Make it their business to introduce their colleagues to people who can help them succeed.
_____ 14. Freely pass along information that might be useful to others.
_____ 15. Relate well to people of diverse backgrounds and interests.

Source: *The Leadership Challenge* by James M Kouzes and Barry Z. Posner (2002), p. 287. Used with permission.

Practice 11   Support Human Diversity

Diversity represents a full spectrum of human differences including race, culture, gender, age, sexual orientation, physical ability, family status, income, and religious or spiritual beliefs. It also includes experience level, working style, and personality type, among other personal and professional differences.

Support for human diversity is a policy in most organizations but the challenge is to actively practice it. Discrimination is clearly against the law yet organizations may not recognize how certain privileges, biases, or prejudices are still practiced toward individuals or groups.

Examine the way thoughts and actions may need to shift within the organization. Create an atmosphere of acceptance, looking for common ground and similarities while accepting and acknowledging differences. Different ways of thinking, acting, and looking at the world add variety and enrich the organization. Show commitment to diversity by taking the following actions:

- ❏ Promote an environment free from racist or sexist jokes or remarks that offend a particular group.
- ❏ Evaluate the effectiveness of diversity management:
  - Are all people treated equitably?
  - Are candidates who may enhance staff diversity sought for new positions? **See Practice 16.**
  - Are staff trained on diversity issues?
  - Are diversity issues a problem at work?
  - What can be done to improve the situation?
- ❏ Offer diversity awareness training for staff.
- ❏ Read articles, books, and references on diversity.
- ❏ Seek opportunities to expand cultural awareness.
- ❏ Understand your own cultural conditioning.

Learn to recognize differences in people to better understand yourself and others. Approaches to assess personality types and behavioral styles can be useful to help understand what influences people's actions and others' responses to those behaviors.

Myers-Briggs Personality Type Indicator (MBTI®)

The Myers-Briggs Personality Type Indicator is a self-report questionnaire that identifies valuable differences between normal, healthy people. This information enhances self-understanding, personal motivations, natural strengths, and potential areas for growth while developing appreciation for others' differences. MBTI® is self-affirming and encourages cooperation (Myers, p. 5).

The MBTI® preferences indicate differences in people that result from how people prefer to:

- Focus attention (extraversion or introversion);
- Take in information (sensing or intuition);
- Make decisions (thinking or feeling);
- Orient toward the external world (judging or perceiving) (Ibid., p. 8). **See Appendix J, *The MBTI® Preferences*, p. 201-202.**

College or university career centers or other counseling facilities provide MBTI® information. The assessment must be administered by a qualified professional.

If you utilize the MBTI® instrument or other personality or behavioral assessments, use these tools for information, not to create negative or positive stereotypes. No one personality type is better than any other. **See Appendix K,** *Behavioral Profiles or Zones,* **p. 203.**

Practice 12

Support Professional and Personal Development

A competent, well informed staff operates with greater independence, authority, self-confidence, and performance. To build competence, provide training and development opportunities for all staff, whether they are working effectively or having performance or behavioral problems.

Consider the following tips to plan training:

- ❑ Identify training needs for individuals, departments, teams, and the organization;
- ❑ Determine training priorities based on the strategic plan, organizational needs, staff needs, budget, and criteria;
- ❑ Determine the best method for training (in-house trainers, consultants, conferences, workshops, retreats, seminars, networking, site visits at other centers, college);
- ❑ Establish a training budget;
- ❑ Gear training to the learner. If a new computer system is installed, everyone needs to know how to use it for their operations, but everyone does not need to know how to trouble shoot it;
- ❑ Challenge employees to take responsibility for tasks they may not have considered. Support staff's willingness to try new things, to possibly fail, and to possibly succeed.

See the following page.

Characteristics of Effective Training

- Provides an opportunity to share life experiences with other adults;
- Allows some control and self-direction in the learning process;
- Establishes a correlation between prior experience and new skill development;
- Encourages active participation and provides the opportunity to do the tasks;
- Has warm, friendly atmosphere receptive to the contributions of those attending;
- Provides for practical application of new material;
- Includes numerous repetitions of the same information in different formats;
- Provides frequent, specific, and accurate feedback;
- Offers an opportunity to ask questions.

Excerpted by permission of the publisher from *The Team Building Tool Kit* (p. 143) by Deborah Harrington-Mackin, © 1994 New Directions Management Services, Inc. Published by AMACOM, division of the American Management Association, New York, NY 10019. All rights reserved. www.amacombooks.org

---

Practice 13

Recognize Accomplishments and Celebrate Successes

Recognize staff contributions and show genuine appreciation for them and their work. Engage in these essentials:

- ❏ Focus on clear standards and goals; give feedback and encouragement which builds trust ((Kouzes and Posner, p. 318-321);

- ❏ Expect the best; model the way and demonstrate how things need to be done; bring out the best in others; high expectations lead to high performance (Ibid., p.321-327);

- ❏ Pay attention; show people you care about them and what they're doing; look for people doing things right; be a caring leader, listen with your eyes and heart; improves morale and builds higher levels of performance (Ibid., p. 327-331);

- ❏ Personalize recognition; avoid a "one-size-fits-all approach" which feels disingenuous, forced and thoughtless; notice achievements and personally deliver praise in a timely manner and in front of peers; say "thank you;" build fires within, not under, people; be thoughtful (Ibid., p. 331 -337).

Staff and Volunteer Appreciation Soup Potluck
Peggy Hunt, Pioneers Park Nature Center Lincoln, NE

This staff and volunteer recognition event is usually held in January. Staff bring soups and volunteers bring the rest (bread, salads, desserts). It is a way to recognize everyone's efforts and have fun.

We give a mug (designed by a local artist) to each volunteer and staff member and I give a special gift to each staff member. It is usually something they can use while either interpreting nature or enjoying the wilderness. Last year, I gave staff laminated tracking cards. The previous year, they received a bandanna with cloud formations printed on it.

Practice 14

Recognize Problems and Find Solutions

Even the most compatible, productive staff will still have problems. Learn to expect it, to recognize problems when they occur, and to take corrective steps to resolve issues. At best, problems provide good opportunities for growth and learning, bringing important issues to light. At worst, unresolved problems can create poor morale, staff dissatisfaction, and staff turnover.

Some personnel problems are severe and require immediate and decisive action by the director. Follow established policies and procedures for addressing these issues. **See Practices 15 and 16.**

A.   Conflicts

Conflicts can create barriers to effective communication, damage trust, and interfere with accomplishing goals. If managed constructively, though, conflict can help build teamwork. Conflict may reveal issues that need to be resolved, cause people to deal with issues they may have avoided, cause people to change behaviors, and stimulate creative thinking and problem solving (Gallaro, et al, p. 152).

Conflict is destructive to people and organizations if issues are ignored, remain hidden, are dealt with indirectly, or are left unresolved. Conflict is best dealt with directly, although postponing action is a useful strategy if a situation is volatile (Ibid.).

Sources of conflict include:

- Resources (time, money, personnel, space, support);
- Personal hidden agendas (advancement, need for acknowledgment, envy, greed);
- Differences in expectations and behavior styles (how people treat each other; how leaders behave; time management; ways of speaking or dressing; territorial issues; cultural differences; formality or informality);
- Differences in opinion (disagreements on approach, how decisions are made);
- Differences in values (family, culture, religion, personal experience, friends, authority) (Gallaro, et al, p. 152-155).

Conflicts occur over large issues and what may appear to be small issues (who makes coffee, stays late to close, works a holiday). Practice open communication, teamwork, collaboration, compromise, and negotiation skills when seeking solutions. **See General Appendix, Appendix A, *The Art of Collaborative Negotiating,* p. 299.**

B.   Performance and Behavioral Problems

Performance and behavioral problems frequently arise at times of personal or organizational crisis. Take constructive steps to identify and resolve these issues.

Although it is sometimes unpleasant and always challenging, a director must see that problems are identified and corrected as quickly as possible. Many directors avoid dealing with these issues because they dread confronting the employee. Staff morale and productivity can be seriously affected if performance and behavioral problems are left unresolved.

Have clearly defined policies and procedures for what is acceptable and unacceptable performance and behavior. Performance standards, a code of ethics, and values statements should define the ways all employees are expected to conduct themselves. **See Practices 5, 15, and 16.**

Also, see Strategic Planning Chapter, Practice 9, *Develop a Values Statement,* p.48 . See General Appendix: Appendix B, *Self-Test on Individual Ethics,* p. 302, Appendix C, *Building Opportunities for Ethical Reflection,* p. 304, and Appendix D, *Steps to Take When Faced With an Ethical Challenge,* p. 306.

III. Establish Policies and Procedures

Practice 15   **Develop Written Personnel Policies**

Develop a personnel policy handbook that contains current policies and procedures. The policies guide personnel decisions and actions and provide legal protection for the organization.

Be careful not to develop more policies than are needed. Too many policies can constrain an organization's flexibility. Keep policies up to date, brief and to the point.

Have an attorney familiar with employment law review all policies to ensure concurrence with applicable federal, state, and local laws. Policies must be approved by the board of directors or other authority. They must also approve any modifications, revisions, and updates, with guidance from the executive director, staff, or the board's personnel committee.

Personnel policy manuals vary from one organization to another. **See Appendix L,** *Personnel Policy Manual,* **p. 204, from the Teton Science School**.

"Employment at will" guides many personnel policies and procedures. **Be sure to read Appendix M,** *Employment at Will,* **p. 206, and Appendix N,** *Employment at Teton Science School,* **p. 209 which includes a sample legal disclaimer.**

Practice 16   **Develop and Implement Standard Personnel Procedures**

A.   Hiring

1.   Identify the Organization's Staffing Needs

An opening for a new position or the departure of a valued staff member are opportune times to look at the staff structure within the organization. This is a good chance to identify staffing needs to better meet strategic priorities and ensure smooth operations.

Recognize these times as opportunities to:

- Review staff practices and procedures;
- Assess what is working and what needs to change;
- Create new staff positions;
- Redefine existing positions.

Don't wait for someone to leave to consider making a change. Identify the organization's staffing needs through ongoing discussion and feedback. Solicit ideas for revising positions and adding new ones from the staff. If the board has a personnel committee, be sure to involve them too. **See the process used to identify staff roles and responsibilities (below).**

Planning for current and future staffing needs is often a part of the strategic planning process. **See Strategic Planning Chapter.**

"Ideal" Staff at a Nature Center
Robert Mercer, Director
Silver Lake Nature Center, Bristol, PA

The Silver Lake Nature Center staff went through a process to help us deal with the growing pains of increased staff. What we learned was a small organization frequently does not have clearly defined functions -- everyone pitches in. As the staff grows, people start to assume someone else will do those little irritating jobs like coordinate the fund raiser or clean the bathrooms.

The staff sat down and generated the following list of functions necessary for our nature center's operations realizing someone must perform and ultimately be responsible for these functions. In an ideal setting, there would be a person or even a department with the necessary expertise in each of these areas.

In the real world, one person may be responsible for many functions. That person should be developing their skills in the function, and systems for performing the roles. When staff increases or changes, these systems are then passed on to the new person to work with and develop.

Accounts Payable	Development Officer	Public Activities
Accounts Receivable	Equipment Manager	Public Relations
Administrator	Events Coordinator	Publications
Animal Keeper	Exhibits - Traveling	Research Coordinator
Bookkeeper	Grounds Manager	School Group Coordinator
Building Manager	Groups - Scouts	Store Manager
Building Displays	Groups - Other	Teacher Training Coordinator
Clerical	Library Manager	
Coordinator of Volunteers	Membership Coordinator	

---

2. Identify the Job and Skills Needed for Each Position

Develop written job descriptions for all staff including regular, temporary, seasonal, full-time, part-time, student, or intern positions. The position description is essential for both the employee and supervisor to have clearly defined duties, responsibilities, and priorities.

If existing staff do not have current job descriptions, make this a priority. If you plan to hire a new position, develop the written job description first. It is needed to advertise and recruit candidates.

To comply with the Americans with Disabilities Act (ADA), be sure to include essential functions and requirements necessary for the position. **See Appendix O,** *ADA Analysis, Position Description,* **p. 210.**

Job descriptions vary from one organization to another. Elements found in most job descriptions also include:

- Job title;
- Name of preparer;
- Date prepared;
- Title of supervisor;
- Position summary;
- List of essential functions and responsibilities;
- Qualifications;
- Education, skills, and/or experience required;
- Special skills or abilities (fluent in Spanish; proficient in donor management software; certified fire manager);
- Physical demands (ability to lift 60 pounds; walk 3 miles);
- Work environment (ability to work outdoors in weather extremes; ability to work in a busy office environment).

Some job descriptions also include:

- Titles and number of people supervised by the position;
- Percentage of time spent on principal duties;
- Other people and/or organizations affected by the position;
- Performance indicators. **See Appendix P,** *Sample Job Descriptions,* **p. 211, and Appendix I,** *Performance Indicators,* **p. 198.**

3. Post and Advertise the Position

Post all position announcements first within the organization to give current staff advance notice of openings and the opportunity to apply before the job is announced externally. For external advertising, consider announcing available positions to targeted audiences where qualified candidates may be found. Be sure to state in advertisements and announcements that the organization is an equal employment opportunity employer.

Send announcements to:

- ANCA members;
- Other environmental organizations;
- Schools, colleges and university departments and placement offices;
- Publications such as AVISO, Chronicle of Philanthropy, JobScan, Job Seeker, National Association for Interpretation, and others. **See Contacts, p. 225.**
- Markets of diverse groups. Most major cities have newspapers for African American and Hispanic groups, for example. Also target publications for women;
- Networks of colleagues, peers, and friends.

4. Develop Search Criteria for Screening Resumes

The process of collecting, screening, and responding to resumes can be overwhelming, especially if the announcement attracted many applicants. Avoid spending time on unqualified applicants by implementing a screening process. Consider the following:

❏ Send a post card or form letter to all applicants, acknowledging receipt of their application. Give them a date when they will hear from you again if they will be asked to interview. No further contact is required if the applicant is not a candidate.

❏ Develop a checklist of specific search criteria based on the job description. **See Appendix Q, *Screening Instrument*, p. 218.**

- ❏ Create a candidate search committee. Ask members to help screen applicants using the criteria developed.
- ❏ Set aside all resumes that fail to meet the minimum requirements or lack professional standards expected for the position (for example, a handwritten resume, typing or spelling mistakes). Keep all resumes on file for six months.
- ❏ Ask the search committee to select their top five to 10 resumes, depending on the position and the number of applicants. Several stages of screening may take place.
- ❏ Keep narrowing down the pool of candidates by further refining the criteria and comparing relative strengths and weaknesses apparent from the resume.

If phone calls are discouraged, be sure to state this in the job announcement. Some people conduct preliminary telephone interviews to screen applicants. This can be an effective way to get to know a candidate but can be time consuming. Use standard questions.

Some directors may choose to respond quickly to outstanding prospects looking for a new challenge rather than use the search committee process. Responding quickly may work best in highly competitive markets where good candidates may be lost to other employers.

5. Develop a Standard Interview Process

Develop a standard process to ensure all candidates are treated equally, fairly, and legally.

a. Prepare

- ❏ Schedule interviews with candidates and anyone involved in the interview (team, panel, several individuals).
- ❏ Do not allow interruptions.
- ❏ Start on time and allow at least 45 minutes.
- ❏ Develop questions from the job description based on skills, knowledge, and abilities needed for the position.
- ❏ Do not make up questions during the interview.

b.   Conduct the Interview

- ❏ Open the interview by welcoming the candidate; be gracious and friendly. Put the candidate at ease.
- ❏ Explain how the interview is structured and who is involved. If using a panel, ask members to briefly introduce themselves. Explain that all candidates will be asked the same questions; they may be asked additional ones generated by their responses; let the candidate know he or she may ask questions; inform the candidate that the interviewer(s) will take notes.
- ❏ Ask prepared questions; take notes; maintain eye contact; remain neutral about the candidate's responses. Clarify information on the candidate's resume if needed. Request permission to contact references.
  - Do not ask questions about age, family, handicaps, marital status, national origin, race or color, religion, or sex. These questions are discriminatory.
  - You may ask candidates if they have been convicted of any crimes. If a background check is standard policy, ask if the candidate is willing to undergo it. A background check is advisable for candidates who will work with children.
  - If interviewing with a panel or a team, distribute questions to each member.
- ❏ Listen to the candidate. Pay attention to body language.
- ❏ Describe the job, duties, responsibilities, priorities, employees supervised (if any), internal and external contacts, and the work environment. Describe the less attractive features of the job too.
- ❏ Invite the candidate to ask questions. Be thorough but brief with replies.
- ❏ Include a field visit, computer literacy test, or a problem-solving component if appropriate.
- ❏ Thank the candidate and be sure the individual knows when a hiring decision will be made.

Interviewing Tips

- During the interview the candidate should do about 80 percent of the talking.
- Avoid discussing job characteristics at the beginning of the interview. This may allow the candidate to tailor his/her answers to your needs.
- Use open-ended questions (e.g., how, what, why, when).
- Pace the interview slowly, giving the candidate plenty of time to talk. Use pauses and silences after the candidate has given an answer to encourage him/her to elaborate.
- Repeat or summarize your interpretation of the candidate's remarks. This will give him/her the opportunity to add to or clarify his/her responses.
- Direct your inquiring to the causes behind the facts rather than searching out specific facts (except with regard to specific training). **This method will also guard against trained interviewees, as the candidate will not be able to use rehearsed answers.**

   For example: You may ask "You indicate familiarity with curriculum design. Explain what that entailed in the Environmental Programs you developed. Was it a team effort or your sole responsibility?"
- Notes should be descriptive and specific (e.g., *reflective, organized responses* as opposed to *good answers*). One comment indicates personality and character; the other really does not say much about the person.

Excerpted from *Recruiting, Interviewing & Selection Process*, (p. 11-12, 1996). **National Audubon Society, Human Resources Department. Used with permission.**

c.   Follow-up

❑   Evaluate the candidate based on the search criteria;

❑   If the candidate is a contender, contact references using the following guidelines:
- Prepare questions in advance. Many former employers will only confirm that the person was employed there, during what time period, title, and final salary;
- Verify employment information provided by the applicant;

- Provide information about the position;
- Ask about the reference's knowledge of the candidate's strengths and skills for the position;
- Ask about any weaknesses the reference may know about the candidate's qualifications for the job;
- Ask if the reference would rehire the candidate if an appropriate position were available.

6. Select and Hire the Best Candidate

❏ Choose a candidate who meets the requirements, has positive references, fits the organization's culture, and is genuinely interested in the position. Consider other organization goals such as increasing diversity.

❏ Offer the position verbally. If the candidate accepts, follow up with an offer in writing.

❏ Detail the terms agreed upon in the appointment letter.
Include: title of position offered; salary; benefits; start date; any other terms both parties have agreed are conditions of employment (paid moving expenses, housing).

❏ If employed "at will," define and explain the terms of employment. **See Appendix M, *Employment at Will*, p. 206.**

B. Employee Orientation

Orientation for new employees helps them see how they fit into the organization and that they are part of it. Orientation should focus on basic information the employee needs to do the job and provide a broad perspective of the organization.

An orientation that involves other staff is a great way to welcome the new person while getting to know his or her colleagues. Involve staff when planning employee orientation. Consider the following:

❏ Welcome by executive director and supervisor;

❏ Make sure the supervisor works with the new employee the first day;

❑ Show location of office or work area;

❑ Introduce new employee to co-workers. Provide organization chart;

❑ Provide a tour of the facility. Show location of rest rooms, supply room, conference room;

❑ Explain telephone and office machine use and any policies about usage;

❑ Provide keys or other access information (alarm codes, radios, cell phones);

❑ Provide a copy of employee handbook or personnel policy manual. Ask employee to review pay procedures, time recording procedures, holidays, vacation, sick leave;

❑ Provide any paperwork to be completed. Address any questions on insurance or other benefits;

❑ Provide copy of job description;

❑ Jointly develop guidelines for employee's first week. Provide specific information such as information to read or review, people to meet, places to visit. Ask a staff member to help the employee by providing guidance and mentoring;

❑ Provide schedule of staff meetings and other required meetings;

❑ Review dress code, housekeeping, safety, emergency information;

❑ Take new employee out to lunch.

C.   Performance Evaluations

Performance evaluations can be dreaded, anxiety producing events feared by even the most successful employee and supervisor. If conducted fairly, openly, and with adequate time to prepare, a performance appraisal can be a highly interactive exchange between employee and supervisor. The evaluation can provide an honest assessment of employee performance from the employee's and the supervisor's perspectives in a constructive way that will help the employee be successful.

Some frequent problems with performance appraisals include:

- Wide variations in ratings from one evaluator to the next, often depending on the personality of the evaluator;
- Managers give better ratings to people they like;
- Employees don't understand the rating they are given;

- Evaluations are general, not specific;
- Managers give average ratings to poor performers;
- Managers forget that the written review is often cited for wrongful discharge cases brought by an employee (Harrington-Mackin, 1994, p. 119-120).

Seek ways to constantly improve skills, knowledge, and results. The performance appraisal is an excellent place to do it.

1. Employee's Role in Evaluation

Supervisors provide employees the self-evaluation form well in advance of scheduling a one-on-one meeting. The employee assesses:

- Major accomplishments and progress made on goals and objectives during the year;
- Recognition, awards, special assignments, or other contributions made by the employee;
- The most important contributions made to the department, team, or organization;
- Additional initiatives, ideas, or suggestions for improvement by the employee;
- New skills, training, education, or professional qualifications earned in the past year;
- New skills or training needs identified;
- Areas of performance improvement identified;
- Recommendations for changes in the employee's department, work area, or team;
- Recommended goals and objectives for the coming year.

The employee completes and returns the evaluation form to the supervisor to complete his or her written assessment of the employee's performance. Make sure the form has room for both employee and supervisor comments.

Employee Performance Evaluation
Evaluation of Goals and Objectives
Delaware Nature Society

I.   Goals and objectives since last evaluation
      Allow one page. Employee lists goals and objectives and notes
      progress.

II.   Future goals and objectives
      List future goals and objective (for coming year).

III. Developmental goals
      Include developmental goals.

IV.   Other comments
      Leave space for employee comments.

Prepared by: Date:
Include a signature line and date

The self-evaluation and performance appraisal allows employees to:

- Provide a self-assessment on performance strengths, weaknesses, difficulties encountered;
- Constructively criticize their own performance and identify areas for improvement;
- Recommend strategies for improved performance;
- Discuss opportunities for growth;
- Ask for support, express concerns, and seek advice.

2.   Supervisor's Role in Evaluation

The supervisor's role in the appraisal process is to gather relevant information about the employee's performance. Seek confidential peer and subordinate appraisals from a representative sample of employees including those supervised. If the employee's work requires frequent interaction with external individuals, consider the value of contacting these sources. **See Appendix R, *Developing Your Team Through Communication*, p. 219, for one organization's approach to gathering peer input.**

Prior to meeting with the employee, the supervisor:

- Provides each employee a self-appraisal form;
- Gathers information to use in the evaluation;
- Reads the employee's self-appraisal;
- Completes a written evaluation of the employee's performance;
- Schedules a time to discuss performance with the employee without interruptions.

During the evaluation, the supervisor:

- Sees his or her role as coach and collaborator with the employee;
- Creates an atmosphere of trust;
- Provides thoughtful, constructive comments, addressing both strengths and weaknesses;
- Listens to the employee's self-appraisal and discusses performance;
- Recognizes accomplishments, achievements, and progress;
- Offers suggestions for improvement;
- Asks for continued commitment to the organization and to improving performance;
- If major performance problems are identified, addresses these issues directly;
- Works to create understanding of the problem and to find collaborative solutions.

Performance appraisals usually assess other criteria including management and administrative abilities, personal attributes, team skills, and interpersonal skills. **See Appendix S, *Individual Assessment,* p. 222-223**.

Some reviews are used to justify salary increases, recommend job changes, identify staffing needs, and identify training needs. Hold the performance appraisal process prior to developing the annual budget so that these financial considerations will be addressed.

3.   Team Evaluations

Teams are evaluated on collective performance and team results. Team evaluations often are conducted by fellow team members who share the same goals or by a team leader. Provide training for team members unfamiliar with conducting performance appraisals prior to the evaluation.

Performance reviews for teams include many of the same guidelines for individuals and supervisors such as gathering peer input, completing a self-assessment, and meeting in person to discuss performance. Team reviews may also include input from outside sources (if the team's work is external), a full team self-appraisal, a review by the team leader, and a review by the executive director.

Benefits to a team review include:

- Members interact and see each other's performance; their review may be more accurate than a supervisor;
- Peer pressure from team members who share the same goals can enhance motivation and improve performance;
- All team members learn to develop assessment skills (Harrington-Mackin, 1994, p. 120).

There are difficulties as well which include:

- Team reviews take more time;
- Distinguishing between team and individual contributions is difficult;
- Some team members are uncomfortable judging or evaluating others;
- Extensive training is needed to become competent giving feedback and functioning as a performance coach (Ibid., p. 120-121).

D.   Disciplinary Action

Develop procedures to follow when employee performance or behavior warrants disciplinary action. As with other personnel policies and procedures, seek the advice of legal counsel.

Some examples of issues requiring disciplinary action include: violation of organizational policy, violent behavior, theft, providing false information on official records, absenteeism, safety violations, unauthorized use of firearms, and harassment of others. These should be identified in the personnel policy manual. **See Appendix L,** *Personnel Policy Manual,* **p. 204.**

When taking disciplinary action:

- ❐ Know the organization's core values, policies and rules. Be consistent and reasonable;
- ❐ If angry, wait a few minutes before talking with the employee;
- ❐ Don't discuss the employee with other staff members. If other staff must be consulted, inquire about the situation and listen without expressing judgment about the employee. Maintain confidentiality;
- ❐ If the organization is an "at-will" employer, you may terminate the relationship at any time, with or without notice, and with or without cause. You may not terminate an at-will employee for an illegal reason such as discrimination. **See Appendix M,** *Employment at Will,* **p. 206.**

Use the following to guide disciplinary actions for performance or behavior problems:

- ❐ Identify the specific problem (or problems). Deal with it quickly and directly;
- ❐ Be sure the employee was informed of the organization's policies and procedures;
- ❐ Check the employee's personnel file for previous disciplinary actions or performance problems;
- ❐ If the offense is serious, determine if there is cause for immediate termination;
- ❐ Meet with the employee to discuss the issue; Determine if the employee understands there is a problem and what the consequences may be. Ask questions. Listen to the employee's perspective. Practice other effective communication skills;
- ❐ If corrective action is needed, determine what would constitute acceptable performance or behavior. Jointly identify the issues and actions that will help the employee get back on track;
- ❐ Keep detailed records;
- ❐ Set a time for follow-up. If employee performance or behavior improves, schedule regular meetings to track employee's continued progress on goals;
- ❐ If performance does not improve, other steps may be needed including steps to terminate.

E.   Grievances

An employee may file a grievance if he or she feels unjustly treated. Each organization handles these complaints differently. Grievances may be handled by human resources staff, the director, the board, or other committee established for this purpose. Include a description of the grievance procedure in the personnel manual.

Address other employee complaints by practicing open communication and the willingness to listen. Encourage employees to express their concerns, and make sure they know they will be heard. This may help diffuse a tense or sensitive situation.

Encourage employees to work out issues with each other by seeking common ground and solutions, rather than looking for a third party to resolve issues. If unable to resolve the problem, the employee's supervisor would need to intervene. Complaints about an employee's supervisor or the director are serious and must also be addressed.

Resolution of Employee Concerns and Complaints

Any time one staff member has a problem with another, they are both encouraged to address the problem openly between themselves. The following process should be used if parties cannot create a solution themselves:

1.   Involve their supervisor;
2.   Discussions with the Executive Director;
3.   Seek solutions outside of the staff.

With unresolved issues with the Executive Director:
1.   The Executive Director and staff member work with the Chairman of the Board;
2.   The problem may be taken before the next Board Executive Committee meeting for discussion and resolution.

From *Teton Science School 1997-1998 Personnel Policy Manual.* p. 22.

F.   Termination

If steps to address performance or behavioral problems have failed, termination may result. Firing an employee is difficult but it cannot always be avoided. At times it is the most appropriate action to take. Develop and follow standard, defensible job termination procedures to use under all circumstances. **See Appendix T, *Standards for Disciplinary Action,* p. 224.**

An employee's job may end voluntarily when he or she submits a resignation letter or gives verbal notice of the intent to leave. Employees may also leave as a result of the employer's request for a resignation, a forced layoff, or the planned ending of a position.

If the organization enforces "at-will employment," make sure there are no other written employment contracts or agreements that may alter the employment relationship.   Be sure to know all applicable employment laws (federal, state, and local) to avoid wrongful termination. **See Appendix M, *Employment at Will,* p. 206, and Appendix N, *Employment at Teton Science School,* p. 209.**

G.   Exit Interviews

Some organizations conduct an exit interview when an employee leaves. Exit interviews are useful to:

*   Bring closure to a relationship with an employee;
*   Ask about the employee's experience and perspective on the organization;
*   Ask about modifications, changes or improvements the employee would recommend;
*   Ask what the employee liked or disliked about working for the organization.

The purpose of an exit interview is to offer the employee an opportunity to reflect on his or her experience and perspective on the organization. An exit interview must be conducted as a safe, non-threatening discussion between the departing employee and the executive director or a director of human resources. If done in this manner, an exit interview can provide candid feedback that may be useful for guiding future organizational policies and actions.

Practice 17   ## Keep Detailed Personnel Records

Detailed personnel records are necessary to document each employee's history with the organization and to meet legal requirements for employers. Compliance with all applicable federal and state employment laws includes keeping appropriate files and other records.

The Americans with Disabilities Act (ADA), Equal Employment Opportunity Commission (EEOC), and the U.S. Department of Justice Immigration and Naturalization Service have specific reporting and record-keeping requirements for employers. Know which laws apply and what the reporting requirements are.

In large organizations with a human resources department, three separate files (a personnel file, a confidential file, and a benefits file) are kept for each employee. Supervisors may access the personnel file but the other two are restricted to human resources staff. Smaller organizations without human resources staff should also create files for each employee. Use the following guidelines.

A. Personnel File

- Employee application;
- I-9 form (if applicable);
- Resume;
- Emergency notification information;
- Job description(s);
- Appointment letter;
- Letters of praise, commendation;
- Awards or recognition;
- Complaint letters;
- Disciplinary action;
- Documentation of coaching, counseling, or warning procedures;
- Performance appraisal for past year; keep all others in a confidential file;
- Resignation letter;
- Termination report;
- Exit interview;
- Any other pertinent employee personnel information.

B.   **Confidential File**

- References;
- Hiring report;
- Complaint letters (older than one year);
- Disciplinary action (older than one year);
- Documentation of any coaching, counseling, or warning (older than one year);
- Performance appraisals (older than one year);
- Vacation, sick leave, other leave reports.

C.   **Benefits File**

- Insurance, pension, beneficiaries, and other benefit information.

All organizations must maintain factual and up-to-date employee files. This information is essential if the organization becomes involved in any employee claims such as discrimination or wrongful termination. Files are also needed for employee references.

References

Arrien, Angeles. *The Four-Fold Way*: *Walking the Paths of the Warrior, Teacher, Healer, and Visionary.* New York, NY: HarperCollins Publishers, Inc, 1993.

Block, Peter. *Flawless Consulting.* New York, NY: Jossey-Bass, Inc., a subsidiary of John Wiley & Sons, Inc., 1981.

_____ *Stewardship: Choosing Service Over Self-Interest.* San Francisco, CA: Berrett-Koehler Publishers, 1996.

Bryson, John M. *Strategic Planning for Public and Nonprofit Organizations.* New York, NY: Jossey-Bass, Inc., a subsidiary of John Wiley & Sons, Inc., 1995.

Covey, Dr. Stephen R. *Principle-Centered Leadership.* © 1990 Stephen R. Covey. Salt Lake City, UT: Franklin Covey Co. Used with permission from Franklin Covey Co., (800) 654-1776.

_____ *The Seven Habits of Highly Effective People.* © 1989 Stephen R. Covey. Salt Lake City, UT: Franklin Covey Co. Used with permission from Franklin Covey Co., (800) 654-1776.

Easton, Sue. *One Size Does Not Fit All.* Cassette tape. Orlando, FL: Easton and Associates, Inc., 1995.

Gallaro, Denise, Knight, Michael E., Lumsden, Gay, and Lumsden, Donald. "Empowerment and Teamwork in the Quality Organization," *The Nonprofit Management Handbook: Operating Policies and Procedures,* Tracy Daniel Connors, Editor. New York: John Wiley & Sons, Inc., 1993.

Harrington-Mackin, Deborah. *Keeping the Team Going.* New York, NY: New Directions Management Services, Inc. AMACOM American Management Association, 1996.

_____ *The Team Building Tool Kit.* New York, NY: New Directions Management Services, Inc. AMACOM American Management Association, 1994.

Katzenbach, Jon R. and Smith, Douglas K. *The Wisdom of Teams*: *Creating the High-Performance Organization.* Boston, MA: Harvard Business School Press, 1993.

Kouzes, James M. and Posner, Barry Z. *The Leadership Challenge.* 3rd Edition. San Francisco, CA: Jossey-Bass, Inc., a subsidiary of John Wiley & Sons, Inc., 2002.

Myers, Isabel Briggs. *Introduction to Type,* 6th Edition. Palo Alto, CA: Consulting Psychologists Press, Inc., 1998.

National Audubon Society. *Recruiting, Interviewing & Selection Process.* Unpublished paper developed by the Human Resources Department of National Audubon Society. New York, NY, 1996.

Robbins, Harvey and Finley, Michael. *Why Teams Don't Work* ©1995. San Francisco, CA: Berrett-Koehler Publishers, Inc. All rights reserved. 800-929-2929.

Rusmore, Barbara, Berthoud, Heather, Russell, Dianne, and Schechtman, Mike. *A Source Book for Executive Directors*, 5th Edition. Takoma Park, MD: Institute for Conservation Leadership, 1997.

The Nature Conservancy. *Employee Notebook.* Unpublished notebook developed by the Human Resources department. Arlington, VA: The Nature Conservancy.

Other Resources

Agyris, Chris. *Intervention Theory and Method: A Behavioral Science View.* Reading, MA: Addison-Wesley, 1970.

Drucker, Peter F. *Managing the Non-Profit Organization.* New York, NY: HarperCollins Publishers, Inc., 1990.

_____ *The Practice of Management.* New York, NY: HarperCollins Publishers, Inc., 1992.

Gelatt, James P. *Managing Nonprofit Organizations in the 21st Century.* (Oryx Press, 2/7/1992), Westport, CT: Greenwood Publishing Group, Inc.

Rohnke, Karl, and Butler, Steve. *Quicksilver.* Dubuque, IA: Kendall/Hunt Publishing Company, 1995.

Scholtes, Peter R., Joiner, Brian L., and Streibel, Barbara J. *The Team Handbook.* 2nd Edition. Madison, WI: Joiner Associates, 1996.

Schutz, Will. *The Human Element.* New York: Jossey-Bass, Inc, a subsidiary of John Wiley & Sons, Inc., 1994.

Appendix A

Types of Teams

Organizational Policy-Making Teams (Multi-functional)
- Identify major areas of concern/opportunity; articulate organizational needs;
- Develop philosophy, policies, direction;
- Establish goals and objectives;
- Formulate implementation plans;
- Identify resources needed to achieve goals;
- Monitor progress, measure and report results; establish time lines and completion target dates;
- Include members from every level of the organization;
- Require long meetings and meet over extended periods of time;
- Are sometimes called Quality Councils;
- Can function as organization's management team if so empowered.

Task-Force or Cross-Functional Teams
- Include between five and eight members; membership based on experience;
- Comprise individuals from two or more different work areas;
- Necessitate long meetings over a short period of time; implement strategic plan for addressing problem/concern/opportunity; others may complete the implementation of the plan;
- Assume investigative, corrective, interactive function;
- Are sometimes called Process Improvement Teams or Product Launch Teams.

Department Improvement Teams (Functional)
- Include only department members;
- Select problems; identify solutions;
- Restrict scope of activity to within department;
- Have short meetings that extend over a long period of time.

Quality Circles
- Include members from functional areas who work together on specific quality, productivity, and service problems;
- Are voluntary in nature;
- Select problem; may not have power and authority to transform ideas into action;
- Received minimal management direction; manager may be left with responsibility for implementation;
- Are often temporary; Serve as forerunner of self-directed work teams.

Self-Directed Work Teams (Functional)
- Comprise an intact team of employees who work together on an ongoing, day-to-day basis and who are responsible for a "whole" work process or segment;
- Assume "ownership" of product or service and are empowered to share various management and leadership functions;
- Are limited to a particular work unit;
- Function semi-autonomously; are responsible for controlling the physical and functional boundaries of their work and for delivering a specified quantity and quality of a product or service within a specified time and at a defined cost.

Appendix A continued

Self-Directed Work Teams (Functional) continued

- Are all cross-trained in a variety of work skills;
- Share and rotate leadership responsibilities; team members have equal input in decisions;
- Accept the concept of multi-skills and job rotation (except for jobs requiring years of training and technical expertise);
- Work together to improve operations, handle day-to-day problems, and plan and control work;
- Set own goals and inspect own work; often create own work and vacation schedules and review performance as a team;
- May prepare own budgets and coordinate work with other departments;
- Usually order materials, keep inventories, and deal with suppliers;
- Are frequently responsible for acquiring new training and maintaining on-the-job training;
- May hire own replacements and assume responsibility for disciplining own members;
- Monitor and review overall process performance.

Self-Managed Teams (Functional)

- Operate with varying degrees of authority and without a visible manager;
- Contract with management to assume management responsibility in addition to performing its specific jobs, including planning, organizing, directing and monitoring;
- Learn and share jobs usually performed by a manager;
- Control own operation;
- Often report in a "skip-level" pattern to managers two or more levels above them who act as integrators/facilitators; may report to "absentee" manager away on special assignment or to a manager with broad responsibility managing several functions;
- Hold weekly team meetings;
- Identify own goals and team direction;
- Persuade others in organization to accept team's goals; schedule and coordinate daily and occasional tasks of the team and individuals;
- Design and conduct cross-training on all tasks;
- Set performance standards for the work team;
- Screen applicants and interview job candidates for the team;
- Hire or make hiring recommendations;
- Provide orientation for new team members;
- Coach and provide feedback on member performance;
- Conduct new team member's evaluations during probationary period;
- Plan and adopt a budget;
- Collect performance data; review results;
- Meet requests from inside and outside the team;
- Identify, analyze, and solve task and relationship problems.

Appendix B

Why Teams Don't Work
There is no single reason.

PROBLEM	SYMPTOM	SOLUTION
Mismatched Needs	People with private agendas working at cross-purposes.	Get hidden agendas on the table by asking what people want, personally, from teaming.
Confused Goals, Cluttered Objectives	People don't know what they're supposed to do, or it makes no sense to them.	Clarify the reason the team exists; define its purpose and expected outcomes.
Unresolved Roles	Team members are uncertain what their job is.	Inform team members what is expected of them.
Bad Decision Making	Teams may be making the right decision, but the wrong way.	Choose a decision making approach appropriate to each decision.
Bad Policies, Stupid Procedures	Team is at the mercy of an employee handbook from hell.	Throw away the book and start making sense.
Personality Conflicts	Team members do not get along.	Learn what members expect and want from one another, what they prefer, how they differ, start valuing and using differences.
Bad Leadership	Leadership is tentative, inconsistent, or stupid.	The leader must learn to serve the team and keep its vision alive or leave leadership to someone else.
Bleary Vision	Leadership has foisted a bill of goods on the team.	Get a better vision or go away.
Anti-Team Culture	The organization is not really committed to the idea of teams.	Team for the right reasons or don't team at all; never force people onto a team.
Insufficient Feedback and Information	Performance is not being measured; team members are groping in the dark.	Create a system of free flow of useful information to and from all team members.
Ill-Conceived Reward Systems	People are being rewarded for the wrong things.	Design rewards that make teams feel safe doing their job; reward teaming as well as individual behaviors.
Lack of Team Trust	The team is not a team because members are unable to commit to it.	Stop being untrustworthy, or disband and reform the team.
Unwillingness to Change	The team knows what to do but will not do it.	Find out what the blockage is; use dynamite or Vaseline to clear it.
The Wrong Tools	The team has been sent to do battle with a slingshot.	Equip the team with the right tools for its tasks, or allow freedom to be creative.

Appendix C

Four Management Paradigms

Scientific management paradigm: "Pay me well." Authoritarian. Leader in control, knows what is best, directs people where to go, what to do. Treats people with fairness. Rewards with pay and benefits. Assumes people are motivated by economic security (p. 176-177).

Human relations paradigm: "Treat me well." Benevolent authoritarian. Takes care of people as long as they comply with what the leader wants. Power lies with leader who knows what is best but treats people with fairness, kindness, courtesy, civility, and decency. Recognizes people's social needs (to be treated well, to be liked and respected, to belong) (p. 177-178).

Human resource paradigm: "Use me well." Human resource approach. Uses and develops staff talent. Leader values cognitive, thinking abilities of staff and delegates more authority and responsibility. Is concerned about efficiency and the contributions of others, making better use of talent, creativity, resourcefulness, ingenuity, and imagination. People seen as economic, social, and psychological beings with talents to be used in creative and constructive ways (p. 178).

Principle-centered leadership: "Let's talk about vision and mission, roles, and goals. I want to make a meaningful contribution." Leader works with the whole person, seeing people as economic, social, psychological, and spiritual beings who want meaning and purpose. Leaders use principles (values, ideas, ideals, norms, and teachings that uplift, ennoble, fulfill, empower, and inspire). Recognize creative energy, resourcefulness, and initiative in people. " People live up to the expectations of them." Make work challenging and fulfilling. Encourage participation in decision-making, encourage self-direction and self-control (p. 178-180).

The principle-centered leadership paradigm "not only embraces the principles of fairness and kindness and makes better use of the talents of people for increased efficiency, but also leads to quantum leaps in personal and organizational effectiveness" (p. 180).

Adapted from pages 176-180 of *Principle-Centered Leadership* by Stephen R. Covey. © 1990 Stephen R. Covey. Reprinted with permission from Franklin Covey Co.

Appendix D

Assessing Staff Management Skills

Communicate Candidly

How candidly do you communicate? Rate each statement below according to this scale:

4	Almost always true
3	True most of the time
2	Seldom true
1	Almost never true

_____ I communicate honestly.
_____ My verbal communications are congruent with my action. I "walk my talk."
_____ I admit my mistakes and imperfections.
_____ When I am wrong, I apologize.
_____ I listen well.
_____ I only make promises I can keep.
_____ I conduct formal employee interviews.
_____ I am candid with prospective employees about the company culture and the job description.
_____ I keep my subordinates informed of what is going on in the organization.
_____ I encourage healthy communication and discourage bickering.
_____ I initiate one-on-one contact with all employees.
_____ I maintain my sense of humor and fun when communicating with employees.
_____ **TOTAL SCORE**

Evaluation
Here's what your score indicates:

41 and above:	You are a candid communicator.
31-40:	Your communication is generally candid, with some exceptions.
21-30:	You could be more candid with your employees. It's worth the effort.
Below 21:	You're not a very candid communicator. This is a good time to work on being more candid.

Source: *A Source Book for Executive Directors*, 5th Edition, 1997. "Human Resources Management" (p. 92).
Produced by the Institute for Conservation Leadership, a nonprofit training, facilitation and consultation organization serving the environmental community. Institute for Conservation Leadership, 6930 Carroll Avenue, Suite 420, Takoma Park, MD 20912. 301-270-2900. icl@icl.org. www.icl.org.

Appendix E

Goal Setting Process
Delaware Nature Society
From Mike Riska, Delaware Nature Society, Hockessin, DE

Prior to budgeting (October), and staff performance evaluations (September/October):

1. Employees meet with the department heads to discuss 5 year goals, current year accomplishments, 1 year goals, and financial considerations related to goals.
2. The department head discusses team goals with director to accept or modify.
3. The department heads present summarized department goals to entire staff at two-day off-site retreat.
4. Goals are presented to specific board committee.
5. Once accepted by board committee, a narrative summary of Society goals by department is distributed to entire board at the November board meeting. Budget is also presented in November.
6. Financial considerations are added into budget to see if they are realistic and do-able.
7. The opportunity for questions and discussion of goals is given during the December board meeting.
8. Staff tie in their goals (individual goals that advance organization goals) for next year into performance evaluation forms. Staff complete these sheets prior to evaluation.
9. Performance evaluation discussion centers on previous year accomplishments in relation to goals.

Appendix F

Goals and Objectives
Delaware Nature Society
From Mike Riska, Delaware Nature Society, Hockessin, DE

Executive Director

1. Implement board approved goals based on 10 year vision.

Fund Development

2. With board and staff: Continue to redirect the organization with focus on maximizing income through memberships, program direction, annual giving, capital development, planned gifts, and marketing.
3. Continue progress on capital development program with 2006 contacts to additional foundations, corporations and individuals with president and board members as appropriate.
4. Work with board leadership and staff to develop board structure for on going capital development programs.
5. Convert former Revel donors to membership/annual giving/Harvest Festival donors.
6. Annually monitor/revise capital development and facilities stewardship plans.

Management

7. Continue to monitor financial condition of DNS and set priorities as necessary.
8. Continue to monitor and focus organization on those tasks related to mission.
9. Insure that new staff has training and support.
10. Continue to insure that all possible organization policies are in place and written.
11. Effectively use remainder of $600,000 for Coverdale.
12. Support personnel committee in the process of securing a successor. Have job description by February 2006.

Land Preservation

13. Use the annual meeting and patrons events as celebrations for the DNS creation of a farmland preservation district.
14. Co-lead forest conservation advocacy effort with advocacy committee member.

Director's Guide to Best Practices

Appendix G

Six Conditions of Empowerment

1. **Win-win agreements:** Psychological/social contract. Recognizes that people are capable of self-direction and self-control and can govern themselves to do whatever is necessary within the guidelines to achieve the desired results. Represents a clear mutual understanding and commitment regarding expectations in 5 areas:

    *   **Desired results:** Overlapping organizational mission, strategy, goals, and job design with personal values, goals, and needs, including timelines.
    *   **Guidelines:** Policies, "no-no's," levels of initiatives, and a few possible procedures.
    *   **Resources:** Financial, human, technical, organizational available to reach desired results; include systems such as information, communication, and training.
    *   **Accountability:** Standards of performance, when to give progress reports.
    *   **Consequences:** Natural organizational and logical personal consequences — financial, psychological, opportunity, perks, scope of responsibility, etc.

2. **Self-supervision:** People supervise themselves in terms of the win-win agreement. Mangers serve as sources of help. Employees evaluate themselves based on the specified criteria in the agreement. Employees feel ownership toward the agreement since they helped create it.

3. **Helpful structures and systems**: Managers establish organizational structures such as strategic plans, hiring, training, professional development, compensation, job design, organizational structure, communication systems, budgeting, information systems. All systems are totally integrated with the win-win agreement and facilitate their fulfillment.

4. **Accountability:** People evaluate themselves. Manager's attitude is helpful, not judgmental. Manager's role may be as a resource, a trainer, or a counselor for career planning and professional development. If trust is high, employees' self-evaluation likely to be more accurate than the manager's would be.

5. **Skills:** Communication, planning and organization, and synergistic problem-solving.

6. **Character:** Traits most critical to establishing win-win agreements are **integrity** (habits are congruent with values, words with deeds, expressions with feelings), **maturity** (courage balanced with consideration) and **abundance mentality** (there is plenty out there for everybody).

Adapted from pages 190-199 of *Principle-Centered Leadership* by Stephen R. Covey. © 1990 Stephen R. Covey. Reprinted with permission from Franklin Covey Co.

Appendix H

Empower Employees

Are you good at empowering employees? Assess yourself by rating each statement below according to this scale:

4	Almost always true
3	True most of the time
2	Seldom true
1	Almost never true

_____ I delegate well and have faith in an employee's ability to handle the delegated task.

_____ I encourage employees to challenge the status quo.

_____ I keep track of and acknowledge employee's creative ideas and contributions.

_____ I actively seek employee involvement.

_____ I schedule regular meeting for employees to brainstorm without a manager.

_____ I set "think agendas" — for example, a problem of the week.

_____ I assign employees to be "boss" or "expert" for a day.

_____ I consistently ask employees for their responses to proposed changes.

_____ I work with subordinates to establish mutually agreed-upon goals and strategies for getting the job done.

_____ I allow subordinates to make mistakes.

_____ I support group activity and peer counseling for problem solving and generating ideas.

_____ I allow subordinates to structure their work in ways that are comfortable and productive for them.

_____ **TOTAL SCORE**

EVALUATION

Here's what your score indicates:

41 and above:	You understand how to empower your employees.
31-40:	You generally do a good job of empowering but miss some opportunities for empowerment.
21-30:	You could empower your employees much more than you do. Try taking a more empowering approach. The results may surprise you.
Below 21:	There's room for a lot of improvement in your empowerment skills. Start working on them today!

Source: *A Source Book for Executive Directors*, 5ᵗʰ Edition, 1997. "Human Resources Management" (p. 91). **Produced by the Institute for Conservation Leadership, a nonprofit training, facilitation and consultation organization serving the environmental community. Institute for Conservation Leadership, 6930 Carroll Avenue, Suite 420, Takoma Park, MD 20912. 301-270-2900. icl@icl.org, www.icl.org**

Director's Guide to Best Practices

Appendix I

Editor's note: Performance indicators are attached to each job description. This establishes a performance agreement with each new employee at the beginning of employment.

Performance Indicators
Special Program Director
Contributed by Ken Voorhis
Great Smoky Mountains Institute, Townsend, TN

Knowledge of Job: Has considerable knowledge of the following: the philosophy and objectives of environmental education and recreation programs; standard resources, materials, practices and facilities utilized in a comprehensive outdoor education and recreation program; the philosophy, goals and objectives of the Great Smoky Mountains Natural History Association and the National Park Service; the principles of supervision, organization and administration of a residential environmental learning center; current literature, trends and developments in the field of environmental education; the practices, procedures, methods, equipment and safety precautions of mountain hiking and camping; wildlife, flora and fauna indigenous to Smoky Mountains region; First Aid techniques; and the geography of the nearby Smoky Mountains National Park. Has general knowledge of the following: the principles of supervision, organization and administration; and current literature, trends and developments in the field of environmental education.

Is able to do the following: plan, direct, coordinate and evaluate the work of subordinate employees; operate a variety of office machines, including popular computer-driven desktop publishing, spreadsheet and file maintenance programs; exercise considerable independent judgment and discretion in applying standards to a variety of work situations; express ideas effectively both orally before large groups and in writing; deal effectively with public officials, civic groups, program participants and the general public; and establish and maintain effective working relationships as necessitated by work assignments.

Quality of Work: Maintains high standards of accuracy in exercising duties and responsibilities. Exercises immediate remedial action to correct any quality deficiencies that occur in areas of responsibility. Maintains high quality communication and interacts with all Institute departments and divisions, co-workers and the general public.

Quantity of Work: Maintains effective and efficient output of all duties and responsibilities as described under "Specific Duties and Responsibilities."

Dependability: Assumes responsibility for doing assigned work and meeting deadlines. Completes assigned work on or before deadlines in accordance with directives, NHA policy, standards and prescribed procedures. Accepts accountability for meeting assigned responsibilities in the technical, human and conceptual areas.

Attendance: Attends work regularly and adheres to NHA policies and procedures regarding absences and tardiness. Provides adequate notice to higher management with respect to vacation time and time-off requests.

Initiative and Enthusiasm: Maintains an enthusiastic, self-reliant and self-starting approach to meet job responsibilities and accountabilities. Strives to anticipate work to be done and initiates proper and acceptable direction for completion of work with a minimum of supervision and instruction.

Judgment: Exercises analytical judgment in areas of responsibility. Identifies problems or situations as they occur and specifies decision objectives. Identifies or assists in identifying alterative solutions to problems or situations. Implements decisions in accordance with prescribed and effective policies and procedures and with a minimum of errors. Seeks expert or experienced advice and researches problems, situations and alternatives before exercising judgment.

Appendix I continued

Cooperation: Accepts supervisory instruction and direction and strives to meet the goals and objectives of same. Questions such instruction and direction when clarification of results or consequences are justified, i.e., poor communications, variance with Institute policy or procedures, etc. Offers suggestions and recommendations to encourage and improve cooperation between all staff persons and departments within the NHA.

Relationships with Others: Shares knowledge with supervisors and staff for mutual and Institute benefit. Contributes to maintaining high morale among all NHA employees. Develops and maintains cooperative and courteous relationships with department employees, staffers and managers in other departments, representatives from organizations, and the general public in order to maintain good will toward the NHA and project a good image. Tactfully and effectively handles requests, suggestions and complaints from other departments and persons in order to maintain good will within the NHA. Interacts effectively with fellow employees, National Park Service employees, professionals and the general public.

Coordination of Work: Plans and organizes daily work routine. Establishes priorities for the completion of work in accordance with sound time management methodology. Avoids duplication of effort. Estimates expected time of completion of elements of work and establishes a personal schedule accordingly. Attends meetings, planning sessions and discussions on time. Implements work activity in accordance with priorities and estimated schedules. Maintains a calendar for meetings, deadlines and events.

Safety and Housekeeping: Adheres to all safety and housekeeping standards established by the NHA and various regulatory agencies. Sees that the standards are not violated. Maintains a clean and orderly workplace.

Planning: Plans, directs and uses information effectively in order to enhance activities and production of the department. Knows and understands the expectations of the NHA regarding the activities of the department and works to see that these expectations are met. Assists in designing and formulating ways, means and timing to achieve the goals and objectives of the department. Within the constraints of NHA policy, assists in formulating the appropriate strategy and tactics for achieving departmental objectives. Assists in organizing, arranging and allocating manpower and other designated resources in an efficient and effective way so as to achieve the goals and objectives of the department.

Organizing: Organizes work and that of subordinate staff well. Ensures that staff members know what results are expected of them and that they are regularly and appropriately informed of all NHA and department matters affecting them and/or of concern to them.

Staffing: Works with other NHA officials and management to select and recommend employment of personnel for the department who are qualified both technically and philosophically to meet the needs of the department and the Institute. Assists in the development and training of department personnel in order to ensure that they are properly inducted, oriented and trained.

Leading: Provides a work environment which encourages clear and open communications. Has a clear and comprehensive understanding of the principles of effective leadership and how such principles are to be applied. Provides adequate feedback to staff so that they know whether their performance levels are satisfactory. Commends and rewards employees for outstanding performance yet does not hesitate to take disciplinary action when necessary. Exercises enthusiasm in influencing and guiding others toward the achievement of departmental goals and objectives.

Controlling: Provides a work environment which is orderly and controlled. Coordinates, audits and controls manpower and other resources efficiently and effectively. Coordinates, audits and controls the utilization of materials and equipment efficiently and effectively. Has a clear and comprehensive understanding of departmental standards, methods and procedures.

Delegating: Assigns additional duties to staff as necessary and/or appropriate in order to meet goals, enhance staff abilities, build confidence on the job and assist staff members in personal growth. Has confidence in staff to meet new or additional expectations.

Director's Guide to Best Practices

Appendix I continued

Decision Making: Uses discretion and judgment to assist in developing and implementing courses of action affecting the department. When a particular policy, procedure or strategy does not appear to be achieving the desired result, moves decisively and definitively to assist in developing and implementing alternatives.

Creativity: Regularly seeks new and improved methodologies, policies and procedures for enhancing the effectiveness of the department. Employs imagination and creativity in the application of duties and responsibilities. Is not adverse to change.

Human Relations: Strives to develop and maintain good rapport with all staff members. Listens to and considers suggestions and complaints and responds appropriately. Maintains the respect and loyalty of staff.

Policy Implementation: Has a clear and comprehensive understanding of NHA policies regarding the department. Adheres to those policies in the discharge of duties and responsibilities and ensures the same from subordinate staff.

Policy Formulation: Keeps abreast of changes in operating philosophies and policies of the NHA and the National Park Service, and continually reviews department policies in order to ensure that any changes in NHA and NPS philosophy or practice are appropriately incorporated. Also understands the relationship between operating policies and practices and department morale and performance. Works to see that established policies enhance same.

Appendix J

The MBTI® Preferences

Where do you prefer to focus your attention? Where do you get energy? The E-I Dichotomy

 Extraversion

People who prefer Extraversion like to focus on the outer world of people and activity. They direct their energy and attention outward and receive energy from interacting with people and from taking action.

Characteristics associated with people who prefer Extraversion:

- Attuned to external environment
- Prefer to communicate by talking
- Work out ideas by talking them through
- Learn best through doing or discussing
- Have broad interests
- Sociable and expressive
- Readily take initiative in work and relationships

 Introversion

People who prefer Introversion like to focus on their own inner world of ideas and experiences. They direct their energy and attention inward and receive energy from reflecting on their thoughts, memories, and feelings.

Characteristics associated with people who prefer Introversion:

- Drawn to their inner world
- Prefer to communicate in writing
- Work out ideas by reflecting on them
- Learn best by reflection, mental "practice"
- Focus in depth on their interests
- Private and contained
- Take initiative when the situation or issue is very important to them

How do you prefer to take in information? The S-N Dichotomy

 Sensing

People who prefer Sensing like to take in information That is real and tangible -- what is actually happening. They are observant about the specifics of what is going on around them and are especially attuned to practical realities.

Characteristics associated with people who prefer Sensing:

- Oriented to present realities
- Factual and concrete
- Focus on what is real and actual
- Observe and remember specifics
- Build carefully and thoroughly toward conclusions
- Understand ideas and theories through practical applications
- Trust experience

 Intuition

People who prefer Intuition like to take in information by seeing the big picture, focusing on the relationships and connections between facts. They want to grasp patterns and are especially attuned to seeing new possibilities.

Characteristics associated with people who prefer Intuition:

- Oriented to future possibilities
- Imaginative and verbally creative
- Focus on the patterns and meanings in data
- Remember specifics when they relate to a pattern
- Move quickly to conclusions, follow hunches
- Want to clarify ideas and theories before putting them into practice
- Trust inspiration

Appendix J Continued

How do you make decisions? The T-F Dichotomy

T **Thinking**	**F** **Feeling**
People who prefer to use Thinking in decision making like to look at the logical consequences of a choice or action. They want to mentally remove themselves from a situation to examine the pros and cons objectively. They are energized by critiquing and analyzing to identify what's wrong with something so they can solve the problem. Their goal is to find a standard or principle that will apply in all similar situations.	People who prefer to use Feeling in decision making like to consider what is important to them and to others involved. They mentally place themselves into the situation to identify with everyone so they can make decisions based on their values about honoring people. They are energized by appreciating and supporting others and look for qualities to praise. Their goal is to create harmony and treat each person as a unique individual.
Characteristics associated with people who prefer Thinking: • Analytical • Use cause-and-effect reasoning • Solve problems with logic • Strive for an objective standard of truth • Reasonable • Can be "tough-minded" • Fair - want everyone treated equally	*Characteristics associated with people who prefer Feeling:* • Empathetic • Guided by personal values • Assess impacts of decisions on people • Strive for harmony and positive interactions • Compassionate • May appear "tender-hearted" • Fair - want everyone treated as an individual

How do you deal with the outer world? The J-P Dichotomy

J **Judging**	**P** **Perceiving**
People who prefer to use their Judging process in the outer world like to live in a planned, orderly way, seeking to regulate and manage their lives. They want to make decisions, come to closure, and move on. Their lives tend to be structured and organized, and they like to have things settled. Sticking to a plan and schedule is very important to them, and they are energized by getting things done.	People who prefer to use their Perceiving process in the outer world like to live in a flexible, spontaneous way, seeking to experience and understand life, rather than control it. Detailed plans and final decisions feel confining to them; they prefer to stay open to new information and last-minute options. They are energized by their resourcefulness in adapting to the demands of the moment.
Characteristics associated with people who prefer Judging: • Scheduled • Organize their lives • Systematic • Methodical • Make short- and long-term plans • Like to have things decided • Try to avoid last-minute stresses	*Characteristics associated with people who prefer Perceiving:* • Spontaneous • Flexible • Casual • Open-ended • Adapt, change course • Like things loose and open to change • Feel energized by last-minute pressures

Appendix K

Behavioral Profiles or Zones

Think of the diagram as a map of a personality universe, with a distinct north, south, east, and west. From left to right it measures assertiveness, from reactive passivity to proactive activity, or from "asking" to "telling." From top to bottom it measures responsiveness, whether we react in a controlled task-oriented fashion (top) or in an emotional people-oriented fashion (bottom). Thus, a "driver" is a combination of task-oriented and proactive. An "expressive" is a combination of proactive and people oriented. An "amiable" is people oriented and reactive, and an "analytical" is a combination of reactive and task-oriented.

Analytical	Driver
Key Value: Work with existing circumstances to promote quality in products and services.	**Key Value**: Shape the environment by overcoming opposition to get immediate results.
Orientation: Thinking	**Orientation**: Action
Time: Past	**Time**: Present
Amiable	Expressive
Key Value: Cooperate with others, make sure people are included and feel good about the process.	**Key Value**: Shape the environment by bringing others into alliance to generate enthusiasm for the results.
Orientation: Relationships	**Orientation**: Intuition
Time: Depends on who they are with at the time	**Time**: Future

Appendix L

Personnel Policy Manual
Table of Contents
Teton Science School, Kelly, WY

Appendix L continued

From Teton Science School *1997-1998 Personnel Policy Manual.* Approved June 23, 1997. Kelly, WY

Appendix M

Employment at Will
Reprinted from Legal-Ease, Spring 1996

Most of us have known or heard of nonprofits that were sued by an employee or former employee. Moreover, insurance experts say that employment-related issues are a main cause of suits against individual members. So it's important to recognize employment law issues. You can avoid lawsuits with just a little advance planning.

Employment Contracts

In Minnesota, employment is *at will* unless special circumstances make it otherwise. At-will employment means that either the employer or the employee may terminate the relationship at any time, with or without notice, and with or without cause. (An employer may not terminate an at-will employee for an *illegal* reason, however, such as discrimination based on state or federal human rights laws).

Certain situations, including the existence of an *employment contract* in some form, may change the at-will relationship. If there is an employment contract, it may be difficult or impossible to terminate an employee or otherwise regulate the conditions of his or her employment.

Sometimes employment contracts are created deliberately; union employees, for instance, usually have contracts. But sometimes an employer creates an employment contract without meaning to.

The Hiring Process. Careless communication during hiring may inadvertently give an employee grounds to argue that there is an employment contract. For example, language in a job announcement may imply that the employment relationship may only be terminated "for cause."

Terms such as "temporary," "permanent," "career path," "long-term growth" or "job security" may seem to promise more than at-will employment.

Similarly, take care during job interviews to avoid statements that may imply a contract. For example, promising employment "as long as you do a good job" or "perform satisfactorily" may be dangerous.

If you use an employment application form, it should state clearly that employment is at will and may be terminated at any time by either party, and that no employment contract is created by statements made during the hiring process. Even more explicit is a statement on the form that only a designated officer of the organization may make any representation to the contrary, and that any such representation must be in writing and signed by the officer.

Offer Letters. Some employers, having chosen someone to fill a position, send a letter formally offering the position. If you offer a job this way, include a statement that the employment relationship is at will.

This is especially important if the applicant is relocating from out-of town. If the relocating employee can show the existence of an employment contract, consummated when he or she accepted the job offer, you may find yourselves liable for relocation costs and lost wages if you terminate the employee. Similarly, if you induce someone to relocate and leave a secure position to work for you, especially someone who is not actively looking for or in need of a new job, the employee may successfully argue "fraudulent inducement" to challenge the otherwise at-will relationship.

Appendix M continued

Signed, Written Contracts. Some nonprofit organizations and their employees actually enter into written, signed agreements. Some agreements even bear the name "employment contract." Often, the organization itself gives the agreement to the employee, requiring his or her signature as a condition of employment. The organization (or the person responsible for hiring and supervision) may believe the "employment contract" is necessary to clarify the terms of employment, such as salary, hours of employment or job responsibilities. What they may not realize, however, is that the "employment contract" may be used by an employee as a promise of employment, provided he or she fulfills all terms of the contract.

Try to clarify terms and conditions of employment without using a signed, written agreement. A job description or a conversation with the employee can set out these details. If the hours of employment are unusual or scattered, a short memo may be appropriate.

If you still think a written agreement or memo is necessary, include a statement that the employment relationship is still at will. Make it clear that the agreement (or memo) simply sets forth the details of the employee's responsibilities (or hours or salary), and that you reserve the right to terminate the employee with or without cause, regardless of compliance (or lack thereof) with the terms of the written agreement.

Some organizations use confidentiality or non-compete agreements. (The first requires employees to keep confidential certain knowledge gained in the course of employment; the latter limits an employee's ability to go to work for a competing organization). Neither is an employment contract, provided it is appropriately worded. Don't avoid these agreements if necessary to protect your organization's interests.

Probationary Periods. A period of "probation" at the beginning of employment may suggest that surviving the probationary period means "permanent" or otherwise secure employment. Any description of a probationary period should clarify that the employment relationship is at will, during and after probation.

Employment Handbooks. Employee handbooks may also be construed to create employment contracts. This doesn't mean you shouldn't use handbooks, however, as they can clarify expected standards of conduct and work rules. But if you adopt an employee handbook, include a clear, specific, conspicuous disclaimer providing that:

1. The handbook is not intended to, and does not, create any contractual obligations;
2. Employment is at will and many be terminated by either party with or without cause, with or without notice;
3. The information and practices set forth in the handbook are simply guides, and the employer may deviate from them at any time, at its discretion; and,
4. The employer reserves the right to change information in the handbook at any time, without advance notice to employees.

The disclaimer should be in CAPITAL LETTERS and/or bold print, and placed at the beginning of the handbook. If it's at the end, it may be difficult to argue that it was conspicuous. If it appears under a specific section of the handbook (e.g., a "Conditions of Termination" section), it will probably not apply to other parts and a contract may be construed to exist relating to conditions outlined elsewhere.

Avoid writing a list of reasons for suspension or discharge. If you must do so, follow the list with a clear statement that it is not inclusive, and that you have the right to suspend or terminate an employee for reasons not on the list, and to use discretion in handling situations described in the list. Avoid vague terms such as "fair," satisfactory"

Appendix M continued

and "reasonable," since they may create an assumption that there must be "cause" before you may take an action such as discipline or discharge. Finally, require your employees to sign and date a statement acknowledging that they received the handbook and that they understand that employment is at-will. As always, consult your attorney at least annually to review changes in the law which may affect your employee handbook.

Performance Evaluations

All employees should be evaluated periodically by their supervisors. Most employees expect, and deserve, performance appraisals, which can improve performance and employee morale.

Generally, a history of positive performance evaluations should not imply existence of an employment contract. Use the guidelines above to govern your actions regarding performance appraisal. Do not promise an employee long-term employment if he or she has a favorable appraisal.

In conducting an evaluation, be candid. This is not the time for "Minnesota nice" unless it's justified by the employee's performance. Try to keep the evaluation process consistent year to year, and from supervisor to supervisor, so you can accurately measure changes in performance. Moreover, specify what an employee must do to address specific problems in performance, and what action you will take if he or she fails to do so (e.g., demotion, probation, termination).

The employee should sign a written evaluation, acknowledging that it was discussed with him or her. Employees need not agree with their evaluations and should be allowed to add their own written comments. File the evaluation in the employee's personnel file, along with documentation of problems or inappropriate events.

Your board should annually evaluate your executive director (president, chief executive, officer, etc.). Some organizations have no such process in place - especially when the executive director is a long-time employee, perhaps even the founder. However, it's in everyone's best interest to initiate an objective performance evaluation process. It gives the executive director concrete goals for the coming year, and gives the board a measure of performance at the end to the year. Evaluation is neither an insult nor a criticism. On the contrary, it may be an opportunity to reward excellent work which would otherwise not have been acknowledged.

The form and content of the executive director's evaluation will vary, depending on the responsibilities of the position and the needs of the organization. The sponsoring organizations of Legal Ease are a good place to start for information or examples of this kind of evaluation.

Consistent performance evaluations will not necessarily prevent an employee from misunderstanding what you expect, nor will they give you immunity from lawsuit or liability in the event a terminated employee sues you. However, the performance evaluation is an important factor considered by the court is such a suit, and it is to your advantage that the evaluation be fair and accurate. In an at-will employment setting, even exemplary performance evaluations will not eliminate the employer's right to terminate at any time, with or without cause. However, the employee may be less likely to sue after termination if the reasons are clearly related to expectations outlined in a performance evaluation.

Legal-Ease is a quarterly newsletter for nonprofit managers and boards published by the Center for Nonprofit Management, University of St. Thomas, 52 Tenth St. S., Minneapolis, MN 55403-2001.

Appendix N

Employment at Teton Science School

This disclaimer is in response to recent trends in Wyoming employment law and Teton Science School's need to control liability risk associated with employee discipline and termination. It is Teton Science School's great desire to protect the long-term future of the school by protecting and maintaining its at-will employment status

Important Notice: Disclaimer and Acknowledgment of Receipt of Handbook

I understand that my employment, compensation and/or benefits can be terminated, with or without cause and with or without notice at the option of either Teton Science School or myself. I also understand that no employee, manager, or supervisor of Teton Science School has any authority to enter into any agreement or make any promises for employment for any specific period of time, or make any statements or promises contrary to this document.

I understand that no conduct or statement, verbal or written, which contradicts this document can constitute an express or implied contract regarding my employment, and I should not rely on any such conduct or statements. I acknowledge receipt of the employee handbook, and I have read and understand its contents, and have had the opportunity to ask any questions I may have about the handbook. I understand that the handbook and all other employment policies, rules or practices of Teton Science School are intended as guides for the efficient and professional performance of my job. Nothing contained in the handbook or any other employment policies, rules or practices shall be construed to be a contract between myself and Teton Science School. Additionally, the handbook and Teton Science School's other employment policies, rules and practices are not to be construed by any employee as containing binding terms and conditions of employment. Teton Science School retains the right to change, contradict or depart from the contents of the handbook and any other employment policy, rule or practice as it deems necessary, with or without notice.

_____

Employee Signature
_____

Date
_____

TSS Supervisor's Signature
_____

Date

Tear out, sign, and return to the Director of Finance (designated personnel administrator) with the Employment Signature Sheet and the Confidential Employee Information Sheet.

_____

From Teton Science School *1997-1998 Personnel Policy Manual*. Approved June 23, 1997. Kelly, WY.

Appendix O

This is a hypothetical position and physical requirements. It is intended to provide an example of considerations in position descriptions to comply with ADA requirements.

ADA ANALYSIS - POSITION DESCRIPTION
POSITION NUMBER: 015668
POSITION TITLE: FISCAL ASSISTANT

ESSENTIAL FUNCTIONS
- Preparation and tracking of all university required forms and requisitions related to expenses and personnel transactions.
- Data entry and maintenance of fund accounting database. Coordination with university controller's office and university foundation.
- Data entry and maintenance of donor records and mailing lists. Coordination with university foundation.
- Filing, typing, preparation of computer generated reports.

MACHINES, TOOLS, AND EQUIPMENT USED
- Typewriter, computer, computer linked scanner, copy machine, fax machine, calculator, telephone.

REQUIRED WORK ENVIRONMENTS
- Job involves mostly sitting. Walking and standing are required only occasionally. A negligible amount of strength is required.
- Work is performed primarily in an internal environment (i.e. office, car, truck) 90% -99% of the time.
- The worker is in a typical office environment and not exposed to adverse environmental conditions 90% - 99% of the time.

REQUIRED PHYSICAL ACTIVITIES
Listed activities relate to essential position functions. Other physical activities to consider are climbing, kneeling, crouching, walking (long distances), characteristics of walking surface, pulling, lifting, handling, repetitive motion, range of vision over 20 inches, and field of vision.
1. Stooping (Required 1%-9% of the time). Bending body downward and forward by bending spine at waist.
2. Twisting (Required 40%-49% of the time). Turning the body partly around from a stationary position such as standing or sitting.
3. Reaching (Required 60%-69% of the time). Extending hand(s) and arms(s) in any direction at shoulder level.
4. Standing (Required 30%-39% of the time). Remaining on one's feet in an upright position without moving. For this position, the standing is dynamic which means moving about while standing.
5. Fingering (Required 70%-79% of the time). Picking, pinching, typing, or otherwise, primarily with fingers rather than the whole hand or arm as in handling.
6. Communicating (Required 90%-99% of the time). Expression or exchanging ideas through verbal/written communication. This activity is important in terms of its necessity to convey information to customers, coworkers, subordinates, and/or supervisors.
7. Hearing (Required 90%-99% of the time). Perceiving the nature of sounds. This factor is important as it relates to the necessity to receive information verbally and/or the need to respond to other sounds in the work environment.
8. Near vision (Required 90%-99% of the time).
9. Color vision (Required 1%-9% of the time). The ability to identify and distinguish colors is required.

Source: Pine Jog Environmental Education Center, College of Education, Florida Atlantic University.

Appendix P: Sample Job Descriptions

Executive Director
Contributed by Gordon Maupin
The Wilderness Center, Wilmot OH

Position Title: Executive Director

General Description:

The Executive Director is the chief executive officer responsible for all phases of the management and operation of a nonprofit (501(c)(3)) nature center. He/she is employed by a volunteer 50 member Board of Trustees.

The Executive Director is supervised by the President of the Wilderness Center, Inc. The President is elected by the Board of Trustees who are in turn elected by the membership.

Duties

Organization

The Executive director is responsible for hiring and termination of the full and part-time paid staff.

The Executive Director supervises the staff. He/she must be familiar with natural sciences, land management, and environmental educational programming and techniques. The Executive Director must also be competent to supervise and administer the business operations of the nonprofit organization.

1. Budget - The Executive Director develops the annual operating budget each year in conjunction with the Treasurer and Financial Secretary. He/She is responsible for operating the Center within the constraints of the budget as approved by the Board of Trustees.

2. Supervision - The Executive Director supervises (directly or indirectly) the paid staff of the Center. This includes annual employee reviews, hiring and dismissal of staff, and administering of personnel policies.

3. Office Management - The Executive Director must stay on top of office operations to see that all phases of the office operate as smoothly and efficiently as possible.

4. Computers - The Executive Director must be familiar with the Center's computer equipment and make decisions regarding purchase, maintenance, and replacement of computer equipment and systems. He/she is also responsible for the selection of software for use at the Center.

5. Committees - The Executive Director serves as an ex officio member of all board committees including Executive Committee (non voting member), Personnel Committee, Budget Committee, Planning Committee, Program Committee, Building and Grounds Committee, Membership Committee, and other committees which may be formed from time to time. If he/she cannot serve on a committee, he is responsible for appointing staff or volunteers to serve in his/her place.

6. Land Management - The Executive Director is responsible for supervising the management of TWC lands.

Appendix P continued

7. Regular Reports - The Executive Director prepares regular written reports to the Executive Committee and the Board of Trustees to keep these bodies apprised of TWC activities.

8. Legal Matters - The Executive Director works with the Center's attorneys concerning all legal work, contracts, tax exemptions and other legal matters related to the Center.

Program

1. Naturalist - The Executive Director serves as a staff naturalist, conducting occasional nature walks, lectures, programs, and answering questions.

2. Special Events - The Executive Director determines what special events the Center will offer. He/she establishes budgets for activities operated by the staff, and works with volunteers on special events operated by the staff.

3. School - The Executive Director supervises the Education Director in working with the Center's school education program. He/she gives general guidelines for lesson and exhibit content, and administrative handling of the school program. He/she also works with the Education Director to determine provisions of school contracts for the educational programming.

4. Programming - The Executive Director works with staff and volunteers to determine the Center's programming for the members and general public.

5. Special Interest Clubs - The Center has several special interest clubs. The Executive Director works with those clubs to see that the relationship between the clubs and the Center remains mutually beneficial.

Planning

1. Land Management - The Executive Director works with the Board of Trustees to establish, and update a comprehensive land management plan for all TWC lands.

2. Facilities - The Executive Director works with the Board of Trustees to develop plans and specifications for TWC facilities.

3. Government Matters - The Executive Director works with area governmental planning agencies to defend the Center's interests and advance the Center's mission.

4. Strategic and Long Range Planning - The Executive Director works with the board, staff and membership to produce strategic and long range plans to ensure the continued success of the organization.

Public Relations

1. Public Relations - The Executive Director performs a wide variety of PR tasks including writing of news releases, working with area media representatives, and developing media plans for promoting the Center and its activities. The Executive Director speaks to community organizations on a frequent basis. The Executive Director is the spokesperson for the Center on any controversial matters.

Appendix P continued

2. Newsletter - The Executive Director edits and/or supervises the production of the Center's monthly *Members' Newsletter* and the quarterly *Teacher Trails*.

3. Annual Report - The Executive Director coordinates the preparation of the Center's Annual Report.

4. Publications - The Executive Director writes and edits other TWC publications such as brochures, newspaper or magazine articles, and radio or television spots.

Fund Raising

1. Bookstore/Birdseed Sale - The Executive Director supervises the operation of the Center's bookstore/gift shop to ensure that it makes an adequate level of profit while contributing to the Center's overall mission. The Executive Director conducts the annual birdseed sale in such a manner as to attract more members and ensure it generates income to support the Center's operations.

2. Fund Raising - The Executive Director works with the Board, staff and volunteers on all fund raising activities of the Center. He/she supervises the development staff to ensure the Center has adequate operating funds.

3. Capital Grants - The Executive Director works with the board and development staff to prepare grant requests for capital funds. The Executive Director works with the board and development staff to decide upon strategies for major fund raising campaigns.

4. Membership Development - All staff members at the Center are responsible for membership development. The Executive Director works with the board, staff, and volunteers to attract more members to the Center. This includes media campaigns, direct mail development, personal contacts and other means of introducing people to the Center.

5. Planned Giving - The Executive Director works with people who may be interested in making planned gifts to the Center.

Education/Experience

The Executive Director will hold a Master's Degree or higher degree in Natural Science, Natural Resources, Environmental Education, or a closely related field. In addition he/she should have experience in the operation of a Nature Center (preferably a 501(c)(3) nonprofit nature center). The job requires a broad knowledge of natural science, working with volunteers, organizational management, land management, fund raising, and supervision of staff.

Appendix P continued

Operations Manager
Contributed by Carolyn Chipman-Evans
Cibolo Nature Center, Boerne, TX

Jobs include, but are not limited to :

- Mail list management, bookkeeping, graphic design, and word processing.

- Office management including filing, organizing, correspondence, oversee maintenance, secretarial duties, message liaison, bulk mail.

- Communication, such as letter writing, phone calls, volunteer coordination, packets to donors, etc.

- Organizing, keeping calendar. Organize press releases. Send out appropriate mail and reports on time.

- Membership management, following through with membership plan, sending reminders, tracking membership, arranging membership drives.

- Policy manual creation: documenting policy and organizing it in a logical form.

- Volunteer Coordinating, helping to interview, schedule and train volunteers, tracking hours and job descriptions, thanking, arranging awards and parties, creating a volunteer policy manual.

- Willing and able to function as a spokesperson for the organization.

  30 hours per week. Hours are flexible, according to your schedule and needs of the Nature Center. Pay starts at ($) per year.

Appendix P continued

Outreach Naturalist
Contributed by Gordon Maupin
The Wilderness Center, Wilmot, OH

The Wilderness Center (TWC or the Center) is a secular, non-profit nature center dedicated to nature education, wildlife conservation, natural history research, and community service. Each year, thousands of people visit to walk the trails, participate in special events, courses, or workshops, or just enjoy being outdoors.

Classes in the natural and physical sciences are led throughout the year, both at TWC and at the schools. Following the Center's educational philosophy, TWC programs teach currently accepted scientific principles, including evolution and a very old universe. Demand is rising for programs at schools and other non-TWC sites.

The Outreach Naturalist position is a full-time position. The Center expects that the position will become self-funding but, if it does not, will continue to fund the position in its operating budget.

Duties include, but are not limited to:

- Implement existing outreach programs (environmental issues, natural history, and astronomy) for all ages, upgrading as and when possible.
- Design and implement additional outreach programs. Design and implement both in-house and outreach adult public programs.
- Oversee all phases of the ongoing outreach program. Maintain materials and equipment; present programs; recruit, train, and schedule volunteer presenters; generate and distribute publicity, etc.
- Assist presenting in-house programs (nature, astronomy).
- Develop and maintain a speaker's bureau of volunteers to present an introductory slide show.
- Assist in all other phases of TWC operations as needed.

Supervision: The Outreach Naturalist works under the supervision of the Education Director. The Outreach Naturalist supervises volunteer presenters.

Qualifications:

- Bachelor's degree in Interpretation, Natural History, or related field. Master's degree desirable.
- Speech, drama, and/or presenting experience highly desirable.
- Computer use (Macintosh) experience desirable, or willingness to learn essential.
- Staff or intern experience in a nature center, outdoor education center, museum, arboretum, zoo, etc. and classroom teaching experience desirable.

Salary and Benefits:

- Salary ($) with yearly merit reviews.
- 85% health insurance and life and disability insurance if qualify for coverage. Contribution to Tax-deferred annuity (TDA) if don't qualify for coverage.
- Tax-deferred annuity plan available.
- Pension plan of 5% of annual salary after one full year of full-time employment.

Appendix P continued

Environmental Education Specialist
Contributed by Judy Miller
Anita Purves Nature Center, Urban IL

Nature of Work: The Environmental Education Specialist is responsible for the coordination of the environmental education program.

Supervision Received: Supervision is received from the Environmental Education/Recreation Manager.

Supervision Exercised: The Environmental Education Specialist directly supervises instructors and volunteers working with the Environmental Education program.

Dimensions and Tasks:

Planning and Programming

1. Plan, coordinate, present and evaluate the school tour and service learning programs.
2. Assist with the development, presentation and evaluation of the Naturalist in the classroom and Assembly programs.
3. Develop, prepare, organize and evaluate curricula for school tour and service learning programs.
4. Develop, prepare and evaluate Educational Loan Box materials.
5. Assist with the planning and presentation of educator workshops.
6. Assist with the planning and presentation of family programs.
7. Assist with the planning and implementation of Nature Center special events.
8. Coordinate Environmental Teen Programs, including the summer Counselor in Training and Junior Counselor program.
9. Coordinate the summer King Camp program.
10. Coordinate the Park District's Environmental Policy Committee.
11. Assist with the care and handling of live exhibits.

Personnel

1. Assist with the daily operations of the Nature Center.
2. Hire, train, supervise and evaluate part-time staff for the school tour and service learning programs.
3. Hire, train, supervise and evaluate Counselor in Training, Junior Counselor and King Camp staff.
4. Recruit, train and supervise school tour and service learning volunteer staff.

Finances

1. Determine and follow program budget.
2. Order and make necessary purchases within budgetary limitations for program areas.
3. Prepare bi-weekly payroll and vouchers.

Appendix P continued

Communication

1. Develop, present and evaluate informational and training materials for the school tour, service learning, Counselor in Training and Junior Counselor and King Camp programs.
2. Design interpretive materials including displays, newsletter articles and multi-media materials.
3. Maintains accurate records and writes reports as necessary.
4. Attends staff meetings.
5. Publicizes programs through media as necessary.

Public Relations

1. Greet and present introductory tours for groups and general public.
2. Answer natural history questions posed by Nature Center visitors.
3. Promote the environmental education programs by working with other environmental groups and agencies.
4. Represent the Park District as necessary or as assigned.
5. Present a positive Park District image by dressing appropriately.

Work Traits

1. Ability to develop, lead and evaluate environmental education programs for different age levels; specifically preschool through high school ages.
2. Ability to communicate effectively, both orally and in writing.
3. Ability to manage a budget.
4. Skills in leadership techniques and management.
5. Enthusiasm and respect for the outdoors.
6. High degree of motivation and initiative.
7. Enjoy working with the general public.
8. Exhibit an ability to work well with others.

Desired Education and Experience

1. A Master's or Bachelor's Degree with a major in Education, Environmental Education, Natural Resources, Outdoor Recreation or related field.
2. Minimum of two years experience in teaching environmental education programs.
3. Demonstrate supervisory and organizational skills.

Appendix Q

Screening Instrument

Naturalist/Interpretive Specialist, Lookout Mountain Nature Center, Golden, CO

Applicant Name_____ Applicant Number_____

Qualifications: Rate each item as indicated in the right-hand points column. A copy of the position announcement is attached for reference.

Point score

1. A minimum of a bachelor's degree in environmental education, interpretation, recreation, education, biology, natural resources, or a related field.

   1=BA
   2=BA in field
   _____ (points)

2. A minimum of two years of experience in interpretive and/or environmental education program design and presentation or any equivalent combination of education and experience.

   1=2yrs
   2=3-5yrs
   3=5+yrs
   _____ (points)

3. Demonstrated ability to conduct and develop on and off-site interpretive and educational programs for children of all ages and adults in cooperation with area educational organizations.

   _____(1-5 points)

4. Demonstrated experience in the development and maintenance of interpretive media (exhibits, way sides, web pages, displays, brochures, visual aids, etc.).

   _____ (1-2 points)

5. Ability to assist with the supervision, recruitment, training, support and provide leadership and technical assistance to seasonal staff and volunteers in delivering interpretive/education program services and interpretive media.

   _____(1-2 points)

6. Written communication and organizational skills.

   _____ (1-2 points)

7. Other (bonus points for special skills and abilities- please highlight these skills in the comments section below).

   _____ (1-2 points)

TOTAL

   _____

Comments:

Appendix R

Developing Your Team Through Communication

Ken Voorhis, Director
Great Smoky Mountains Institute
Great Smoky Mountains National Park, Townsend, TN

Abstract: Good internal communication is important for developing the effectiveness and magic that a good team can possess. A model for developing a peer review process that encourages staff to give one another valuable input in a non-threatening way is discussed. Other ideas for enhancing communication among staff members are presented.

Key Words: Communication, staff training and development, evaluation, feedback

The Art of Communication

What is one critical component that can deeply affect your program, mission, and staff effectiveness in either a positive or negative way? I am speaking of communication, the art in which interpreters are expected to excel. We work tirelessly to evaluate, polish, and improve our communication with our visitors. Do we give the same attention to our communication with those who we work with day to day? Is our communication within our staff allowing us to develop as a "team", that is, effectively working together toward the same objectives? Excellent communication amongst our staff is critical to developing an effective team approach and the magic that such a group can work.

Unfortunately good communication between staff members is not something that usually occurs without some effort. A variety of factors work against good communication. We are very busy. Schedules often preclude ability to communicate equally with everyone. Perceptions of mission, visitors, management, priorities etc. can be quite varied. Individual needs, backgrounds, prejudices, stereotypes, and values can limit our abilities to communicate as well. One could probably continue with a long list of reasons why communication can be difficult. One could also probably come up with a variety of examples within her/his situation where staff conflict and associated decrease in the effectiveness of your team's ability to serve its mission was caused by poor staff communication.

Building Communication

Great Smoky Mountains Institute is a residential environmental education center. People are involved in our programs 24 hours a day, often seven days a week. A number of our staff live on site. They are somewhat isolated and often spend much of their personal time with each other as well. Most are very dedicated, excited to be working here and living within the National Park. Teamwork is something we encourage within our participants. It is something we are proud of within our staff and the magic that the team works is highly dependent upon good communication. Communication is something we plan for and continually work to improve. When it breaks down we have problems that often could have been easily avoided.

Creating an atmosphere where communication is encouraged and supported is certainly an important responsibility of all managers. Managers who ask for input, advice and suggestions are more likely to have employees who are willing to approach them with concerns. Those who react negatively or defensively to such feedback are less likely to hear about problems or concerns until it is too late and are often in the business of damage control rather than being able to avoid potential conflicts.

Everyone connects with some people more easily than others. We rarely have the opportunity to choose the people that we work with and so have to adapt to various personalities. Knowing who we can communicate with well and those with whom there are potential communication problems is important. Formalized personality or leadership surveys can be helpful for staff to begin to view how other people view others, how they think and make decisions and how they can best be approached. We have effectively used such surveys and even simple games that help us understand each other's personalities better.

Meetings can often become a burden to staff with busy schedules but planned effectively they can be an important place for communicating critical messages beyond the essential meeting objectives and enhancing communication within the group. We have a weekly Monday morning meeting and an evaluative meeting at the end of each program. There is often a great deal of information and logistics to cover at the Monday meetings but staff know what to expect and come prepared for the week. Staff are encouraged to let management know about issues that the staff would like to discuss at these meetings. To take some of the drudgery out of logistic-type meetings we occasionally try to leave time for a "fun" activity. We actually ask staff to come with several of these activities and write them with their name on a slip of paper. The activities are supposed to be fun, interactive and perhaps something that they could use in a program. When time allows we pull a slip from a jar and the staff member whose idea it is leads us through the activity. While there are often moans about having more important things to do, once involved the group usually has a good time and the levity leaves them more ready to move on to the next task and feeling like a team.

The Peer Review Process - A Model
The idea that I most want to share here is not as commonplace as the above mentioned ideas. It is a formalized peer review that has become an important part of our continued effort at increasing communication, building our team, and enhancing the magic that we share as a whole. It is a fairly simple process to implement but requires commitment by the staff and orientation to its purpose. These reviews are conducted twice each session, once at the mid-point, and once near the end.

Several weeks before a Peer Review, sheets are distributed to each staff member listing each staff member's name and a column in which to write Strengths, and one for Areas to Improve. There is also a space to write strengths and areas to improve for our overall program. Staff are instructed ahead of time that this is an opportunity for us to help each other grow and to encourage one another. It is done anonymously, so that staff can be frank, but is not a place for telling each other off. It is to be done in a supportive atmosphere. When writing areas to improve staff are asked to write it in the way they would like such a comment put to them. Staff then write short phrases in each area, trying to think of something for each person but not to the extent that they are having to dig things up. Each person is also expected to write several comments in each area concerning his or herself.

After the reviews are gathered, our office manager types up a sheet with each person's strengths and areas to improve. The next stop is actually the hard part but helps complete the process and really works to build the team. We gather for a peer review session in which all of the reviews will be read to the entire group. To avoid inappropriate or petty comments I do read all of the reviews ahead of time. I have sometimes had to seek clarification but have rarely needed to ask someone to reword a comment.

The peer reviews are mixed up and a volunteer chooses one and reads the comments to the person to whom it is addressed. That person then chooses one and we continue until all are read. We usually applaud or give hugs to the person whose review has just been finished. The ground rules for the presentation of the reviews is that there will be no additional comments or further discussion at that time. After the review staff are encouraged to get with one of the supervisors if they need clarification or are disturbed about certain comments. Rarely is this necessary.

People are usually hardest on themselves and are not surprised at the comments made. If there is a misunderstanding or conflict the supervisor can add clarification and if necessary seek out the individuals that need to further discuss an issue. We normally have far more strengths to share about one another than areas to improve.

When first presented with the idea of peer reviews staff have various reactions. Some have suggested that they are adults and should be able to talk about these things face to face. In a perfect world that may be true but in reality most people avoid conflict and even appreciation is given in small doses. We ask that staff give it a try before making a judgment and although it is not necessarily comfortable for everyone, the majority of people have come around to valuing the input that is gained. Presenting the reviews in a large group can be unnerving but serves several purposes. First, knowing that they will be read aloud keeps people honest and supportive in their comments. Second, experiencing such a process as a group builds empathy with one another and helps bond the group. Thirdly, hearing the whole group's comments about an individual helps one to hear strengths for that person that may not have been appreciated before and to view areas to improve from the whole group's perspective.

I asked our staff to write a few comments about the peer review process and will share some of them here: "Gives a chance to tell people about the good things they do. Sometimes those are the things that you forgot to let them know." "Sometimes it is difficult to tell these things to a person face to face." "The reviews can bring out important points about our program and each other that need airing and clarifying." "They are especially good for evaluating teaching methods and other professional areas that don't normally come up in conversation." "Gives you a chance to mention little things that you might not have wanted to make a big deal about." "They are esteem boosts as well as constructive criticism. It is an excellent tool to use especially when a staff doesn't get along." "Good to get something in writing so you can look back once in a while to see if you are improving or not." "Since I have been here, reviews have been a real 'feel good' kind of thing, it helps to renew you a bit." "A bit stressful, hard to look forward to criticism but is relieving to learn that your worst fears are primarily self inflicted. Creates a supportive atmosphere."

Conclusion
Good teamwork means good communication. A good manager will evaluate the communication effectiveness of his/her staff and develop ways to further enhance that communication. The peer review process has been something that has worked well in our situation. It has become a tool that allows individuals to improve based on input from their co-workers. It allows us to encourage one another, helping us to grow as individuals and enhancing group cohesion. The effectiveness and value of the process can vary greatly depending on the personalities and issues involved and we continue to adapt it to meet specific situations.

Our jobs require us to be good at communicating our message with others. If we give as much attention to communicating among ourselves the communication of our message to our visitors should be enhanced as well.

Director's Guide to Best Practices

Appendix S

Individual Assessment

Please Print   **Date**

Identification Section		
Name	Social Security Number	
Present position	Birth Date	Hire Date
Department/Division	Date assigned to current position	
Immediate previous position	Current grade	Foreign language
Assessed by	Reviewed by	

Education & Training Section (School, Degree, Date where appropriate)		
Undergraduate	Associate	Associate
Other significant		

Current Achievement Level - Use arrow to indicate relative position on scale; → improving, ← diminishing, ✓ stable: NA (centered) if time on job is inadequate for rating

1	2	3	4	5	6	7	8	9	10
Unacceptable									Highest

Current capabilities: In the boxes below, rate the individual on each item from 1 (definite strength) to 5 (definite weakness); "NA" if unable to assess, unknown or not relevant. Next circle the 5 most prominent individual strengths and (X) up to 5 developmental needs.

Managerial/Administrative Abilities	Personal Attributes	Interpersonal Skills
❏ Raises appropriate issues ❏ Ability to identify and deal with causes of problems ❏ Ability to manage change ❏ Audit quality of work ❏ Accuracy of work ❏ Organizes effectively ❏ Decisive ❏ Handles details well ❏ Computer skills ❏ Identifies and deals with conflicts ❏ Office management skills	❏ Hardworking ❏ Innovative; creative ❏ Takes initiative; self starter ❏ Mental ability ❏ Resilient; bounces back after failure ❏ Analytical ❏ Flexible, open minded ❏ Self-confident ❏ Integrity/Ethics ❏ Other _____	❏ Team Builder ❏ Works well with superiors ❏ Works well with peers ❏ Sells ideas effectively ❏ Writes effectively ❏ Listens and considers ideas of others ❏ "Values" orientation ❏ Clear in verbal communication ❏ Other _____

Appendix S continued

Career Path Plan for the Next Three Years

Most appropriate next move (Be specific)	Now	Short-term 6-18 months	Long-term 3 years	Comments
Other possible moves				

Above columns Now, Short-term, and Long-term grouped under: Approximate Readiness

Individual's Development for Next 12-18 Months: Major output of the process; please give thoughtful consideration to completing this section.

_____
_____
_____
_____
_____
_____
_____
_____

Individual's Objectives/Aspirations and Views - Ex: Long-term career aspirations, expectations in current position or next position, individual motivators, and other personal values.

_____
_____
_____
_____
_____

Special Comments - List any characteristics which have distinguished the individual's career.

_____
_____
_____

From Aullwood Audubon Center and Farm, Dayton, OH. Reprinted with permission.

Director's Guide to Best Practices

Appendix T

STANDARDS FOR DISCIPLINARY ACTION

The **STANDARDS FOR DISCIPLINARY ACTION** shall be used by supervisors to assure uniformity in treatments in the most common disciplinary problems. The list of offenses is not exclusive. It is meant to be illustrative of the most common disciplinary problems.

A   Actions that may cause immediate dismissal:
1.   Sabotage: Participation in an act of destruction or attempted destruction of University property or equipment which obstructs University operation.
2.   Falsification of records: The willful and deliberate misrepresentation, falsification or omission of any fact whether verbal, written, or communicated in some other medium.
3.   Conviction of a crime which would affect adversely the employee's ability or availability to perform the duties of the job or the University's ability to carry out its mission.
4.   Theft of any property of the University or of any other person or entity.
5.   Strike or concerted activity

B.   Actions that may cause an immediate three day suspension on the first occurrence and dismissal on the second occurrence.
1.   Insubordination: A deliberate and inexcusable refusal or failure to obey a reasonable order which relates to an employee's job function.
2.   Drinking on the job or reporting to work under the influence of alcohol. An employee exhibiting a pattern of alcohol abuse to the extent that it affects work performance is a problem drinker. A problem drinker shall not be subject to disciplinary action unless the employee has refused to recognize the condition, failed to cooperate by not seeking help or treatment has proved unsuccessful.
3.   Reporting to work under the influence or use of non-prescribed drugs.
4.   An intentional battery on another person.
5.   Possession, sale, distribution of illegal drugs on University property or on the job. Possession, sale, or distribution of alcoholic beverages except authorized events.

C.   The following is a sample list of actions which may cause oral reprimand or written reprimand on the first occurrence leading to three day suspension and dismissal with repeated occurrence.
1.   Unauthorized use of state property, equipment or personnel.
2.   Threatening or abusive language directed toward another. Offensive language regardless of intent.
3.   Sexual harassment.
4.   A pattern of absences whether necessary or excused.
5.   Unauthorized distribution and solicitation.

Source: Adapted from Rules of the Department of Education, Division of Universities, Florida Atlantic University. Rule 6C5-5.014 of the Florida Administrative Code. University Support Personnel System (USPS) Employee Standards and Disciplinary Procedures.

Contacts

AVISO
American Association of Museums
1575 Eye St. NW, Suite 400
Washington, DC 20005-1105
202-289-1818
202-289-6578
aaminfo@aam-us.org
www.aam-us.org

The Chronicle of Philanthropy
1255 Twenty-third St., NW
Washington, DC 20037
202-466-1200
202-466-2078 (fax)
www.philanthropy.com

JobScan
Student Conservation Association
P.O. Box 550
Charlestown, NH 03603
603-543-1700 or 603-543-1828
earthwork@sca-inc.org
www.sca-inc.org

Job Seeker
28672 County EW
Warrens, WI 54666
608 378-4290
608 378-4290 (fax)
jobseeker@tomah.com
www.tomah.com/jobseeker

National Association for Interpretation
P.O. Box 2246
Fort Collins, CO 80522
888-900-8283 or 970-484-8283
970-484-8179 (fax)
jobsnai@aol.com (Job Listings)
www.interpnet.com

Contacts continued

National Audubon Society
Human Resources
700 Broadway
New York, NY 10003
212-979-3010
212-979-3016 (fax)

The Nature Conservancy
4245 North Fairfax Drive, Suite 100
Arlington, VA 22203-1605
703-841-5300
703-247-3721 (Job Hotline)
www.tnc.org

Reviewers

Andy Brown, Battle Creek Nature Center, Prince Frederick, MD
Peggy Hunt, Pioneers Park Nature Center, Lincoln, NE
Greg Lee*, Dodge Nature Center, West St. Paul, MN
Robert Mercer, Silver Lake Nature Center, Bristol, PA
Carl Palmer*, Ogden Nature Center, Ogden, UT
Corky Potter, Shavers Creek Environmental Center, University Park, PA
Tim Sandsmark*, Greenway and Nature Center of Pueblo, Pueblo, CO
Pat Welch, Pine Jog Environmental Education Center, West Palm Beach, FL
Jim Yaich*, Jamestown Audubon Nature Center, Jamestown, NY

*   Former director

CHAPTER 5: FUNDRAISING AND DEVELOPMENT

Generating Financial and Organizational Support

Funding is necessary to advance the organization's mission and achieve goals established during strategic planning. Funds are essential to ensure growth, stability and longevity of any organization.

To produce sufficient resources to support an organization, most directors develop an income mix that may include earned income (fees, services, contracts), interest income (from endowments or other investments), and charitable contributions (donations, gifts, grants, and support).

This section focuses on developing, cultivating, and maintaining charitable contributions. Directors, board members, development staff, and volunteers will benefit from learning and incorporating these practices to increase financial and organizational support.

For governmental organizations, this information will be useful to agency administrators as well as "Friends" groups created to generate additional financial and community support. **See Boards Chapter.**

Integrated Development

An integrated development program combines short and long term fundraising through annual, capital and planned giving programs

Annual giving produces income for operations through donors committed to making annual contributions to your organization. *Capital giving* targets funds for special projects and capital needs such as buildings and facilities. *Planned giving* concentrates on large, permanent gifts for long term support such as bequests.

This chapter focuses on annual giving and does not cover capital campaigns and planned giving programs. All are essential to a developing a completely integrated fundraising program.

Fundraising Policies

The board of directors makes policy decisions for how funds will be raised, processed, managed, and used. This is done through board committees (finance and development) for a vote by the full board. The director and development staff advise and recommend policies.

The board of directors may choose to define and set policies for various types of gifts. Policy decisions may include how funds should be invested or what percentage of interest from restricted funds may be budgeted annually.

One policy might state, for example, that all planned gifts (bequests, estate sales, sale of property, etc.) are permanently restricted for an endowment fund. This policy may be a way to solicit and promote planned giving.

> An *unrestricted gift* is a gift made without any condition or designation (p. 124).
>
> A *temporarily restricted gift* is temporarily restricted for a particular purpose but which when spent becomes an unrestricted gift for accounting purposes and is at that time reported as income (p. 118).
>
> A *permanently restricted gift* usually becomes part of an endowment, the interest from which is restricted for use as specified by the donor (p. 92).
>
> From *AFP Fundraising Dictionary Online*. Used with permission.

James M. Greenfield in "Fund Raising Overview" provides an excellent guide for a fund development policy manual in *The Nonprofit Management Handbook*. **See References, p. 275.**

See Appendix A, *National Charities Information Bureau Standards in Philanthropy*, p. 277-278, for policy and fund accountability information.

Ethics in Fundraising

Development activities provide frequent opportunities to inform, educate and involve numerous people in your organization's mission. Those engaged in fund development must represent the organization with the highest ethical standards and practices expected from the organization and the fundraising profession.

Ethical dilemmas may occur over decisions to solicit or accept gifts from certain donors or prospects. A donor's wishes may be outside the organization's mission or the donor may wish to influence the organization's direction. Ultimately, ethical decisions in fundraising are resolved by good judgment, discussion, and through policies which guide these decisions.

The Association of Fundraising Professionals (formerly National Society of Fund Raising Executives*) developed the "Code of Ethical Principles and Standards of Professional Practice" for development professionals. The principles and practices stated in this document represent the highest standards to be modeled in any fundraising activities.

"A Donor Bill of Rights" was a collaborative effort by the American Association of Fund Raising Counsel, the Association of Healthcare Philanthropy, the Counsel for Advancement and Support of Education, and AFP. The bill states what donors have the right to expect from organizations they support and is a model for all development activities.

See Appendix B, *Code of Ethical Principles and Standards of Professional Practice*, p. 279, and Appendix C, *A Donor Bill of Rights,* p. 281.

* Some references in this chapter include previous NSFRE publications.

Legal Requirements for Reporting Donations

State and federal regulations require nonprofit organizations to record and acknowledge charitable donations and contributions. Check with an accountant who specializes in nonprofits or consult a tax attorney to make sure you understand and comply with current federal and state reporting requirements. **See box below.**

Updates on tax law changes and accounting rules may be found in *The Chronicle of Philanthropy*, the *Nonprofit Times* or through membership in professional organizations such as the Association of Fundraising Professionals. **See Contacts, p. 297.**

A Potential Checklist of Accountability
By *Independent Sector*, Washington, DC. Used with permission.

Key question for grant makers and grant seekers: *How can an organization take steps that will help it maintain the public's trust?*

By making information about the organization easily available to any member of the public upon request, in recognition of the nonprofit organization's special responsibility to the public for openness in their activities:

- Current IRS form 990 (including all parts and schedules, except contributors list with amounts, which is protected under the Privacy Act;
- IRS Form 1023 (the organization's original application for recognition for tax exempt status);
- Annual report (often contains some or all of the following items):

  - ❑ Most recent financial audit report;
  - ❑ List of contributors, at least large contributors (amounts of contributions may be disclosed only with permission of contributor — some organizations list contributors within amount ranges); donor request for anonymity should be honored;
  - ❑ Governing documents: vision and mission statements, code of ethics/statements of values, standards of practice, operation or accountability, including conflict-of-interest and affirmative action or other inclusiveness policies;
  - ❑ List of board members and officers (usually listed in annual report; form 990 includes compensation of top employees and officers); staff roster;
  - ❑ Long range plan outline based on vision and mission statements;
  - ❑ Any current reports on program accomplishments;
  - ❑ Any ongoing evaluation procedures for assessing effectiveness for the organization, employees, managers and trustees, or outline for a process of self assessment which the organization encourages, including summary of ethics audit process.

Independent Sector **is a national leadership forum working to encourage giving, volunteering, not-for-profit initiative and citizen action. Copyright © 1997 Independent Sector.**

Other Development Guidelines

A director leads and advocates fund development to ensure the financial soundness and continuity of the organization. Established fundraising practices that generate annual, capital and planned gifts that are based on strong ethical principles and practices are the keys to success. Protect donor rights and incorporate sound business and fund management practices to build donor confidence in the organization's credibility.

Fundraising and development is challenging and requires a sustained commitment to develop relationships with donors and supporters. Short term fundraising successes are important, but to guarantee the stability and longevity of programs and mission, planned steady growth is essential.

Remember to use your organization's site, buildings, facilities and programs to inspire current and prospective donors. Seeing the organization's work firsthand inspires people to want to give.

It's My Nature Center Too

Not long ago, I was working with one of my members who happened to be a civil engineer. He was helping determine what we needed to do to repair the dam on our small lake. As I was thanking him for his generous contribution of professional advice, he said, "Hey it's no problem, it's my nature center too."

Those were among the nicest words I have ever heard from a member of my nature center. This member summarized the atmosphere I have spent a career trying to create. He expressed his feeling of ownership of our organization.

Perhaps the most important thing anyone can do for a nature center is to instill this feeling of ownership in as many people as possible. Once you have established this feeling in the community, the funds needed to make your organization successful will appear one way or another. Some you'll earn through hard work. Others will just show up with little effort on your part. The key is for people to feel as if they are a part of what you are doing.

Gordon Maupin, The Wilderness Center, Wilmot, OH

Checklist of Recommended Practices

I. Build a Development Team

- ❐ Practice 1   Demonstrate Development Leadership
- ❐ Practice 2   Coordinate Fundraising with Others
- ❐ Practice 3   Engage Board Members in Fundraising
- ❐ Practice 4   Build Development Capability with Staff
- ❐ Practice 5   Enlist Key Volunteers
- ❐ Practice 6   Hire Consultants When Needed

II. Plan for Development

- ❐ Practice 7   Tie Goals to Mission, Strategic Plans and Programs
- ❐ Practice 8   Know and Understand Your Constituency
- ❐ Practice 9   Keep Fundraising Principles in Mind
- ❐ Practice 10   Identify and Target Funding Sources
- ❐ Practice 11   Select the Appropriate Solicitation Strategy

III. Create Goals and Strategies

- ❐ Practice 12   Produce an Annual Development Plan
- ❐ Practice 13   Establish an Annual Giving Program
- ❐ Practice 14   Develop Individual Support Through Members, Contributors, and Major Donors
- ❐ Practice 15   Develop Institutional Support Through Foundations, Businesses, and Other Organizations
- ❐ Practice 16   Conduct Special Events
- ❐ Practice 17   Generate Additional Funds Through Earned Income

IV. Establish Ongoing Systems

- ❐ Practice 18   Thank Donors for Their Contributions
- ❐ Practice 19   Process Donations Promptly
- ❐ Practice 20   Keep Accurate Membership and Donor Records
- ❐ Practice 21   Recognize Donor Support
- ❐ Practice 22   Produce Development Reports
- ❐ Practice 23   Evaluate Fundraising Strategies

Recommended Practices

I. Build a Development Team

Practice 1

Demonstrate Development Leadership

The executive director's development role is to:

❑ Be the primary fundraising strategist;

❑ Provide leadership to volunteers (including board members) and staff, keeping them focused on the mission and vision, recognizing their fundraising efforts, and resolving disputes;

❑ Work closely with the director of development or other key development person;

❑ Represent the organization at all major fundraising events and gatherings;

❑ Make solicitation/cultivation calls and visits to major donors and prospects (Adapted from NSFRE, *Self-Study Survey Course on Fundraising,* p. 4:10).

In some small to medium-size organizations, the director handles most development responsibilities. This approach requires support staff to manage record keeping and other important fundraising details.

Practice 2

Coordinate Fundraising with Others

Fund development is "... a highly coordinated and cooperative program designed to yield maximum public support for nonprofit organizations" (Greenfield, 1993, p. 442). It requires exceptional coordination between various people and departments within an organization as well as numerous people outside. A partial list includes the following:

• Executive director;

• Board members and committees, especially development and finance;

• Volunteers;

• Staff (development, finance, program, marketing, public

- relations, administrative, site managers, grounds managers);
- Consultants;
- Members and other contributors;
- Major donors;
- Corporate and foundation representatives;
- Government entities;
- Businesses and local vendors;
- Media.

Practice 3

Engage Board Members in Fundraising

Board members are essential leaders and partners in any organization's development program. In fact, one of the board's chief responsibilities is to ensure the organization has adequate funds invested and managed responsibly (Greenfield, 1993, p. 441).

Most board members are expected to give both time and money. They "set the pace" for giving by others (Doty and Cox, p. 502) through their own financial and volunteer contributions.

Board members introduce the organization to new fundraising contacts (NSFRE, *Self-Study Survey Course on Fundraising,* 4:27), becoming "ambassadors to the professions, to the business community, and to personal friends who are in a position to lend their support to a good cause" (Doty and Cox, p. 502).

Choosing capable board members to fund raise is the nominating committee's responsibility. The director must be actively involved in this process as well as motivating and involving board members in fundraising on an ongoing basis. **See Boards Chapter.**

Practice 4

Build Development Capability with Staff

The adage "everyone is a fund raiser" is true for most nonprofit organizations. Staff members play important roles in fundraising, representing the organization to a variety of people on a daily basis. Each contact is an opportunity to create a positive impression resulting in increased members, donors and organizational support. Every organization may not need nor be able to afford a full development department and professional staff. Some directors may wish to add development staff or train existing personnel to assume these responsibilities and duties. All organizations can benefit from understanding the complexities of a development program and need someone — generally staff — to handle all the details.

You may want to use this section to evaluate the effectiveness of your development program, identify skills and experience needed in staff, target candidates for positions you plan to fill, or to better understand challenges development staff face and your role in helping them succeed.

A.   Director of Development

A director of development is responsible for planning and managing the fund development program. This position reports to the executive director and works closely with the board.

The NSFRE *Self-Study Survey Course on Fundraising* lists the following duties of a development director:

- Sees that fundraising is done in an ethical manner, is cost-effective, efficient, and meets goals on time;
- Provides leadership and guidance to staff, volunteers, donors and the community on philanthropy;
- Is people oriented while able to coordinate and manage great detail;
- Understands nonprofit organizations;
- Facilitates group processes, understands individual motivations, motivates volunteers and takes action to see they follow through;
- Reports to the board, analyzes development data, and facilitates discussions with the board that lead to action (Adapted from NSFRE, *Self-Study Survey Course on Fundraising*, p. 4:7-4:8).

Tips for Recruiting a Development Director

Look for the following knowledge, skills, and experience when recruiting a development director:

- Familiarity with trends (in the community, in your field of specialization, in the development profession);
- Personnel and financial management experience;
- Thorough knowledge of nonprofit organizations and governing boards;
- Knowledge and experience in ethics and tax law basics;
- Volunteer management and training expertise;
- Excellent marketing, public relations, and communications skills;
- Skilled at constituency development and cultivation;
- Experienced with fund development planning and evaluation;
- Accomplished in all fundraising activities including:
    - Proposal writing;
    - Face-to-face solicitation;
    - Phone solicitation;
    - Direct mail;
    - Special events;
    - Planned giving;
    - Capital campaigns;
    - Prospect identification, research and qualification;
    - Human relations, individual dynamics, and group dynamics;
    - Gift processing, accounting, management, and reporting;
    - Donor relations, recognition, and acknowledgment.

Adapted from *NSFRE Self-Study Survey Course on Fundraising*, p. 4:7- 4:9. Used with permission.

Development directors' salaries vary considerably depending on geographic location and years of experience. As "senior management positions" who work closely with the executive director and board, development directors often command higher salaries than other staff positions (CompassPoint, FAQ #6).

Some directors may choose to hire a candidate with excellent communication skills (written and verbal) and the ability to work well with a variety of people, but who lacks development experience. Professional development training would be necessary.

B.   Other Development Positions

Other positions may be needed to conduct fundraising activities in addition to or instead of a director of development. Titles for these positions include development officer, development coordinator, development assistant, capital campaign director, planned giving officer, or administrative assistant to coordinate development activities.

Some organizations hire a development coordinator or assistant to manage fundraising instead of hiring a development director. This may be a cost-saving decision appropriate to the size of the organization's fundraising efforts. Many fundraising activities may be successfully planned and conducted with staff in these roles.

The need for varied and sometimes specialized positions (capital campaign director, planned giving officer) often depends on program size and development needs.

Since fundraising is information-intensive work, someone needs to make sure all the details are handled smoothly and competently. If development is the responsibility of the executive director and board, support staff is needed to provide "backup support" (Klein, p. 34).

Development staff:

- Keep membership and donor records;
- Handle annual membership renewals;
- Draft acknowledgment letters;
- Draft solicitation letters;
- Prepare grant proposals;
- Coordinate special events;
- Research prospects;
- Assist board members with solicitation meetings.

Practice 5   Enlist Key Volunteers

Volunteers play an important role in fundraising. In many organizations, volunteers "take charge," directing and motivating other volunteers and staff to proceed with fundraising (Greenfield, 1993, p. 445). Volunteers provide important links to the community and to potential funding sources.

In fundraising, voluntary leadership "requires dedication, advocacy, personal sacrifice, and serving as an example to others" (Greenfield, 1993, p. 445). To be successful, fundraising volunteers need training and support to understand the mission, goals, "personality and operating style" of the organization (Ibid.).

Volunteers in leadership roles bring certain qualities to fundraising. Jim Lord in *The Raising of Money* identifies four:

1.   **Affluence** — the ability to make a substantial contribution.
2.   **Influence** — the ability to attract others to volunteer and make substantial contributions.
3.   **Availability** — the willingness to give priority attention to the program.
4.   **Team spirit** — the willingness to provide voluntary leadership *and* to accept professional direction (Lord, p. 26).

Commitment to the cause is seen by some as essential (Greenfield, 1993, p. 445) and by others as "helpful" but not a requirement for volunteering (Lord, p. 26). Influential people not associated with your cause can be recruited and their interest developed through education and training.

Recruiting a volunteer not tied closely to your mission can send a powerful message to the community of your organization's broad appeal. "The most successful organizations are those who make their campaign the *community's* campaign — and who pass the torch of leadership and ownership to those who can make things happen for the organization" (Lord, p. 27).

Practice 6

Hire Consultants When Needed

A consultant may be needed to plan and implement various parts of a fundraising program or campaign. It is common practice to contract professionals for this purpose. But consultants are not recommended for actually soliciting gifts from donors (Doty and Cox, p. 505). This responsibility is better handled by a board member, trained volunteer, or the director.

Most states regulate the activities of fund raisers who solicit and handle contributions. Check with the state consumer services department or the state attorney general's office for information.

Consultants provide services such as board training, overall organizational development planning, feasibility studies, capital campaign or event planning, or materials such as brochures and annual reports. A standard written contract is essential to specify what is to be done, the time frame, and specific costs.

The Association of Fundraising Professionals recommends consultants be paid fees rather than on a contingency basis (as a percentage of funds raised). **See Appendix B, *Code of Ethical Principles and Standards of Professional Practice, #4), p. 279. See Appendix D, *How to Pick the Right Fundraising Consultant*, p. 282.**

II.   Plan for Development

Practice 7

Tie Goals to Mission, Strategic Plans and Programs

Fundraising based on the organization's mission and tied to programs and community needs identified in the strategic plan creates a strong, unified message to those whose support you seek.

Having a vision and clearly defined mission, knowing how the mission relates to the constituency, identifying strategies to achieve the mission, and determining the cost of programs and activities creates a compelling fundraising "case" to present the public.

A case statement contains "the reasons why an organization both needs and merits philanthropic support, usually by outlining the organization's programs, current needs, and plans" (Levy, p. 28).

A strategic plan which details priorities and costs of programs and initiatives (including staff, facilities, equipment, and other needs) can be a shopping list for generating philanthropic support (Greenfield, 1996, p. 5). **See Strategic Planning Chapter.**

Practice 8

Know and Understand Your Constituency

Knowing and understanding your constituency — members, donors, or prospective supporters — is an essential part of a successful fund development program. Other development planning steps depend on this information.

Listen to your community to know what they care about. "If we can find out what's on *their* minds and where *they're* going, we'll be in a strong position to shape our offering accordingly" (Lord, p. 11). Otherwise, you will be guessing your constituency's level of interest and willingness to support your mission and programs.

Consider the following marketing tips for development:

❏   Target your audience and identify methods to reach them;
❏   Determine what the audience values about you;
❏   Define your programs in terms the audience understands;
❏   Learn who your audience is: age, gender, income level; also lifestyle, who else they support;
❏   Learn who your "competition" is;
❏   Emphasize quality in all you do;
❏   Tailor communications to specific audiences;
❏   Communicate in person whenever possible;
❏   Use the media — print, radio, television, film — and the internet to your advantage;
❏   Develop a distinctive identity: use your logo on all visual communications.

Get to know and understand the language of marketing as it relates to fund development. The NSFRE *Self-Study Survey Course on Fund Raising* includes elements of marketing significant for member and donor acquisition, communication of organizational plans and programs, and volunteer recruitment (NSFRE, *Self-Study Survey Course on Fund Raising*, p. 1:13-14). **See the following page.**

Elements of Marketing

Products. "If you meet the audience's need and are recognized by the audience, then you have a quality product and are well positioned."

Public(s). "You are successful when you know and understand your public and how your products benefit them."

Research. "... find out what you need to know about your public(s): who they are, what they need and want, how they receive information, and which target audiences have the highest priority (current and likely) for various products (service, giving, volunteering)."

Price. "... how much you charge (fees for services) or ask for (donations to consider, volunteer time)."

Production and distribution. "... how well you can meet demand and where the product is available."

Communication. "...how you use public relations and public information within the community; what you do to motivate people to respond. Good communication is a result of how you position yourself by clarifying your distinct niche and how you tailor the message to various audiences."

Cultivation (constituency development). "... what you do to maintain and expand the audience's commitment to your organization and its programs, and what you do to encourage donors to give again at higher levels."

Documenting your activities. "...involves writing a plan, implementing the plan, monitoring your progress, and evaluating your performance."

Adapted from "Laying the Foundation for Fund Development", *NSFRE Self-Study Survey Course on Fund Raising*, 1995, 1:13-1:14.

Practice 9

Keep Fundraising Principles in Mind

A. Why People Give

People give money to organizations for a variety of reasons. Some give because they care about the issues the organization addresses or like the approach taken. Others give because being affiliated with the organization makes them feel good. Some people like the newsletter or a premium being offered to join (Klein, p. 16).

The Association of Fundraising Professionals identifies reasons why people give:

- To identify with a worthy cause or goal;
- To give something back;

- To gain tax benefits and financial-planning benefits;
- To respond to the person asking;
- To gain immortality;
- To express deep emotion (such as joy through a commemorative gift or grief through a memorial gift);
- To help or care for others;
- To diminish negative feelings (guilt, fear, anger) (Adapted from NSFRE *Self-Study Survey Course on Fund Raising*, p. 6:6).

B.   Why People Should Give to You

A fund development program " ... unites *people* with the *purposes* of the nonprofit organization" (Greenfield, 1993, p. 446). Focus on what your organization has to offer the community to appeal to prospective donors.

Too often, organizations focus on their "needs" for money to fund buildings, equipment, staff, or other parts of their programs. Instead, produce solutions, answers, capabilities, and opportunities for the community, and the community will respond (Lord, p. 3-4).

C.   How People Give

The decision to give may be made spontaneously or through careful planning (NSFRE, *Self-Study Survey Course on Fund Raising*, p. 6:6). Gifts may be outright gifts of cash, securities, real estate (without rights retained), or in-kind donations. Other gifts are planned and include bequests, real estate (with retained rights), life insurance, charitable remainder trusts, charitable gift annuities, or charitable lead trusts (Williams, p. 16).

D.   How to Build Support

Building a fundraising program is a long term process that requires time, commitment, organizational credibility, and sustained relationships with others. Ongoing relationships with individual donors, foundation and corporate representatives, members, and the community are essential to strengthen and build a development program. People give to people, not to institutions.

But providing personal attention to all donors and prospects is impossible. Donors with giving histories that show potential to give more and prospects capable of making large gifts deserve your attention (Greenfield, 1993, p. 445).

This means concentrating attention on major donors while never forgetting the membership and community as a whole. Plan and participate in membership programs. Seek public relations opportunities in the community to build organizational credibility. Members come from your community and are the organization's foundation. It is important not to forget them.

E. Maintaining Confidentiality

Respecting donors' privacy and confidentiality is part of building donor relationships and trust. Anonymous gifts must remain unnamed, and staff and volunteers who handle donor records must be held accountable for maintaining confidentiality.

F. What You Need to Know about Asking

Kim Klein in *Fundraising for Social Change* says fear is why most people are reluctant to ask for money, even for the causes, issues and organizations they believe in most. The reasons most people --and you -- may fear asking for money include:

1. Rejection (being turned down);
2. Offending a friend by asking for a donation;
3. Feeling obligated to donate to causes of those who donate to yours.

Practice 10   Identify and Target Funding Sources

Typical funding sources for most organizations come either from individuals or institutions. Individuals include members, one-time contributors, and major donors. Institutions may be businesses or corporations, foundations, government entities, clubs or community groups. Special events target both individuals and institutions. Earned income is included as a major source of additional funding. **See Practice 14 for detailed strategies for each funding source.**

A.   Individuals

Individuals represent the greatest overall giving to nonprofit organizations compared to foundation and corporate contributions. In 2005, individuals represented nearly 85 percent of charitable giving in the United States *(Source: Giving USA Foundation , 2005)*.

1.   Members

Members provide basic annual support and are the backbone of an organization. They are distinguished from other donors because membership implies "... the individual is *receiving certain benefits* and *holding certain responsibilities* as a result of having given a financial gift or paid annual dues" (Clark, p. 485).

Membership often includes benefits such as a one year newsletter subscription, free or discounted admission to facilities and programs, discounts at stores, invitations to special programs, eligibility to volunteer, eligibility to vote, or qualification to serve as a board member (Clark, p. 486-487).

Tax Deductibility of Membership Benefits

"Certain types of benefits customarily provided to members in exchange for membership payments ... of $75 or less may be disregarded."

"Free admission to members-only events" and "rights or privileges that can be exercised frequently during the membership period" are limited from the regulations restricting tax deductibility of membership fees.

United States Department of the Treasury, Legal Regulations

Check current laws with a tax accountant or nonprofit attorney prior to adopting any development policies.

Membership dues are a primary source of income in many organizations and are used to cover annual operating expenses (Greenfield, 1996, p. 48). Membership dues to qualified non-profit organizations are deductible, subject to current tax laws. **See the box above and on the following page.**

Costs of membership programs include:

- Direct costs for membership recruitment and renewal.
- Printing and postage for communication with members; also, membership cards, a membership directory, invitations to events.
- Member services such as support for board and committee meetings, newsletters, annual reports, and premiums (Greenfield, 1996, p. 48).

Benefits, Premiums, and Tax Deductions

The Internal Revenue Service (IRS) requires "full disclosure" to donors as to how much of their contribution may be claimed as a tax deduction. Benefits and premiums offered to donors affect this tax benefit.

It is the donor's responsibility to report to IRS only the eligible amount, but it is the organization's job to tell the donor how to properly adjust their gift to reflect the value of the benefits for tax purposes.

Be sure all development policies are reviewed by a tax accountant or attorney familiar with current federal laws. **See p. 275, Other Resources, *The Charity's Guide to Charitable Contributions*, by Pamela McAllister**.

Donor clubs consist of members who contribute at higher levels than the general membership and typically receive additional benefits. Giving clubs are a way to generate increased annual support, identify prospective major donors, and build deeper commitment to the organization.

2. Contributors

Individuals who make a one-time gift or donate to a special event, program or activity may be called *contributors* or project donors. These donations are generally tracked separately and classified as a subcategory in individual giving.

3. Major Donors

Major donors are identified as individuals who contribute significant gifts to an organization. Major donor prospects are those who have the ability to make large gifts. Each organization must decide what constitutes "major." For most organizations, a $500 gift signifies an individual's ability to contribute at a greater level than general membership. Consistent giving at this level is a certain indicator of a donor's ability to make a larger contribution.

B. Institutions

1. Foundations

Charitable foundations may be independent, company sponsored, community, operating or family foundations (NSFRE, *Self-Study Survey Course on Fund Raising,* p. 6:22). In 2005, foundations represented 11.5 percent of charitable giving in the United States (*Source: Giving USA* Foundation).

Foundations often have application guidelines that identify their interests, criterion for support, deadlines, and report requirements. They provide seed money for new projects, finance multi-year demonstration projects, back experimental programs, or fuel initiatives such as joint ventures between several organizations. Few foundations support operations.

An excellent source for foundation information is The Grantmanship Center. Other sources are *The Foundation Directory*, *The Chronicle of Philanthropy*, and the *NonProfit Times*. **See Contacts, p. 296.**

2. Businesses and Corporations

Support from local or regional businesses and corporations is an important source of funding. Corporate contributions represented nearly 5.3 percent of all charitable gifts in the United States in 2005 (Source: Giving USA Foundation).

Businesses and corporations may contribute cash, donate in-kind services, provide equipment and materials, sponsor programs, offer employee matching gifts, or offer other important sources of annual and capital funds. Charitable foundations of large corporations can be a source for major contributions.

Both corporations and businesses are excellent sources for board members and for volunteers to help with other organizational efforts (fundraising, special events, projects).

3.   Government Entities

Funding from government entities may range from local, county, state and federal agencies to quasi-governmental organizations such as conservation, water, or environmental districts. Identify agencies and entities in your area to uncover new funding sources.

Government support is usually either:

- Direct (grants, research and development funds, purchase-of-service contracts);
- Indirect (tax exemptions, reduced mailing rates, etc.), (NSFRE, *Self-Study Survey Course on Fund Raising,* p. 6:23, from Michael Seltzer, *Securing Your Organization's Future,* 1987, p. 291-321).

4.   Clubs, Community Groups and Other Associations

There are a variety of social, community, service or other groups in most communities. Some are:

- Lions, Rotary, and Kiwanis Clubs;
- Chambers of Commerce;
- Junior League;
- Men's and women's social clubs;
- Professional associations (business men and women, architects, landscape architects, engineers);
- Garden clubs;
- Native plant societies;
- Wildflower associations;
- Hiking clubs; trail associations;
- Bicycle clubs;
- Pack and paddle groups.
- Photography clubs.

C.   Special Events

Special events are a popular way to bring in additional funds for an organization. Events attract members, business and corporate sponsors, nonmembers and the public at large to participate in a community oriented activity or special gathering. Special events can be highly successful, generating significant operating support from a broad audience.

Special events require thorough planning and participation (staff, volunteers, sponsors, members, the public) to be successful. Events lacking fundraising goals may produce a fun event that provides exposure for the organization, but it may not produce much money.

D. Earned Income

Income from fees, services, merchandise, and other sources of earned income is a viable and important part of the funding mix. Although not considered a form of fundraising (earned income is money exchanged for goods or services), it is a major source of financial support for many nonprofit organizations. Some cover a significant portion of their annual operating expenses through earned income.

Practice 11

Select the Appropriate Solicitation Strategy

Which solicitation strategy you use depends on who will be solicited, who will solicit, and the level of support requested. Personal solicitation is 16 times more effective than mail, but it is impossible to achieve with all members and donors (NSFRE, *Self-Study Survey Course on Fund Raising,* p. 6:7, from Greenfield, *Fundraising: Evaluating and Managing the Fund Development Process).*

A. Personal Solicitation

Personal solicitation is:

- Most effective when conducted by a peer of the prospect;
- Recommended for top prospects;
- Limited by the number of volunteers available to participate and by the director's time;
- May take place with a team of two or more volunteers, with a volunteer and the executive director making the call, or with a board member and development director (NSFRE, *Self-Study Survey Course on Fund Raising,* p. 6:8 - 6:9).

B. Mail Solicitation

Mail solicitation invites the recipient to become a supporter. It is:

- Sent to prospect lists to generate memberships and contributions;
- A way to reach a large number of people;
- Best if letters are customized and personalized (shows knowledge of current or previous donors, levels of giving);
- Impersonal unless the recipient is known.

Direct mail is a specialized type of mail solicitation that:

- Includes a series of solicitation letters with planned follow up, renewal and upgrade letters to build support over several years (Greenfield, 1996, p. 37);
- Is best if mailed to lists with a minimum of 5,000 names;
- Usually takes at least three years to become profitable; (Ibid., p. 36);
- Requires years of experience to master (NSFRE, *Self-Study Survey Course on Fund Raising,* p. 6:11);
- Reaches the largest number of people but is the most impersonal, least efficient way to generate support;
- Has low response rates (between .5% and 1.0% to first time requests for new members) (Ibid., p. 6:11), but response depends on the quality of the mailing lists.

Successful direct mail has a minimum response rate of one percent and an average gift size of $20 or more (Greenfield, 1996, p. 40).

Important Elements of Direct Mail

Outer envelope: If it doesn't "survive initial screening (less than five seconds)," the letter won't get opened.

Appeal letter: It must capture the reader's attention in 15 seconds. Four-page letters get a better response than one page letters. The first paragraph and the "P.S." messages are "key attention getters."

Enclosure: A brochure, reprinted newspaper article or flyer may have a positive affect on someone unfamiliar with the organization; these add to the cost of producing and mailing (printing costs, postage).

Response card: A response card makes it easy for the recipient to reply; include the prospect's name preprinted, checkoff boxes suggesting gift amount, and a place to request information.

Reply envelope: This makes it easy for the donor to return a contribution.

From NSFRE, *Self-Study Survey Course on Fund Raising,* p. 6:13-6:14

C. Telephone Solicitation

Telephone solicitation is:

- Useful for membership renewals, upgrading donors, and to cultivate existing major donors;
- Least effective for recruiting new members. Cold calls to nondonor prospects are "expensive and inefficient" (Greenfield, 1996, p. 81);
- More personal than mail solicitations. Can be used in combination with mailings;
- Frequently conducted by phone banks of trained volunteers or paid callers (NSFRE, *Self-Study Survey Course on Fund Raising,* p. 6:10).

Be cautious if choosing telephone solicitation. Some sources recommend it over mail solicitations because response rates are better. However, many people are offended by calls asking for money. Consider testing a sample market before launching a major fundraising effort based on telephone solicitations.

III. Create Goals and Strategies

Practice 12   **Produce an Annual Development Plan**

Planning is necessary for successful long term fundraising. Knowing why funds are needed, how much and in what period of time is fundamental to operating a successful fundraising program.

Base the annual development plan on the strategic plan and mission (NSFRE, *Self-Study Survey Course on Fund Raising,* p. 1:29). If strategic planning has not occurred, base the development plan on goals established in the long range or annual operating plan.

A. Budget

Develop annual goals and budget with those responsible for carrying out the fundraising. This may include board members, staff, volunteers, donors and the director.

A development team (even in a small organization) is crucial to the annual budget planning process. They assess if the organization is ready and has the capacity to reach the annual goals (Ibid., p. 1:31). The assessment takes place *before* the annual budget is finalized to develop realistic yet challenging fundraising goals.

The development team projects income by analyzing donors' giving histories, identifying new prospects, and recommending strategies for soliciting donors. In addition, they estimate fundraising costs and project the financial resources needed to reach the goals in the proposed annual budget.

B.   Information Needs

To develop a realistic annual development plan, take the following steps (from Doty and Cox, p. 495-498, and NSFRE, *Self-Study Survey Course on Fund Raising,* p. 1:29):

- ❑   Identify the fundraising goal from the preliminary budget planning process;
- ❑   Evaluate past fundraising efforts and the results from those efforts (from reports and analysis); look at the past 3-5 years, if data is available (Doty and Cox, p. 497);
- ❑   Identify the gift potential of current donors (from records kept);
- ❑   Research and identify prospective donors;
- ❑   Identify other sources of funds (special events, earned income, endowment funds);
- ❑   Look at the difference between anticipated revenue and desired funds to determine if goals are realistic;
- ❑   Identify staff and volunteer time needed and available for fundraising;
- ❑   Identify expenses and resource needs to conduct fundraising (money, equipment, office space, materials);
- ❑   Finalize annual fundraising goals;
- ❑   Assign responsibilities for meeting fundraising goals (Executive Director, Director of Development, board members, volunteers, other staff);
- ❑   Create a work plan and time line for the year.

Donor record keeping, analysis and reporting as well as prospect identification is a year round endeavor. An organization with a staffed development program will be better equipped to handle a greater volume of research but all programs benefit from development being a continuous process.

C.   What to Include in the Plan

The NSFRE *Self-Study Survey Course on Fund Raising* recommends a written development plan that complements the annual budget and includes:

- A statement of the fundraising purpose;
- Strategic and financial goals;
- Policies, if any, related to those goals;
- Cultivation strategies;
- Solicitation strategies for targeted market segments;
- Time frames for development;
- People responsible for reaching fundraising goals. (NSFRE, *Self-Study Survey Course on Fund Raising*, p. 1:31). **See Appendix E,** *Fundraising Readiness: How Does Your Agency Stack Up?*, **p. 283.**

Fundraising Tips

When I was first given the responsibility to raise funds for my organization (I had no training or experience in this area), my most useful resource was the local newspaper. Any time anyone gave anything to anyone, I clipped the article and started a file on the donor.

Before too long, I had a pretty good idea who gave what (or how much) to whom, why the gift was made, and at what time of year the donor made the gifts. This is basic research which is at the heart of any development plan.

Jim Yaich, Former Director
Jamestown Audubon Nature Center, Jamestown, NY

Practice 13   Establish an Annual Giving Program

Annual giving offers donors the opportunity to "support a mission that matches their interests, needs, or values" and brings yearly, renewable support for the organization (NSFRE, *Self-Study Survey Course on Fund Raising,* p. 6:1).

The purpose of annual giving is to provide operating income (both unrestricted and restricted) and to:

- Acquire donors;
- Renew donor support annually;
- Cultivate donors to increase giving levels;
- Build donor loyalty;
- Identify and involve leaders;
- Identify major gift prospects (NSFRE, *Self-Study Survey Course on Fund Raising,* p. 6:2).

Annual giving does not occur just once a year. Rather, plan and schedule ongoing fundraising to provide a continuous source of operating funds for programs, projects and activities year round.

Funding sources for annual giving include individuals, institutions (or organizations), and special events (Clark, p. 499-500; NSFRE, *Self-Study Survey Course on Fund Raising,* p. 6:4).

Practice 14 — Develop Individual Support Through Members, Contributors, and Major Donors

A. Members

1. Establish Membership Dues Categories and Benefits

Dues categories vary from one organization to another. Look at other organization's memberships and the associated benefits offered to members. Benefits may include a newsletter, free admission, discounts at shops or programs, or other premiums. **See Appendix F,** *Sample Membership Categories,* **p. 286.**

2. Recruit New Members

a. Mail Solicitation

- ❑ **See direct mail, p. 252**, for letters, inserts, envelopes, response cards, and expected results;
- ❑ Track results of each mailing sent including time of year, costs, and response.

b.   On-site Recruitment

☐   Prominently display membership brochures and envelopes to recruit members on-site (offices, gift shop, trails, other buildings);

☐   Promote membership at all programs, classes, meetings, and workshops sponsored;

☐   Train staff and volunteers to promote membership and answer inquiries;

☐   Include a membership brochure in all informational mailings sent.

c.   Off-site Recruitment

☐   Place brochures in prominent locations throughout your community (major attractions, chamber of commerce, tourist areas);

☐   Target locations where people may visit who share similar interests to those of your organization;

☐   Bring membership brochures to all outreach events attended by staff;

☐   Ask staff to take membership brochures to any conferences, programs, or seminars they attend.

d.   Members Recruiting Others

☐   Ask members to recruit others. Consider organizing a contest with prizes for those who bring in the most members. This requires highly motivated members willing to participate (Clark, p. 490).

e.   Advertising

☐   Promote the organization through local newspapers and other publications;

☐   Look for free advertising and other opportunities to promote programs and activities at your facility ("Things to Do" columns, television and radio interviews, etc.);

☐   Create budget for annual advertising expense;

☐   Place advertising in targeted markets.

Tips for Recruiting Members

- Assess the competition. Does your organization provide a distinctive niche to attract members? If it is similar to others in your area, would an umbrella organization be possible?
- Identify people or groups who are interested in your mission. Look at surveys or polls conducted in your area or conduct one of your own.
- Consider list exchanges, rental or purchase. List purchase can be very expensive.

Adapted from "Membership Development" by Constance Clark in *The Nonprofit Management Handbook*, p. 489.

3.   Renew Members

- ❑ Renew members prior to their expiration date at the anniversary of their original membership gift. Some organizations begin sending reminders four months before membership expires (Clark, p. 492);
- ❑ Send a one page renewal letter that is "friendly, appreciative, and relaxed" and reiterates the reasons for renewing (benefits, prestige, importance of mission), (Clark, p. 492-493);
- ❑ Read and respond to all membership letters and notes. Listen and respond to all calls;
- ❑ It is less expensive to renew a member than to find a new one. Make sure members feel valued by the organization;
- ❑ Plan for several reminder letters. Create a category in your records for lapsed members. Try them again during a special appeal or again next year before dropping them from your lists;
- ❑ Renew throughout the year to spread out the volume of letters, checks, and record keeping.

B.   Contributors

Individuals who contribute during a special event, campaign, or for a special project are considered contributors. Once a contribution is received, the individual may be asked to become a member, solicited during special appeals, or asked to support other funding opportunities. Some organizations automatically add contributors to mailing lists although there is a difference between a membership gift and a one-time gift or project contribution.

❑   Add contributors to your donor records and mailing list. Include donors who gave memorial gifts, honorary gifts in someone's name, or a one-time gift for a special fund raiser (land purchase, a building fund, an education program);

❑   Include contributors in mailings sent to members (newsletter, announcements, special appeals);

❑   Develop special appeals and membership letters for this group of donors to encourage their support.

Special Appeals

Plan a separate solicitation — an *annual appeal* — to your membership requesting additional support for the organization. The annual or *special appeal* supplements income from memberships and other contributions. It is a planned mailing, scheduled for a time of year when donors are most receptive to making a contribution (fall, year end, and spring are usual times for special appeal letters).

* Personalize appeal letters to donor club members and major donors. When possible, acknowledge their past giving and ask them to give again at that level or higher.
* "Dear Member" letters are more cost effective for the general membership. These non-personalized letters may be printed in quantity.
* Make the appeal timely, asking members to support an important seasonal program, activity, or aspect of your operations.
* Project special appeal income during annual development planning. Set a goal.
* Project and budget expenses to produce the mailing during annual development planning. Consider design, printing costs, inserts, envelopes, response card, return envelope, postage.
* Also consider staff time needed to produce the mailing, process and acknowledge the gifts.

C.   Major Donors

Each organization determines what size gift will constitute a major donor. A small organization may have far different criteria from a larger one. The level at which a gift is considered major may be $100, $1,000, $10,000, or more.

Major donors require special attention and care to earn and keep their support. Successful major donor development depends on

---

building relationships to gain the donor's trust, counsel, active involvement and financial support.

Doty and Cox define donor cultivation as "... the art of gradually developing personal links between the organization and its constituency" (Doty and Cox, p. 507). This is not always easy to do. Addressing the needs of a donor may be time consuming, demanding, and frustrating, especially if the donor's wishes stray from your mission.

Identify major donors and prospective major donors by doing the following:

- Analyze donor records to look for consistent patterns of giving at a level greater than general membership;
- Create a master list of major donors by giving levels;
- Identify individuals known and unknown to the organization.

To build relationships with major donors and generate their financial support:

- Make donor cultivation a top priority;
- Schedule monthly visits and calls to major contributors. "If three people commit themselves to having lunch twice a month with different major donors (or donors targeted for major upgrading), at the end of the first year, 72 supporters will have been flattered and their commitment heightened" (Doty and Cox, p. 507);
- Involve your board members and key staff members in donor cultivation visits and calls;
- Think of major donors at times other than when you need financial support. Donors will appreciate being thought of as more than the money they contribute;
- Send short notes, articles of interest, or make brief telephone calls to share news with the donor;
- Keep a list of donors to contact. Make sure it is visible and easily accessible (keep it in a top desk drawer or some other place you regularly use). Development staff are usually quick to remind you to contact major donors;

❑ Document each call, visit or contact for the donor's file. **See Appendix G,** *Techniques to Nurture Your Donors,* **p. 287.**

Plan major donor solicitations throughout the year when donors are available and receptive to calls and visits. Remember the following:

❑ Develop ideas and proposals for the donor to consider based on your knowledge of their interests, ability to give, and willingness to give;

❑ Timing is important. Some donors prefer year-end giving while others prefer pre-tax or post-tax times. Structure your request to fit their needs;

❑ Put together the best solicitation team. This may be a board member, a volunteer, the director, or a combination;

❑ Make sure all who make the donor visit are prepared. Review the donor's giving history, interests, and background; thoroughly review the proposal to be submitted. **See Appendix H,** *Major Donor Solicitation: Using Team Work for Success,* **p. 288.**

Donor Clubs

Members who contribute at or above a certain level each year may become members of a donor club. These members receive added benefits and premiums above those given to general members. To establish a donor club:

❑ Identify members at various giving levels ($50, $100, $250, $500, $1,000). Determine if enough members already contribute at these levels to begin a club;

❑ Project how much money can be generated from the members of the club;

❑ Determine the costs of establishing the club (printing, mailings, special events, premiums);

❑ Identify a club name that provides a "separate, meaningful, and prestigious identity" (Greenfield, 1996, p. 57); **See Appendix F,** *Sample Membership Categories,* **Friends of Teton Science School, p. 286.**

❑ Select giving-level names that symbolize something distinctive about the organization and the donor's affiliation with it;

❑ Develop "progressive benefits and privileges to aid commitment and lead to opportunities for expanding donor interest and involvement" (Greenfield, 1996, p. 57). Consider special programs, field trips, parties, dinners or events that are planned and offered just for these members;

❑ Develop premiums for each donor group to thank and acknowledge their support;

❑ Develop a brochure that describes the club's purpose, programs, and special benefits to current and future donors (Greenfield, 1996, p. 58);

❑ Promote the club in newsletters, advertising, and through targeted mailings;

❑ Develop a plan for ongoing recognition of club members (donor walls, plaques, certificates);

❑ Develop a written policy statement for the club.

Practice 15 **Develop Institutional Support Through Foundations, Businesses, and Other Organizations**

The National Society of Fund Raising Executives recommends a seven-step process to develop and nurture institutional or organizational support (adapted from NSFRE, *Self Study Survey Course in Fund Raising*, p. 6:26-6:27).

1. **Research**: identify prospects, be thorough, but don't let research hold you back from personal contact and relationship building; narrow your prospects to sources that match your organization's needs;

2. **Inquire/approach/involve**: make contact through a letter of inquiry, personal call, invitation to visit your site or facility, invitation to join your board, or a request to speak at a program you are offering;

3. **Develop request**: define and describe the project that best matches the organization's funding guidelines with your mission;

4. **Solicit**: ask in the way most suited to the prospect (in person, through a proposal, by phone);

5. **Follow-through**: check to make sure request was received and all information requested was provided; offer to meet to discuss the proposal; after a gift is received, keep the donor involved and informed;

6. **Report**: if funder has reporting requirements, meet the deadlines, and report the results of the grant;

7. **Repeat**: always be looking for the next opportunity to engage this same prospect (even if they turned you down) in something else.

The decision to affiliate or associate your organization with a particular entity — a foundation, business, corporation, or an individual — is an issue to be determined by the board. The board of directors will want to establish policies for soliciting and accepting donations if they have not already done this. **See Boards Chapter.**

A.   Foundations

Foundations are an important source of funding for many organizations but few regularly support annual operations. Look to foundations to fund projects, activities, or personnel that fall outside the annual operating budget. Foundations are also an excellent source for capital or project funds.

Successful long term relationships with foundations depend on meeting or exceeding stated goals and objectives, fulfilling conditions in the grant, keeping to the schedule, and submitting reports and other requirements on time. Credibility with foundations is enhanced by the success of each endeavor undertaken.

Also, remember some foundations fund a project or activity for a year or more and then move on to other programs of interest. Some prefer starting projects and expect organizations to find other funds to sustain them.

Development strategies for building foundation support include:

❒   Research the foundation's areas of interest and giving history. Utilize the Grantsmanship Center, the Foundation Directories, and current information from the *NonProfit Times* and *The Chronicle of Philanthropy*. Use the internet to search for foundations web sites; **See Contacts, p. 296**;

❒   Request and analyze foundation proposal guidelines to identify the foundation's interests and requirements to submit a proposal;

❒   Look for the overlap between the foundation's interests and your organization. Be creative but realistic: a frivolous proposal not fully developed will damage the organization's credibility;

❒   Approach the foundation (call, send a letter of inquiry, make an appointment to visit);

❒   Develop the proposal, a budget, and support materials. **Read Appendix I, *Tips for Writing Effective Grant Proposals*, p. 291, and Appendix J, *Grant Seeker's Checklist*, p. 292.**

B.   Businesses and Corporations

A good way to involve the community in your organization is by seeking business and corporate donations and sponsorships. Local businesses and major corporate employers often are looking for ways to become involved in the community and demonstrate their community responsibility. They may also be a good source for potential board members, to sponsor events, promote programs and activities, and to provide in-kind services and materials.

To generate business support:

❑   Get to know the local business owners in your community. Do business with them whenever possible;

❑   Involve members of the business community on your board of directors;

❑   Join a local business council or chamber of commerce; attend meetings and share information about your organization and its programs;

❑   Ask a local business to donate a service or product. Acknowledge the gift in a prominent location;

❑   Seek business sponsors for a special event, program, or activity at your facility. Again, acknowledge prominently;

❑   Recruit employees to volunteer with the organization;

❑   Ask a local business to provide meeting space, conference facilities, or a training location. Acknowledge the sponsor with a gift (a plaque, photo, certificate of appreciation) that may be displayed at the business;

❑   Stay current on business trends and develop ways to link your programs with their interests (a link from their web site to yours). Read newspapers for tips on community issues of interest to local businesses;

❑   Develop networks with business leaders to provide tips on "hot" topics and interests that may be matched with your organization's goals. Recent trends include community partnerships, employer supported volunteer work, adopt-a-project, and adult/child mentoring programs.

Corporations are a good source for larger gifts, especially if they have a corporate giving program. Some corporations have foundations established to manage funding requests.

Some national or multinational corporations have local subsidiaries that donate funds to the community. They tend to favor communities where employees live and where the company has a major presence. Corporations also may have "discretionary funds" handled by top executives who make personal decisions about where and how much to give.

To develop corporate support:

❑ Seek top-level corporate representatives for your board;

❑ Research corporate interests carefully to determine if their interests may be matched to yours. Be creative. Corporations contain people with many different interests. Investigate before you ask;

❑ If a corporation has a foundation, use the same strategies with the corporate foundation as you would with a private one. If developing a proposal, review guidelines in **Appendix I, *Tips for Writing Effective Grant Proposals,* p. 291,** for suitable language in a corporate proposal compared to a foundation proposal;

❑ See if the corporation has an employee matching gift program. Promote your organization to employees and their children. Mention matching gift programs in all published materials you distribute.

C. Clubs, Community Groups, and Other Associations

Communities contain numerous groups whose purposes include providing services, community support, recreation and a host of other societal needs. Many clubs, groups and other organizations are a good source of financial support.

To generate support from organized groups in the community:

❑ Identify and develop a mailing list of clubs, community groups, and other organizations in your community;

❑ Develop a targeted mailing seeking organizational memberships, project donations, individual memberships, or just to introduce yourself and the organization to the group;

❏ Provide them something they need. Groups often look for speakers and field trips for their members. If this fits your mission, consider offering your services and facilities for a program. Promote membership at the event;

❏ Offer meeting space for community groups;

❏ Ask an organization or club to sponsor an event or program. Advertise their sponsorship when promoting the event;

❏ Concentrate your fundraising efforts on those with the potential to provide financial support. Some clubs and organizations are more philanthropic than others;

❏ Cultivate groups for other strategic reasons (partnerships, collaboration, marketing).

Practice 16   Conduct Special Events

When organizations think of ways to raise money, special event ideas abound. A special event sounds like fun, has the potential to attract many people, and lets you avoid the potential discomfort of asking a donor for money face to face.

In all fundraising endeavors and especially special events, develop clearly defined fundraising goals. Create a special events committee, a detailed list of tasks, prepare a budget, and develop a time line (Klein, p. 149-152). **See Appendix K, *Planning a Special Event* p. 294.**

Special events require significant staff and administrative support to plan, coordinate, and carry out the event. To generate income for the organization, an event must be able to pay for staff time, operating expenses, any up-front costs (promotion costs, facility rental, entertainment, food, etc.), and other direct expenses.

For many organizations, a special event can be " ... the worst possible use of staff and volunteer energy, time, and commitment" (Doty and Cox, p. 510). Many hours of planning and coordination must go into a special event and sometimes, the payoff is small.

Special events may be highly successful and generate a significant portion of an organization's annual operating income. Events are sometimes tied to seasonal occurrences (October Fest), annual events (Earth Day, Summer Solstice), to local or historical events (honoring a patron's birthday), and to numerous other special occasions.

The following questions from "Annual Giving Programs" by Doty and Cox in *The Nonprofit Management Handbook* may help guide your decision to sponsor a special event.

1. What is the event's primary purpose? Is it fundraising or something else? Be wary of trying to accomplish too many things with one event.
2. Is there an existing event to which a fundraising component could be added, for example, an annual luncheon honoring businesses?
3. Are there volunteers anxious to take responsibility? The event will still need staff support, but be sure volunteers "own" at least part of the event.
4. Will organizing the event foreclose the opportunity to do something more "profitable?" (Doty and Cox, p. 510).

Also consider these questions:

1. Is the event appropriate to the organization? Ask: "If people knew nothing about our organization except that it had sponsored this event, what would their opinion be? If the answer is 'neutral' or 'good,' then the event is appropriate."
2. Is the event in keeping with your organization's image? Consider sponsoring something related to your mission or overall purpose.
3. Do you have adequate money to pay for costs of the event? Consider cash flow problems if up-front money is needed.
4. Can the event be repeated? Creating a tradition in your community has positive long term benefits for the organization (Klein, p. 147-149).

See the following page for two very different experiences with special events.

Special Event Auction at Teton Science School

Anna Wolf, 1998 Auction Coordinator and Jack Shea, Executive Director
Teton Science School, Kelly, WY

Every August for the last 20 years, Teton Science School (TSS) has sponsored its annual fundraising auction. Businesses and individuals in our community donate goods and/or experiences which are offered to the public at both live and silent auctions. Donations to the auction help TSS support its education programs.

The auction has a highly developed volunteer committee and a part-time staff. Major responsibilities are volunteer coordination, procurement and storage of auction items, organization of paperwork, and follow up. Volunteer committees are formed into small groups who report to other volunteers and to the auction coordinator. Volunteers begin soliciting donations by June 15 and have all donations in by August 1. The volunteer committee work includes: coordinating hospitality, publicity, invitations, raffles and auction acquisitions, arranging vacation getaways, and follow-up such as generating thank you letters. Caterers and businesses support the auction with delicious donations and spectacular food displays. The auction has a cash bar with servers provided the day of the auction.

Unique goods, services, vacation getaways, and once in a lifetime experiences are offered during both Silent and Live auctions. Past auctions have featured snowmobiles, guided fishing trips on numerous rivers, getaways to Ireland, Cape Cod, New York and Florida, handmade furniture, artwork, antiques, and many more intriguing items.

The tradition of our auction has helped the Teton Science School continue to offer excellence in educational programs. The average net proceeds for the last two years has been $70,000. The cost to the school is around $15,000.

A Not-So-Special Event
Robert Mercer, Director, Silver Lake Nature Center, Bristol, PA

One of the most challenging decisions a director faces is canceling a long time annual event. The Silver Lake Nature Center had been holding a "Nature Fair" for 15 years. The event required hundreds of volunteer hours, an inordinate amount of staff time, and netted a small amount of money ($2,500). For five years, I recommended we cancel the event, but the resistance was strong. The most common argument was "So what if it doesn't raise money. It's a great public relations event."

The death knell sounded after I gathered data such as the cost of staff time and factored in the cost of volunteerism. Most importantly, I quantified the "public relations value" by tracking memberships - new and renewed - during the event. Volunteers conducted surveys to ask participants how long they had been coming for this event and what other programs they attended. The facts were clear. The "Fair" was neither a fund raiser nor a public relations event.

Practice 17

Generate Additional Funds Through Earned Income

Earned income is a viable source of additional revenue for many organizations. Although not considered a form of fundraising, earned income is a significant source of money that helps diversify the organization's funding mix.

Earned income is typically generated from goods and services. It may include fees, sale of products or materials, or other income such as royalties from books or publications.

Consider the following as possible sources of funds:

- Admission fees;
- Program fees;
- Contract fees;
- Sale of membership lists;
- Gift shop or merchandising sales;
- Concessions;
- Facility rental (meetings, retreats, training sessions, organizational meetings, etc.);
- Building rental for parties, weddings, other services;
- Paid company outings.

Contracts

Contracts for services are considered a very important part of fund development at Ijams Nature Center.

Through a contract with the City of Knoxville, the nature center chairs the Water Quality Forum made up of agencies and organizations involved in regional water quality issues. Originally created by the city in 1989, the group meets quarterly to discuss and develop strategies for cleaning up pollution in the local creeks and the Tennessee River.

The city funds a staff position at the nature center as part of the contract, and the nature center provides water quality programs for the community. This includes an annual river clean-up, an adopt-a-creek program, and a storm drain stenciling effort.

The contract fits well with the nature center's annual and strategic objectives and funds a much-needed staff position. The City of Knoxville benefits by having water quality issues addressed and by meeting some National Pollution Discharge Eliminating System permit requirements through the nature center's work.

Ijams Nature Center, Knoxville, TN

IV.   Establish Ongoing Systems

Practice 18   **Thank Donors for Their Contributions**

Thanking donors is the most important part of any fundraising effort, large or small. It is the one thing organizations must never fail to do and which should always come first. Donors can never be thanked enough.

Development ultimately depends on *stewardship,* or the way gifts are used, managed, and invested according to the donor's wishes. Stewardship begins with saying "thank you" the day the gift is received (Lord, p. 92). Personal letters, calls, or visits are most effective with major donors.

See Appendix G, *Techniques to Nurture Your Donors,* p. 287.

Practice 19   **Process Donations Promptly**

Make sure all gifts are processed promptly. To do this, develop a system to process each gift from the time the check arrives until it is recorded, deposited, receipted and acknowledged to the donor (NSFRE, *Self Study Survey Course in Fund Raising*, p. 2:13).

Avoid common fundraising mistakes such as misplaced checks, inaccurate or incomplete records, lost deposits, accounting errors, failure to thank and acknowledge a donation by establishing routine procedures for handling contributions.

See the following page.

Sample Gift Processing System

Handle and Process the Check
- ❑ Designate who will handle and process all donor checks, records, and deposits.
- ❑ For consistency and accountability, limit who handles checks and records donor information.
- ❑ Plan a "checks and balances" system with two people who open checks, record information, and prepare bank deposit information.
- ❑ Stamp checks with organization bank account information. Deposit is prepared after recording the gift.

Record the Gift
- ❑ Record the gift in the donor file (computer database, computer spreadsheet, or other manual system).
- ❑ Look for changes in personal information (name, address, etc.) and update records.
- ❑ Designate gift amount to proper fund account (for example: membership renewal, special event, pledge payment, endowment fund, etc.).
- ❑ Generate a receipt.

Acknowledge the Gift
- ❑ Generate an appropriate acknowledgment letter or card with the gift amount and purpose of the gift stated in the letter. This will document the gift for the donor's income tax purposes.
- ❑ The letter should be in the executive director's name or from the person who solicited the donor. Personalize acknowledgment letters with the name and address of the donor and with a handwritten postscript at the bottom.
- ❑ Multiple thank you letters for major gifts are appropriate and expected. The board chair, development director, volunteer who solicited the gift, or the program director whose program benefits from the gift all may send thank you notes or letters.
- ❑ Acknowledge all gifts. For those less than $10.00, a post card is sufficient.

Prepare Reports
- ❑ Depending on development program size, reports may be prepared daily, weekly, monthly or by event. Reports provide an opportunity to analyze the results of a renewal letter, special appeal, newsletter appeal, campaign, etc.
- ❑ Review reports with staff, board members and committee members to share results and evaluate efforts.

Deposit the Gift
- ❑ Prepare bank deposit after recording all donor and gift information.
- ❑ If checks will not be deposited immediately, place in a locked safe, box or cabinet until the deposit is made.

Practice 20 **Keep Accurate Membership and Donor Records**

Accurate records help sustain a fund development program. An accurate membership list is needed to renew, solicit, upgrade and deliver promised benefits to your supporters (Klein, p. 160).

Many organizations use their in-house computers with database programs maintained by staff. This is preferred unless your membership is very large. External mail houses may be contracted to maintain the membership list and handle mailings.

Great sources for current database information are found in the Grantsmanship Center publications, the *NonProfit Times*, and *The Chronicle of Philanthropy*. **See Contacts, p. 296.**

Managing Donor Records

Make sure donor records are accurate. Attention to the spelling (and pronunciation) of donor names is essential in all correspondence. Make sure board members, volunteers, and staff also recognize the importance of this.

Use donor database software to track and manage detailed donor and membership records. Most software can be modified for the user with multiple tracking fields. Annual giving, capital campaign gifts, and planned gifts all may be recorded as well as more detailed information on the individual or institution. Check The NonProfit Times and the Chronicle of Philanthropy for updates on software. **See Contacts, p. 297. See p. 298 for free Ebase software.**

Most database programs are compatible with word processing software but be sure to check. Renewals, upgrade letters, special appeals, labels, email updates and other correspondence all may be prepared and sent directly from the database.

Include the following information in donor records:

- Name (include nickname);
- Salutation;
- Address (home and business); e-mail address;
- Phone and fax numbers (home and business);
- Business title;
- Spouse's name (note different last name, if applicable);
- Children's names;
- Giving history;
- Renewal date;
- Affiliations;
- Special interests.

Update the database and track it for accuracy. In general, databases are best managed by one or few people to provide consistency in data entry and to prevent mistakes.

Practice 21

Recognize Donor Support

Donor recognition extends beyond the initial letter or call of thanks. Consider the following ideas for ongoing donor appreciation:

☐   If membership is small, print member names by category in one issue of your newsletter or in the annual report. Acknowledge major donors in the newsletter each issue;

☐   Highlight members in your newsletter or publicly at your building or facility. Public recognition lets others know you appreciate donors;

☐   Annual meetings are a great place to recognize donor support. Present awards or other symbols of appreciation to members at these big events;

☐   Major gifts deserve media attention, if the donor is agreeable. Inform newspapers, television and radio stations about big gifts. The media may feature your organization and the donor in the story;

☐   Create a donor wall to acknowledge major contributions to everyone who visits;

☐   Think of naming opportunities: benches, seats, walls, boardwalks, exhibits, trails, buildings. There are endless possibilities;

☐   Scholarships are a great way to create a long-lasting way to recognize a donor or a memorial gift;

☐   Be creative with gift ideas beyond the certificates and plaques that are standard forms of recognition.

Practice 22

Produce Development Reports

Produce progress and summary reports for all development efforts. Board members, staff, volunteers, members and donors all want to know the programs, projects, and activities made possible through their efforts and contributions. Donors can keep track of the progress their investment made possible (Greenfield, 1996, p. 134).

Development reports are a very powerful way to motivate board members, staff and yourself to keep up with development activities. The numbers reflect the successes and failures of development efforts. **See "Reporting and Fiscal Fundamentals" in Appendix A, *NCIB Standards in Philanthropy*, p. 278.**

Practice 23 **Evaluate Fundraising Strategies**

Annual giving is ongoing and often the same approaches or strategies are repeated year after year. When something works once or twice, we want to do it again.

The downside is that ideas can "quickly become stale and uninteresting" to audiences (Greenfield, 1996, p. 133). To keep the audience's attention requires offering them stimulating and exciting projects they can support. Tying fundraising goals to strategic planning makes sure this occurs.

So does evaluating the effectiveness of fundraising efforts. By looking at what works and what doesn't, an organization can alter its strategies and take corrective actions to produce better results.

For anyone seeking tips on evaluating all aspects of your development program, *Fund Raising Cost Effectiveness* by James M. Greenfield is an excellent resource. **See References, p. 275.**

References

Clark, Constance. "Membership Development," *The Nonprofit Management Handbook: Operating Policies and Procedures.* Tracy Daniel Connors, Editor. New York: John Wiley & Sons, Inc., 1993.

CompassPoint references are from their web site at www.compasspoint.org. Copyright 1999. All rights reserved. For more information, contact: CompassPoint Nonprofit Services, 706 Mission Street, 5th Floor, San Francisco, CA, 94103-3113. 415-541-9000.
Fundraising FAQ # 6: What should we look for in a director of development and what is the typical salary range?

Doty, Nan D., and Cox, Barbara M. "Annual Giving Programs," *The Nonprofit Management Handbook*, Tracy Daniel Connors, Editor. New York: John Wiley & Sons, Inc., 1993.

Greenfield, James M. "Fund-Raising Overview," *The Nonprofit Management Handbook*, Tracy Daniel Connors, Editor. New York: John Wiley & Sons, Inc., 1993.

___ *Fund-Raising Cost Effectiveness.* New York: John Wiley & Sons, Inc., 1996.

___ *Fund-Raising: Evaluating and Managing the Fund Development Process.* New York: John Wiley & Sons, Inc., 1991.

Giving USA. New York: American Association of Fund Raising Counsel Trust for Philanthropy, 1996.

Klein, Kim. *Fundraising for Social Change.* Oakland, CA: Chardon Press, 1988. *Fundraising for Social Change* is currently in its 4th Edition (2000). www.chardonpress.com.

Legal Regulations. Washington, DC: United States Department of the Treasury Department, 1996.

Levy, Barbara R., Editor. *AFP Fundraising Dictionary.* Alexandria, VA: Association of Fundraising Professionals, 2003. www.afpnet.org/resource_center.

Lord, James Gregory. *The Raising of Money.* Cleveland, OH: Third Sector Press, 1996.

A Potential Checklist of Accountability. Washington, DC: Independent Sector, 1997.

Self-Study Survey Course on Fund Raising. Alexandria, VA: National Society of Fund Raising Executives, 1995.

Seltzer, Michael. *Securing Your Organization's Future.* New York: Foundation Center, 1987.

Williams, M. Jane, Editor. *Big Gifts* . Farmington Hills, MI: The Gale Group, 1991.www.gale-edit.com.

Other Resources

Fundraising for Nature Centers: A Collection of Funding Strategies, Volume 1. Dayton, OH: Association of Nature Center Administrators.

Greenfield, James M. *Fund-Raising Fundamentals.* New York: John Wiley & Sons, Inc., 1994.

McAllister, Pamela. *The Charity's Guide to Charitable Contributions.* Seattle, WA: Conlee-Gibbs Publishing, 1998. 800-788-8665. www.exemptlaw.com.

Participants Manual. *Survey Course on Fund Raising.* Alexandria, VA: National Society of Fund Raising Executives, 1994.

Appendix A

National Charities Information Bureau (NCIB) Standards in Philanthropy.
Governance, Policy and Program Fundamentals

1. **Board Governance:**
    The board is responsible for policy setting, fiscal guidance, and ongoing governance, and should regularly review the organization's policies, programs and operations. The board should have:

    a. An independent volunteer membership;
    b. A minimum of 5 voting members;
    c. An individual attendance policy;
    d. Specific terms of office for its officers and members;
    e. In-person, face-to-face meetings, at least twice a year, evenly spaced, with a majority of voting members in attendance at each meeting;
    f. No fees to members for board service, but payments may be made for costs incurred as a result of board participation;
    g. No more than one paid staff person member, usually the chief staff officer, who shall not chair the board or serve as treasurer;
    h. Policy guidelines to avoid material conflicts of interest involving board or staff;
    I. No material conflicts of interest involving board or staff;
    j. A policy promoting pluralism and diversity within the organization's board, staff, and constituencies.

2. **Purpose:**
    The organization's purpose, approved by the board, should be formally and specifically stated.

3. **Programs:**
    The organization's activities should be consistent with its statement of purpose.

4. **Information:**
    Promotion, fundraising, and public information should describe accurately the organization's identity, purpose, programs, and financial needs.

5. **Financial Support and Related Activities:**
    The board is accountable for all authorized activities generating financial support on the organization's behalf:

    a. Fundraising practices should encourage voluntary giving and should not apply unwarranted pressure;
    b. Descriptive and financial information for all substantial income and for all revenue-generating activities conducted by the organization should be disclosed on request;
    c. Basic descriptive and financial information for income derived from authorized commercial activities involving the organization's name, which are conducted by for-profit organizations, should be available. All public promotion of such commercial activity should either include this information or indicate that it is available from the organization.

Appendix A continued

6. **Use of Funds:**
   The organization's use of funds should reflect consideration of current and future needs and resources in planning for program continuity. The organization should:

   a. Spend at least 60% of annual expenses for program activities;
   b. Insure that fundraising expenses, in relation to fundraising results, are reasonable over time;
   c. Have net assets available for the following fiscal year not usually more than twice the current year's expenses or the next year's budget, whichever is higher;
   d. Not have a persistent and/or increasing deficit in unrestricted net assets.

Reporting and Fiscal Fundamentals

7. **Annual Reporting:**
   An annual report should be available on request, and should include:

   a. An explicit narrative description of the organization's major activities, presented in the same major categories and covering the same fiscal period as the audited financial statements;
   b. A list of board members;
   c. Audited financial statements or, at a minimum, a comprehensive financial summary that:
      1) Identifies all revenues in significant categories;
      2) Reports expenses in the same program, management/general, and fundraising categories as in the audited financial statements, and;
      3) Reports all ending balances. (When the annual report does not include the full audited financial statements, it should indicate that they are available on request.)

8. **Accountability:**
   An organization should supply on request complete financial statements which:

   a. Are prepared in conformity with generally accepted accounting principles (GAAP), accompanied by a report of an independent certified public accountant, and reviewed by the board; and
   b. Fully disclose economic resources and obligations, including transactions with related parties and affiliated organizations, significant events affecting finances, and significant categories of income and expense; and should also supply
   c. A statement of functional allocation of expenses, in addition to such statements required by generally accepted accounting principles to be included among the financial statements;
   d. Combined financial statements for a national organization operating with affiliates prepared in the foregoing manner.

9. **Budget:**
   The organization should prepare a detailed annual budget consistent with the major classifications in the audited financial statements, and approved by the board.

The National Charities Information Bureau has promoted informed giving since 1918. NCIB uses the above nine standards to evaluate national organizations who fund raise and accept contributions. They may be contacted at 19 Union Square West; New York, NY, 10003-3395; 212-929-6300; www.give.org or info@nationalcharities.org.

Appendix B

Code of Ethical Principles and Standards of Professional Practice

Code of Ethical Principles
Adopted 1964; Amended October 2004

The Association of Fundraising Professionals (AFP) exists to foster the development and growth of fundraising professionals and the profession, to promote high ethical standards in the fundraising profession and to preserve and enhance philanthropy and volunteerism.

Members of the AFP are motivated by an inner drive to improve the quality of life through the causes they serve. They serve the ideal of philanthropy; are committed to the preservation and enhancement of volunteerism; and hold stewardship of these concepts as the overriding principle of their professional life. They recognize their responsibility to ensure that needed resources are vigorously and ethically sought and that the intent of the donor is honestly fulfilled. To these ends, AFP members embrace certain values that they strive to uphold in performing their responsibilities for generating philanthropic support.

AFP members aspire to:

- practice their profession with integrity, honesty, truthfulness and adherence to the absolute obligation to safeguard the public trust;
- act according to the highest standards and visions of their organization, profession and conscience;
- put philanthropic mission above personal gain;
- inspire others through their own sense of dedication and high purpose;
- improve their professional knowledge and skills, so that their performance will better serve others;
- demonstrate concern for the interests and well being of individuals affected by their actions;
- value the privacy, freedom of choice and interests of all those affected by their actions;
- foster cultural diversity and pluralistic values, and treat all people with dignity and respect;
- affirm, through personal giving, a commitment to philanthropy and its role in society;
- adhere to the spirit as well as the letter of all applicable laws and regulations;
- advocate within their organizations, adherence to all applicable laws and regulations;
- avoid even the appearance of any criminal offence or professional misconduct;
- bring credit to the fundraising profession by their public demeanor;
- encourage colleagues to embrace and practice these ethical principles and standards of professional practice; and
- be aware of the codes of ethics promulgated by other professional organizations that serve philanthropy.

Standards of Professional Practice

Furthermore, while striving to act according to the above values, AFP members agree to abide by the AFP Standards of Professional Practice, which are adopted and incorporated into the AFP Code of Ethical Principles. Violation of the Standard may subject the member to disciplinary sanctions, including expulsion, as provided in the AFP Ethics Enforcement Procedures.

Director's Guide to Best Practices

Professional Obligations

1. Members shall not engage in activities that harm the member's organization, clients, or profession.
2. Members shall not engage in activities that conflict with their fiduciary, ethical, and legal obligations to their organizations and their clients.
3. Members shall effectively disclose all potential and actual conflicts of interest; such disclosure does not preclude or imply ethical impropriety.
4. Members shall not exploit any relationship with a donor, prospect, volunteer or employee for the benefit of the member or the member's organization.
5. Members shall comply with all applicable local, state, provincial, federal, civil and criminal laws.
6. Members recognize their individual boundaries of competence and are forthcoming and truthful about their professional experience and qualifications.

Solicitation and Use of Charitable Funds

7. Members shall take care to ensure that all solicitation materials are accurate and correctly reflect the organization's mission and use of solicited funds.
8. Members shall take care to ensure that donors receive informed, accurate and ethical advice about the value and tax implications of contributions.
9. Members shall take care to ensure that contributions are used in accordance with donors' intentions.
10. Members shall take care to ensure proper stewardship of charitable contributions, including timely reports on the use and management of funds.
11. Members shall obtain explicit consent by the donor before altering the conditions of contributions.

Presentation of Information

12. Members shall not disclose privileged or confidential information to unauthorized parties.
13. Members shall adhere to the principle that all donor and prospect information created by, or on behalf of, an organization is the property of that organization and shall not be transferred or utilized except on behalf of that organization.
14. Members shall give donors the opportunity to have their names removed from lists that are sold to, rented to, or exchanged with other organizations.
15. Members shall, when stating fundraising results, use accurate and consistent accounting methods that conform to the appropriate guidelines adopted by the American Institute of Certified Public Accountants (AICPA)* for the type of organization involved. (*In countries outside of the United States, comparable authority should be utilized.)

Compensation

16. Members shall not accept compensation that is based on a percentage of contributions; nor shall they accept finder's fees.
17. Members may accept performance-based compensation, such as bonuses, provided such bonuses are in accord with prevailing practices within the members' own organizations, and are not based on a percentage of contributions.
18. Members shall not pay finder's fees, commissions or percentage compensation based on contributions, and shall take care to discourage their organizations from making such payments.

Reprinted with permission.

Appendix C

A Donor Bill of Rights

PHILANTHROPY is based on voluntary action for the common good. It is a tradition of giving and sharing that is primary to the quality of life. To assure that philanthropy merits the respect and trust of the general public, and that donors and prospective donors can have full confidence in the not-for-profit organizations and causes they are asked to support, we declare that all donors have these rights:

I. *To be informed of the organization's mission, of the way the organization intends to use donated resources, and of its capacity to use donations effectively for their intended purposes.*

II. *To be informed of the identity of those serving on the organization's governing board, and to expect the board to exercise prudent judgment in its stewardship responsibilities.*

III. *To have access to the organization's most recent financial statements.*

IV. *To be assured their gifts will be used for the purposes for which they were given.*

V. *To receive appropriate acknowledgment and recognition.*

VI. *To be assured that information about their donations is handled with respect and with confidentiality to the extent provided by law.*

VII. *To expect that all relationships with individuals representing organizations of interest to the donor will be professional in nature.*

VIII. *To be informed whether those seeking donations are volunteers, employees of the organization or hired solicitors.*

IX. *To have the opportunity for their names to be deleted from mailing lists that an organization may intend to share.*

X. *To feel free to ask questions when making a donation and to receive prompt, truthful and forthright answers.*

DEVELOPED BY
American Association of Fund Raising Counsel (AAFRC)
Association for Healthcare Philanthropy (AHP)

Council for Advancement and Support of Education (CASE)

Association of Fundraising Professionals (AFP)

ENDORSED BY
Independent Sector
National Catholic Development Conference (NCDC)
National Committee on Planned Giving (NCPG)
National Council for Resource Development (CRD)
United Way of America

Reprinted with permission.

Director's Guide to Best Practices

Appendix D

How to Pick the Right Fundraising Consultant

The best way to seek out firms to interview is to check with organizations similar to yours and find out which ones they have used. Find out from other nonprofits in your area who the best local consultants are. Sometimes it is an advantage to choose a firm that knows your community well. Don't hire any fundraising consultants until you find that they have satisfied customers.

Consult present or former clients of the firms you are considering and ask the following questions:

- What is your evaluation of the firm's services?
- How realistic did the firm's cost estimates turn out to be?
- Would you engage that particular firm again?
- Did the firm achieve the organization's fundraising objective?
- Did the firm achieve any of the following for the organization: improvement of the organization's program, increased involvement of influential leadership, an improved public image of the institution and/or improvement of the extent to which administrators and board members work well together?

Some important questions to ask the firm:

- What is the fundraising background of the firm's key executives before they became consultants?
- Has the firm consulted with institutions or agencies similar to ours? What is your track record with those groups?
- How will the firm bill our organization for services?
- Will our organization have to pay out-of-pocket expenses? If so, how will they be billed; in advance or when they're incurred?
- Will the firm provide general plans for our organization's effort, including cost estimates and a schedule of events?
- Will the firm conduct a feasibility study?
- Where are the firm's permanent offices? If they are far away, how often will the staff visit our organization? What costs are involved in these visits? Is the firm familiar with our community? Has it done business here before?

Adapted from *Big Gifts (The Nature Center Handbook) Student Resource.* **Edited by M. Jane Williams. Copyright ©
1991 The Gale Group. All rights reserved. Reprinted by permission of The Gale Group. www.gale-edit.com**

Appendix E

Fundraising Readiness: How Does Your Agency Stack Up?
By Brigette Sarabi
Copyright © 1997 The Grantmanship Center. Reprinted with permission.

Hastily patching together a fundraising scheme to deal with some impending fiscal crisis is an all-too-common approach to an all-too-common problem. Unfortunately, however, donors don't write big checks just because your organization finds itself in a bind.

More probably, they'll wonder how you got in this fix in the first place. Poor management? Bad business practices? Ineptitude?

That's why the best place to start building a successful fundraising plan is from a position of strength, not desperation. Just as individuals should have a physical exam every now and then, organizations too need a regular check-up. The "Organizational Assets & Liabilities Checklist" on the following pages is a simple tool to help accomplish that. It's an exercise you should perform before embarking on a full-scale fundraising campaign.

Start by establishing an ad hoc organizational assessment team that includes leadership from both staff and board. Make sure administrative, financial, and program people are included so that all sectors of the organization have some investment in the effort. Together, spend time going over the checklist and filling it out.

The simple format calls for yes-or-no answers, but don't worry if you occasionally find yourself somewhere in the middle (the dreaded "sort-of" column). That's okay; your answers will still point out areas that need attention.

After completing the checklist, you should have a pretty good picture of the organization's general health and business practices. This information can be used to guide your planning efforts.

It's a first step toward maximizing strengths and remedying weaknesses - and making yourselves more attractive to prospective donors.

Brigette Sarabi developed The Grantsmanship Center's Strategic Fundraising Workshop. In addition to training for the Center, she works as a fundraising and management consultant in the Pacific Northwest.

Appendix E continued

ORGANIZATIONAL ASSETS AND LIABILITIES CHECKLIST

FINANCES	YES	NO
Do you have an annual budget, approved and monitored by the board, which includes all program and management expenses and all sources and uses of funds?	☐	☐
Does your agency prepare monthly financial statements which compare actual revenues and expenses to the approved budget?	☐	☐
Does your agency follow accounting practices which conform to standard practice?	☐	☐
Is an independent audit or review of the agency's financial condition conducted annually?	☐	☐
Is a written statement of the organization's financial position (i.e., a financial statement) available to potential funders and donors?	☐	☐
Can you identify which programs are running at a surplus or loss and why?	☐	☐
Can you identify your primary funding sources and whether or not they are secure for the next few years?	☐	☐
Do you differentiate between restricted and unrestricted income?	☐	☐
Are you running a deficit?	☐	☐
If you have a deficit, do you have a plan to eliminate it within the next fiscal year?	☐	☐
Do you have a financial surplus?	☐	☐
If you have a surplus, is it unrestricted money?	☐	☐
And is it repeatable?	☐	☐
Do you receive more than 30% of your operating budget from one source?	☐	☐
If yes, is the money unrestricted?	☐	☐
If yes, is this funding renewable over the mid-to-long term?	☐	☐

PERSONNEL	YES	NO
Do you have an adequate number of active board members?	☐	☐
Do you have board members who are recognized leaders in the community?	☐	☐
Does the board provide clear leadership within the organization?	☐	☐
Does the board participate in fundraising?	☐	☐
Do board members have relationships that can help leverage additional resources for the organization?	☐	☐
Is the board stable? (e.g., is there orderly turnover of board members, with adequate training of new board members?)	☐	☐

Appendix E continued

PERSONNEL continued	YES	NO
Do you have a stable volunteer base?	☐	☐
Can volunteers be used more effectively to meet the personnel needs of your organization? (e.g., if staff has been cut, can volunteers fill part or all of the gap?)	☐	☐
Do you have adequate staff to implement current programs?	☐	☐
Do you have adequate administrative and support staff?	☐	☐
Do you have adequate fundraising staff?	☐	☐
Is there staff leadership that works effectively with the board to implement goals and objectives?	☐	☐
Do you have dynamic program staff who could assist in fundraising (as motivators, recruiters, speakers)?	☐	☐

CREDIBILITY	YES	NO
Do you have documented evidence of community support?	☐	☐
• community leaders on board of directors?	☐	☐
• receive financial contributions from individuals?	☐	☐
• receive cash or in-kind donations from local businesses?	☐	☐
• a large number of people accessing your services?	☐	☐
• recognition by the press, government, other agencies?	☐	☐
• an active volunteer base involved with the agency?	☐	☐
• positive testimonials form clients, members, volunteers, etc.?	☐	☐
Have you had documented program success?	☐	☐
• Can you demonstrate the results of the services you provide (e.g., changes in your clients as a result of services)?	☐	☐
• Is there continuity in the successful provision of these services (e.g., history plus track record)?	☐	☐
Is there evidence of good organizational health?	☐	☐
• Is the organization financially stable?	☐	☐
• Does the board give money, as well as time, to the organization?	☐	☐
• Are you getting funds from a diverse array of funders/donors?	☐	☐

Appendix F

Sample Membership Categories

Friends of Aullwood
Aullwood Audubon Center and Farm
Dayton, OH

Memberships

Friend	$45
Contributing	$60
Sustainer	$125
Sponsor	$250
Patron	$500
Corporate	Various Levels

Benefits
Friends
Receive Aullwood newsletter, bimonthly, free general admission, 10% discount on gift items in Aullwood's Book & Gift Shops, free admission to Flights of Fancy Festival (April), free admission to Aullwood Apple Fest (September), discounted fees on children and adult workshops and/or classes, discounted feeds on natural history travel, special invitations to events throughout the year, the gratification of supporting environmental education programs at Aullwood.

Contributing $60
All benefits above plus two complimentary passes for free general admission for your friends.

Sustainer $125
All benefits above plus two complimentary guest passes to the Wildlife Festival and 10% discount on books in Aullwood's Book & Gift Ships.

Sponsor $250
All benefits above plus four additional complimentary guest passes to Wildlife Festival and Roger Tory Peterson's *Field Guide to Eastern Bird Songs* (double cassette)

Patron $500
All benefits above plus 20% discount on gifts in Aullwood's Book & Gift Shops and two free admissions to the Quilt Preview Party

Corporate Memberships Various Levels
Aullwood offers many special benefits for the corporate sponsors including benefits for employees. For details, contact Ardith Hamilton or Charity Krueger at 937-890-7360.

http://aullwood.center.audubon.org/aacffoa.html

Cibolo Nature Center
Boerne, TX

Memberships

Acorn	$25 Individual
	$35 Family
	$13 Student
	$20 Senior
Naturalist	$50
Supporter	$100
Guardian	$250
Champion	$500
Steward	$1,000

Benefits
Acorn
Newsletter, calendar of events, 10% event/workshop discount, 10% shopping discount.
Naturalist
All benefits above plus CNC Guide to the Great Outdoors
Supporter
All benefits above plus CNC Note Cards and name in annual report
Guardian
All benefits above plus two season passes to Songs & Stories
Champion
All benefits above plus annual pass to all Land Stewardship Programs
Steward
All benefits above plus name on donor plaque.

www.cibolo.org/join

Appendix G

Techniques to Nurture Your Donors

Little do donors know how much time you, as a fund raiser, spend attempting to nudge them toward more frequent and larger gifts. Yet, whether or not they have any inkling of your intentions, many seem to quit giving right after their first gift. Simply put, they *lapse*.

So how do you keep your donors from lapsing? First, be sure not to send known annual-only donors all your annual appeals during the year. You will be wasting your resources.

At the same time, your most aggressive upgrade attempts should be aimed at those who have given a number of gifts, all of the same amount. The longer the same-amount gift history, the fewer the lapses when an upgrade is aggressively sought. The shorter the same-amount gift history, the greater the lapses.

Also, test reducing the number of appeals you send to your multiple-gifts-per-year-donors. Your net income will likely increase — and the number of lapses will decrease.

In my opinion, over-appealing, over-upgrading and over-aggressiveness are major maladies of fundraising today. As long as fund raisers continue to be overly aggressive, they will reap what they have sown — declining donor bases and declining response rates (which conversely mean higher lapses rates).

Most importantly, fund raisers must nurture donors to reduce the odds of their lapsing. It is simply a matter of using multiple methods to *thank, praise* and *reward* donors for achievement! Generally, fund raisers should spend more time finding ways to *thank* donors, and less time dreaming up additional appeals.

Here then are fourteen techniques to successfully nurture donors:

1. Acknowledge donor gifts by letter or mini-letter, especially at the $10-and-over level. Vary the letters. Monitor the results.
2. Add handwritten P.S.'s to selected acknowledgment letters.
3. Recognize all gift upgrades with special letters. This generates enormous good will.
4. Acknowledge *all* donor letters and notes, including short remarks like "Keep up the good work."
5. Honor donor requests. Yet try not to take "no" for an answer.
6. Make surprise phone calls of thanks.
7. Send small surprise gifts of recognition, like pins, plaques and special purchases.
8. Invite donors to attend your annual meeting. Have an acknowledgment program when they arrive.
9. Ask donors to an annual open house.
10. Recognize cumulative gift achievement.
11. Recognize the number of years of consistent giving achievements.
12. Mail special annual reports to donors. Include a cover letter. In the report, describe your mail program and its accomplishment. Also, praise donor groups. Mention the number of donors in each giving group. Share some statistics. Include a return envelope.
13. Thank donors again in each appeal they receive.
14. Devote one-third of your newsletter to the need for funds and the recognition of donors. Tell your donors why you mail multiple appeals. Aim some copy to readers who have lapsed.

By Don Kuhn, CFRE (Ret.), NSFRE member and consultant, May Development Services, Greenwich, CT.
Reprinted with permission from the author.

Appendix H

Major Donor Solicitation:
Using Team Work for Success
Developed for
Pine Jog Environmental Education Center, West Palm Beach, FL
by Norma Jeanne Byrd, Consultant

This outline details duties and responsibilities of volunteers and staff involved in major donor solicitations. It includes a step-by-step process that will help guarantee success.

I.   Responsibilities Before the Visit

    A.   Board Members
1. Submit detailed information on prospects to development staff.
2. Recommend strategies for approaching prospects (individual meeting at home or office, group meeting with several prospects) and who should initiate contact.
3. Make calls, arrange meetings and appointments.
4. Review all prospect information and case statement.

    B.   Executive Director
1. Coordinate appointments and meetings with board members and prospects.
2. Plan major initiatives, events, and proposals with development staff.
3. Send confirmation letter with appointment time to prospect.
4. Include materials for prospect to review prior to meeting.
5. Review all prospect information prior to meeting.

    C.   Development Staff
1. Research prospects.
2. Create permanent prospect and donor files; make copies available for board members and executive director prior to visit.
3. Gather and prepare solicitation and information materials.
4. Assist with scheduling and coordination.
5. Provide confirmation letters for board and director.
6. Provide training for board and staff.
7. Plan and organize events.

II.   Conducting the Visit

    A.   Board Members
1. One or more board members visit the prospect(s) with Executive Director.
2. Bring complete set of materials previously sent in case prospect has misplaced the others.
3. Provide introductions, create comfortable atmosphere (whether in prospect's home, business or neutral setting).
4. Be sociable in the first few minutes to establish rapport. Be yourself and be relaxed.
5. If visit is with previous or current donor, acknowledge their past or current support.
6. Bring the discussion around to the point of the meeting. Speak about your experience with the organization. Speak from your heart first and from your head second (ie: let them know why the center is important to you before filling them in with the facts and figures).
7. Be passionate but brief.

    B.   Executive Director
1. Go with board members on prospect calls to provide specific information on programs, projects, staffing, budgets, costs and future plans. If your relationship with the prospect

is stronger than the board member's, you serve as the "bridge" between prospect and the board member.

    2.   Make the "case" to the prospect. Speak with passion, commitment, and knowledge.

  C.   Both Board Member and Executive Director

    1.   Listen to the prospect. Don't do all the talking.

    2.   Ask prospects leading questions to encourage their ideas. Give prospects lots of opportunities to talk about what interests them.

    3.   Keep the meeting on track.

    4.   Don't avoid the purpose of the meeting which is to generate financial support!

    5.   Determine from the conversation and tone of the meeting if the time is right to ask for a gift or if more time is needed to get to know each other.

    6.   Be specific with your request. If you determine an "ask" is appropriate, ask for a specific amount.

    7.   Remain positive and encouraging if you don't receive an immediate "YES" response. Rarely does a prospect commit on the spot.

    8.   Know when it is time to close the meeting.

  D.   Working with Each Other

    1.   Contribute equally and naturally to the meeting.

    2.   Be sure that one doesn't dominate the other when working as a team. If you tend to talk over others, just be aware of it and remember to listen to the prospect and each other for clues to how the visit is going.

  E.   What to Notice

    1.   Body language: observe eye contact, restlessness or nervousness (by them, not you!), smiles and laughter, arm crossing, attitude changes, responses to ideas as they are presented.

    2.   Details of the physical setting. Much can be learned about a prospect by observation of the surroundings. You may see awards, photos, acknowledgments from others, books of interest, etc. Take note.

    3.   These visits can never be totally scripted. Think of the visit as a dance where you in turn both lead and follow. Remember: often what *isn't* said is just as important as what *is*.

III.   Ending the Meeting

  A.   Length of meeting: 15 minutes to no more than an hour.

  B.   End meeting on upbeat, positive note and summarize what you will do to follow up (send materials, proposal, schedule a field trip, etc.).

  C.   Executive director: Always acknowledge and thank the board members who are volunteering their time. The prospect will respect this.

  D.   Look for opportunities from the meeting (even if it didn't go the way you expected).

IV.   What You Should Know After the Meeting

  A.   What interested the prospect?

  B.   If it wasn't stated, what is the appropriate gift range to request?

  C.   Are any additional materials/information needed for the prospect?

  D.   Should a formal request or proposal be sent following the meeting?

  E.   When will you hear from the prospect?

V.   After the Visit

  A.   Both Board Member and Executive Director

    1.   Jot down notes and impressions of the meeting immediately.

    2.   Provide this information to development staff for permanent files.

Appendix H continued

        3.   File a prospect/donor visit report within 1-3 days.

        4.   Keep track of new information gained from the visit (interests expressed, questions or concerns they had about the organization, any barriers or impediments to developing this person as a long term supporter, what interested them most or produced a positive reaction when discussed).

        5.   Send thank you note or letter and provide copies for files.

        6.   If proposal requested, mention in note to prospect that it will arrive under separate cover.

        7.   Request staff to send follow-up information and support materials.

    B.   Development Staff

        1.   Keep schedule of all meetings and appointments.

        2.   Up-date files with prospect/donor visits reports.

        3.   If reports not submitted in timely manner, issue reminders.

        4.   If requested, send follow-up materials and information.

        5.   Develop proposals based on what was discussed at the visit.

        6.   If subsequent meetings are required, follow through and arrange with prospect, board member and director.

        7.   Track and manage all prospect/donor correspondence in permanent files.

VI.   Response to Gift or Pledge

    A.   Executive director: Call donor to thank for major gift. Notify board member.

    B.   Board member: Call donor to thank if a major gift is received. Send personal thank you note.

    C.   Development staff: Send thank you immediately or no later than 3 days from receipt of gift. If pledge received, follow up with a pledge reminder letter at schedule agreed upon for pledge payment.

VII.   Ongoing Relationships with Donors

    A.   Calls and visits

    B.   Providing up-dates

    C.   Encouraging authentic involvement

    D.   Invitations to special events

    E.   Other opportunities

Appendix I

Tips for Writing Effective Grant Proposals

Let's assume you know your organization's target for a funding proposal, how much you are asking for, and the purpose of the grant request. Now it's time to sit down and start writing the proposal. Following are tips offered by grant proposal experts:

- Keep the request short, no longer than two or three pages. Most prospects are overwhelmed with paper and you don't want to get lost in the shuffle.

- If writing to a foundation, talk in terms of a gift. If writing to a corporation, write in terms of an investment. The two organization types have different mindsets; foundations are in the business of giving money away while corporations try to make money. Use language that fits your prospect.

- Make your request's verb tense positive instead of conditional. For example, instead of writing "if you would consider," write "your gift will" or "your gift can."

- Study other agencies the group has funded. Call colleagues who obtained gifts or grants from the group to find out why their proposals were successful.

- Study all materials available on the foundation or funding group to get a sense of their philosophy and general overall interests. Focus on aspects of your project that are in tune with that philosophy.

- Write in clear, concise form. Avoid burdensome language and jargon.

- Short sentences make your proposal easier to read. Break the subject matter into bite-size pieces.

- Underline your request.

- Talk about opportunities, not problems.

- Cite the relevance of the gift to the donor. Show how the gift is as important to the donor as it is to the recipient.

- Credentials are important. Make sure the organization knows your group is qualified to do what you are proposing.

- Follow grant application directions provided by the funding organization. Their requirements are usually clear.

- Proofread your proposal carefully. Make sure all information presented is accurate and relevant, and that information throughout corresponds.

- Say "thank you" whether or not your proposal is funded. If such acknowledgment is not given, the donor group may not be interested in funding you the next time a request is made. Handwritten notes are good.

Sources: Nike B. Whitcomb, President, Nike B. Whitcomb Associates, 54 West Hubbard Street, Suite 402, Chicago, IL 60610. (312)346-9018. Lucille D. Fallon, Director of Corporate/Foundation Relations, Michigan State University, 4700 South Hagadorn, East Lansing, MI 48823. (517)355-8257.

This article is being reprinted from *Successful Fund Raising* with the permission of Stevenson Consultants, Inc. *Successful Fund Raising* is a monthly newsletter designed to provide its subscribers with ideas, strategies and management topics that will strengthen their fund-raising efforts. To receive a free sample issue, simply call, write or fax your request to Stevenson Consultants, Inc., PO Box 4528, Sioux City, IA 51104. Phone (712) 239-3010. Fax (712) 239-2166.

Appendix J

Grant Seeker's Checklist

☐   Before starting the application process, be clear about what you want to accomplish. Draw up a long-range plan that projects goals at least five years ahead.

☐   Research potential funders thoroughly - a cursory look through a foundation directory isn't good enough. Then apply what you've learned. Don't ignore a funder's guidelines in the hopes of "fitting" your proposal in their niche.

☐   Only preview successful applications from grant seekers whose projects are similar to yours. You'll not only get some good ideas, but an understanding of the competition, too.

☐   Once you verify available funding, divide your efforts into three further phases: writing the proposal, marketing, and management.

☐   Writing the proposal should take only about 40% of your time. Try to get program officials to review a 3-5 page summary of your plan first, to make sure you're on the right track.

☐   Basic rules of proposal writing: don't ask for more than you need; take your time writing the proposal; never lie; never use the same application twice; be up-front about asking for money; and don't waste time getting to the point.

☐   Don't overlook marketing. It should take at least 10% of your time. Make sure your organization will appeal to a potential funder, try to look professional, and involve key community figures where possible.

☐   Management is vital. You must be able to demonstrate that you have the management skills and experience that can deliver success.

☐   Know the funder. It's been estimated that your chances of success improve by as much as 300% when you make contact with the funder before and during the proposal writing process. Don't ask for hidden agendas, but find out about general trends or new ideas the funder is currently interested in.

☐   Always work to a timetable. Make sure you have enough time to complete your application so it meets the funder's deadlines. If you don't have time to do it properly, don't compete for the grant at all.

☐   Give thought to the idea of cooperation. Many funders, particularly federal agencies, like applications where more than one organization is involved. If you submit a cooperative proposal, remember to make sure that there is both a formal and informal relationship between grantees.

☐   When dealing with any funder, but especially federal agencies, remember to read the instructions before applying. It sounds simple, but federal competitions live by two rules: 1) The agency is always right, and 2) When in doubt, refer to rule 1.

☐   Don't just tell the funder about the existence of the problem you intend to solve. Prove it with statistics, case studies, testimony, and any other measurable data.

Appendix J continued

☐   Know your budget. It's probably the first thing a funder will look at in your proposal. It needs to be realistic and give credibility to your entire proposal. Present the budget separately from the rest of the application, make sure the figures are correct and that the budget accurately reflects your needs. Keep a record of how you arrived at your costs.

☐   A few other writing hints: 1) Avoid filling your proposal with jargon; 2) Begin each section with a strong, clear sentence; 3) Don't go overboard, but do try to make your proposal interesting to read; 4) Check with the funder to see if there's a preferred format, type style, etc.

☐   If your proposal doesn't win support, keep calm. Never berate funding officials or grant reviewers. Try to get more information and ask whether it would be worth submitting another application in the future. Go back over your proposal with care and see if you can find places where it might have been stronger.

☐   The key to a strong proposal is proving the likelihood that it will achieve its goals. Result areas should always be clearly determined and measurement indicators should be outlined. It may not be easy to do, but the value of having clear performance standards can't be underestimated.

☐   Remember that often the key to a strong proposal is simplicity. Don't waste words. Funders are looking for a proposal that will succeed, so keep things clear, factual, supportable, and professional.

☐   Don't give in to pressure. A rushed proposal rarely wins. Keep a file with standard information enclosed and updated, like staff resumes and community statistical data, so you can concentrate on the specific grant information needed when the time to apply arrives.

☐   When dealing with foundation or corporate funders, don't underestimate the importance of the original contact letter. Make it as strong as possible and keep it to the point.

Reprinted from the *Federal Assistance Monitor*, CD Publications, Silver Spring, MD. To order call: 1-800-666-6380. Used with permission.

Appendix K

Planning a Special Event

Distribute and use this form with board members and staff to outline and guide planning steps.

Event Name:_____ Event Date:_____
Use on all invitations and announcements.
Event Location: _____ Lead Organizer(s):_____
Staff Support: _____

Income Strategies

1. How will you generate income (sponsors, pledges, contributions, tickets, etc.)? List all sources.

2. How will you collect income (in advance, during event, personal solicitations, letters)?

3. What is the follow-up for the event? Letters? Calls? Personal visits? Who will write and sign letters? Who will track income?

4. Are incentives (raffles, door prizes, silent auction) planned as part of the event? If yes, list ideas. If items for raffles, door prizes, silent auction, etc. are not already owned by the organization, who will solicit these donations? Track donations?

5. Are sponsors sought to pay up-front costs of the event?

6. How will contributors be acknowledged? An event program? Published in newsletter? Personal letters? Special gifts?

Board, Staff or Volunteer Responsibilities. Who will:

1. Plan and organize the event?
2. Identify prospects to invite? Establish a target number of prospective donors/participants from each board member. Also seek prospect ideas from established donors.
3. Identify gift potential: list potential and realistic target gift amount based on previous giving, giving to other organizations, interest level, known information.
4. Determine desired number of participants for the event?
5. Secure the event facility, food/drinks, entertainment, keynote, speakers, exhibits?
6. Develop invitations, event program, and other materials?
7. Follow-up: prepare letters with specific gift request, sign, write personal notes, send promised materials, etc. Arrange follow-up calls, visits.

Appendix K continued

Time allowed for each phase:

1. Planning/Organizing _____
2. Prospect ID _____
3. Gift potential ID _____
4. Invitation list _____
5. Event logistics _____
6. Materials _____
7. Follow-up _____

Board/Staff/Volunteer Name	Responsibility	Estimated Time
_____	_____	_____
_____	_____	_____
_____	_____	_____
_____	_____	_____

Budget: Complete early in the planning process to determine feasibility and project income goals.

Expenses

Expenses		Revenue Projections	
Facility rental	$_____	Gross goal	$_____
Equipment rental	$_____		
Prizes/incentives	$_____		
Food/refreshments	$_____	Budgeted expenses	$_____
Promotional material	$_____		
Printing	$_____		
Postage	$_____	Net goal .	$_____
Fees/honoraria, etc.	$_____		
Travel	$_____		
Other	$_____		
Total	$_____		

Sponsor information Complete for each sponsor identified.

Sponsor name: _____

Address: _____

Contact person: _____ Phone: _____

Type of support offered _____

Contacts

Aspen Publishers, Inc.
200 Orchard Ridge Drive, Suite 200
Gaithersburg, MD 20878
800-234-1660 (customer service)
800-638-8437 (orders)
800-901-9075 (fax)
www.aspenpublishers.com

Resources for Global Sustainability, Inc.
Environmental Grantmaking Foundation
PO Box 3665
Cary, NC 27519-3665
800-724-1857
919-329-8273
orders@environmentalgrants.com
www.environmentalgrants.com

The Foundation Directory
The Foundation Center
79 Fifth Avenue
New York, NY 10003
212-620-4230
http://.fdncentr.org

The Grantsmanship Center.
P.O. Box 17220
1125 W. Sixth St., Fifth Floor
Los Angeles, CA 90017
212-482-9860
213-482-9863 (fax)
www.tgci.com
Sign up online for a free subscription to *The Grantsmanship Center Magazine.*

Contacts continued

Subscriptions

The Chronicle of Philanthropy
1255 23rd Street NW, Suite 700
Washington, DC 20037
202-466-1200
help@philanthropy.com
www.philanthropy.com

The NonProfit Times
201 Littleton Road - 2nd Floor
Morris Plains, NJ 07950
973-401-0202
973-401-0404 (fax)
www.nptimes.com
The *NonProfit Times* is offered free to full time U.S. nonprofit executives.

Membership Organizations

Association of Fundraising Professionals (AFP)
1101 King Street, Suite 700
Alexandria, VA 22314
800-666-3863
703-684-0410
703-684-0540 (fax)
www.afpnet.org

Independent Sector
1200 18th Street, NW, Suite 200
Washington, DC 20036
202-467-6100
202-467-6101 (fax)
www.independentsector.org

Contacts continued

Software

Ebase donor database software is available free to nonprofit organizations. Visit their web site at www.ebase.org. Ebase uses FileMaker Pro software and can be used with either Windows or Macintosh operating systems.

Reviewers

Andy Brown, Battle Creek Nature Center, Prince Frederick, MD
Lynn Corliss, Center for Coastal Ecology, Beaufort, SC
Peggy Hunt, Pioneers Park Nature Center, Lincoln, NE
Greg Lee*, Dodge Nature Center, West St. Paul, MN
Bob Marye*, Louisiana Nature Center, New Orleans, LA
Robert Mercer, Silver Lake Nature Center, Bristol, PA
Cindy O'Connor, Wetlands Institute, Stone Harbor, NJ
Carl Palmer*, Ogden Nature Center, Ogden, UT
Tim Sandsmark*, Greenway and Nature Center of Pueblo, Pueblo, CO
Jack Shea, Teton Science School, Kelly, WY
Bo Townsend*, Ijams Nature Center, Knoxville, TN
Christine Turnbull*, The Friends of Hunt Hill Audubon Sanctuary, Inc., Sarona, WI
Robert Venner, DeGraaf Nature Center, Holland, MI
Doug Weeks, Waterman Conservation Education Center, Apalachin, NY
Pat Welch, Pine Jog Environmental Education Center, West Palm Beach, FL
Brian Winslow, Asbury Woods Nature Center, Erie, PA
Jim Yaich*, Jamestown Audubon Nature Center, Jamestown, NY

* Former director

GENERAL APPENDIX

Appendix A

The Art of Collaborative Negotiating
by Andrew E. Schwartz

President of A. E. Schwartz & Associates, Waverly, Massachusetts
Reprinted with permission from NONPROFIT WORLD, Vol. 12, No. 4
Published by The Society for Nonprofit Organizations.

It is difficult to imagine a more crucial skill for nonprofit managers than that of negotiating. Without solid negotiating abilities, you will inevitably make serious mistakes in dealing with people at all levels, both inside and outside your organization.

As a negotiator, you must concern yourself with substantive issues and your continuing relationships with people. If you push too much, you may create hard feelings. If you are overly concerned about getting along with others, you may lose ground for your organization.

Collaborative negotiation is a problem-solving approach that looks for a workable solution and explores everyone's needs until all are satisfied. With collaborative negotiation, both sides can collectively find solutions that go beyond the scope of the individual parties involved. Personal relationships can improve rather than deteriorate. To put this powerful technique to work for you, follow these steps:

1. Embrace a Win-Win Strategy
The first step is to accept a "win-win" philosophy of negotiation. The idea is that you give the other party something it wants, and the same is done for you. The win-win technique involves managing the outcome by clearly assessing your needs as well as the other side's needs and establishing a strategy to achieve both.

2. Prepare
This often-neglected initial step in negotiation is extremely important. Every successful negotiation is one part face-to-face discussion and nine parts homework. During the preparation stage, you should perform the following tasks:

- Assign people to a negotiating team, and specify team members' roles.
- Clearly define objectives on each issue.
- Develop a hierarchy of acceptable positions on the issues.
- Create solid, reasonable arguments to support each position.
- Anticipate the positions and rebuttals of the other party.
- Develop and coordinate strategies to use at the negotiating table. Devise some simple signals the negotiating team can use to communicate during negotiations.

3. Develop a BOA
Anticipate the fact that you may not be able to reach an agreement. Not every negotiation concludes with a handshake and a resolution of all issues. Developing a good BOA -- best optimal alternative -- gives you a huge advantage. If you can walk away from negotiations and be happy with your alternatives, you have strong bargaining power. Be sure to reveal your BOA to the other side at some point during the negotiations. It makes them realize you really do have options. These options let you reject bad agreements and walk away from fruitless negotiations.

4. Set a Deadline
Too frequently, negotiations drag on with no end in sight. One way to avoid interminable negotiations is to establish a firm, specific deadline in advance. A deadline forces everyone to use time economically and to concentrate on key points.

Be sure the deadline is appropriate for the issues involved. The more complex the issues, the more time the negotiations will require. Even in complex negotiations, however, a deadline is invaluable.

5. Acknowledge the Other Person's Position
Negotiating doesn't require that the two of you hold similar positions of authority. It doesn't demand that you like each other. But it does require that you accept the validity of the other person's view.

6. Set an Accepting Tone
Begin negotiations with a statement that solicits agreement on the general problem. Continue this positive tone throughout the negotiation process. If you have something negative to say during negotiations, phrase it in a positive way or preface it with a positive statement.

7. Pinpoint the Goal
Before any sort of bargaining can begin, you and your counterpart must agree on the aim of negotiations. You must define the who-what-where-when-how-and-why of the issue and have an idea of the objectives and dimension of a solution.

8. Find Areas of Agreement
Next, you and the other side must identify your mutual interests. Before you can resolve your differences, you

Appendix A continued

must find a common ground where meaningful negotiations can begin. Asking everyone to focus on a mutually desired result will build trust, reduce anxiety, and encourage open communication.

9. Brainstorm Ideas
Most negotiations could use a dash of imaginative thinking. The best agreements for all concerned are often not considered because nobody has thought of them. Premature criticism and closure kill creative thinking. In order to foster creativity and imagination, set aside some time during negotiations to examine different and unusual approaches.

During this period, permit everyone to think out loud without committing to any one idea. To encourage discussion, make it clear that criticism and ridicule will not be tolerated during this brainstorming process.

10. Maintain a Question and Answer Exchange
The heart of any negotiation is the ongoing dialogue during which negotiators discover each other's feelings and attitudes. A question and answer exchange enables you to separate actual from fancied needs, isolate the real obstacles, and identify what approach to use in obtaining agreement. Ask specific, open-ended questions, and probe areas of conflict to uncover as much information as possible. Your own answers and statements must be equally candid.

11. Develop Proposals and Compromises
The next step is to generate proposals and compromises in which everyone wins something. Start by resolving a small difference, and build from there. Concede minor points that your counterpart considers major. Swap concessions until a partial or total resolution of the larger issue is reached. Should a deadlock occur on one topic, move on to another and resolve that one. Agreement in one area softens disagreement in a related area and releases new ideas that lead to settlement. The trick is to keep the proposals and counter proposals coming and the forward momentum continuing until all possible segments of the issue have been resolved.

12. Summarize Each Topic
Frequent summaries ensure that everyone is proceeding in the same direction and will ultimately reach the same destination. Ask the other side for a brief rehash of what you've covered so far -- points of agreement, areas of disagreement, concessions, and conclusions. Jot down important points. These notes can prove invaluable during the final stages of negotiation.

13. Keep Options Open
Never box yourself or the other side into a corner. A public stance coupled with a threat or ultimatum are the two most common ingredients in a cornering strategy. Try not to take a public position that will prove impossible to retract without losing face. Avoid the disasters of threats and ultimatums.

14. Don't Give Up
Even when there seems to be no hope for a meeting of the minds, hang in there. Negotiations are cyclical, and what is steadfast today may be negotiable tomorrow. Given time to rethink their positions and adjust to new ideas, people often soften their rigid postures. So don't press the issue. Give yourself and others a few days away from the bargaining table to relax and review what has transpired; then meet again.

TIPS TO MASTERING THE ART OF NEGOTIATION

As the above steps make clear, successful negotiating involves trading off between getting along with people and getting what you want. All negotiators face this dilemma: "How can I get what I really desire and yet maintain a friendly relationship with the other side?" Here are tips to achieving these seemingly contradictory objectives and mastering the art of negotiation:

1. Gain the Other Person's Trust
No matter how logical and factual you are, the other party will doubt your credibility. Good faith commences with symbolic acts such as shaking hands, maintaining eye contact, and pulling out a chair for someone, and is maintained by consistent honesty. If you want others to level with you, level with them. Although you may occasionally feel that bluffing could help your position, don't do it. It's not worth the gamble. The consequences can be disastrous if your hand is called.

2. Look at Both Sides
Each of us has a unique perception of the reality we face. In negotiations, most of us judge ourselves as more reasonable and accommodating than the other side. The other side has the same perception of us. Be aware of these dangerous misconceptions, and consciously deal with them. Otherwise, hostilities can escalate and ruin your negotiations.

3. Focus on the Issues
Remember that the other side is not your enemy. Like you, they have legitimate desires and needs that the negotiations should fulfill. The objective is to negotiate the disagreements on issues -- not to focus on the personalities of negotiators. Concentrate on direct, fair, and honest dealings leading toward a partnership. Providing the other side with satisfying results fosters good will, continues amicable relationships, and achieves a strong commitment on their part to implement the agreement.

4. Volunteer to Do the Paperwork
Paperwork is not fun, but those who take the notes, write the memos, and prepare the reports are usually more pleased with the final results. Most negotiators first agree on general terms, with the specifics worked out in writing. If you do the writing, you can communicate the details

Appendix A continued

from your perspective. This is a powerful position. Don't surrender it to the other side.

5. Handle Objections Tactfully

The negotiation process isn't a debate. Arguing and scoring points only encourage the other side to maintain a rigid position in order to save face. If an objection is well-founded and rational, accept it and allow the individual to proceed to other points that may be more favorable to your views. If an objection is irrational, accept it temporarily. Then move on to other topics that may enable those on the other side to see for themselves that their thinking was illogical.

6. Use the Power of Silence

You don't have to talk all the time or even most of the time. Effective negotiators have learned the art of active listening. Silence does not mean you are stupid, ill-prepared, rude, or asleep. One of the greatest compliments you can give others is to listen to what they are saying. Practice listening, understanding, and appreciating other people's positions and motivations.

Stop the impulse to interrupt and make your points. Instead, restate and paraphrase to clarify what has been said.

7. Look Beyond the Words

Look for the meaning beyond the literal words people say. Observe body language that can provide telling cues. People's gestures convey feelings in numerous ways. You open your hands if you're ready to cooperate, for instance, and clench them if you're fighting for self-control. If you're nervous, you clear your throat. If frustrated, you rub the back of your neck. To show acceptance, you touch another. You convey "no" by buttoning your coat.

8. Practice Good Communication Skills

Remember, how you say things is as important as what you say. Follow these principles of good communication:

- Introduce any new or foreign concepts early in the negotiation. Use repetition to familiarize the other party with the concept. Before long, the concept will be recognized and often accepted.
- Use props whenever possible. People place much more value on what they see than what they hear.
- Make it a habit to rephrase or restate a negative response.
- Be aware of what you saying and doing. Watch your body language, mannerisms, tone of voice, and voice inflection. Humor is especially troublesome; it can be interpreted as flippant or sarcastic. Only through self-observation can you be certain you are conveying the message you want.
- Never attack someone's principles. Distinguish the principle from the body of your argument.
- Regularly express appreciation of the other party's time and efforts to reach a mutually acceptable agreement.
- Always end a meeting on a positive note.

KEYS TO SUCCESS

Collaborative negotiation is the supreme test of your human-relations skill and management maturity. It also is the only way to achieve consensus and commitment -- the real objectives of any settlement. Being able to create a successful, collaborative negotiation process will be invaluable to your management success.

Reprinted with permission from The Society for Nonprofit Organizations, a nonprofit membership organization that provides information and resources to the nonprofit sector. Publishers of *Nonprofit World Journal*, 6314 Odana Road, Suite 1, Madison, WI 53719-1141. 800-424-7367.

Appendix B

Self-Test on Individual Ethics

A guide for employees to use privately in assessing their own actions.

Reprinted with permission from Independent Sector, Washington, DC.

Commitment Beyond Self

- Am I faithful to the public service mission of my organization in fulfilling my responsibilities?

- Do I participate in volunteer and charitable giving opportunities offered to me as a member of my organization?

- Do I demonstrate a sense of cooperation for the benefit of the whole organization?

- Do I strive for excellence in fulfilling my organization's responsibilities?

Obedience to the Laws

- Do I know and follow existing federal, state and local laws as well as rules of my organization?

- Do I raise questions when I'm not sure about the laws or rules but wonder whether laws might apply?

Commitment Beyond the Law

- Can I articulate my organization's mission and recognize my own role in achieving this mission?

- Do I follow not only the rules of law, but also the spirit of the law?

Commitment to the Public Good

- In my organization's operations, am I true to my organization's standards put forward in public announcements?

- Am I responsive to public inquiries about my organization's activities and finances?

- Do I work at my organization partly as a way of making a personal contribution of time and effort to the public good?

Respect for the Worth and Dignity of Individuals

- In my own actions, do I always see other human beings as individuals who bring something of value to our work place and to our discussions?

- Do I always recognize that every other person has his or her own right to personal dignity and do I respect that in all of my actions?

Tolerance, Diversity and Social Justice

- Do I fully recognize that if we are to deal effectively with current and future challenges that we need the special skills, knowledge and perspectives of a broad variety of individuals with differing attitudes, outlooks and cultural backgrounds?

- When I encounter personal conflict, do I work to channel that energy in constructive ways?

- Do I strive to recognize and understand differences in communication styles between genders and between cultural backgrounds?

- Do I communicate (verbally and nonverbally) the equal value of all persons, even though they may differ in appearance, style, customs, talent and technical skill?

Accountability to the Public

- Am I familiar with my organization's operations and activities in my area of responsibility? Do I take initiative to learn what I do not know?

- Do I act responsibly and responsively to all inquiries about my organization?

- Do I know to whom to refer matters about which I have no knowledge? If not, do I take initiative to find out?

Openness and Honesty

- Do I routinely take an open and honest position?

- Am I meticulously accurate in collecting and reporting information?

- Do I disclose to my organization any personal conflicts of interest that might affect the work that I do for my organization?

Prudent Application of Resources

- Am I familiar with, and do I follow, my organization's personnel and travel policies?

- Do I act always to conserve my organization's resources?

- Do I stay within assigned budgets?

- Do I always refrain from temptations to use my organization's resources and supplies for personal use?

Independent Sector is a national leadership forum working to encourage giving, volunteering, not-for-profit initiative and citizen action. Copyright © 1997 Independent Sector.

Appendix C

Building Opportunities for Ethical Reflection
Reprinted with permission from Independent Sector, Washington, DC.

How can an organization maintain a reflective, evaluative stance toward itself in order to monitor its own behavior both for ethics and effectiveness?

Build opportunities for reflection into the "ongoing" life of the organization.

Here are some possibilities that you may find useful as you consider the particular qualities of you organization.

- Use questions as a focus during a board retreat, or incorporated into a workshop for volunteers, staff or board members or in a retreat or workshop for your entire organization.

- Send questions ahead of time for any forum you wish to use to address ethics, so members may come with the reflection process already under way.

- Create opportunities for individuals to reflect privately, in small peer groups (i.e. board members, administrators, volunteers, staff) and in small and large groups that represent the organization as a whole. Each level of reflection will surface different perspectives and insights.

- Incorporate an "ethics section" into your organization's newsletter highlighting a different value or ethical behavior each month, including key reflection questions relevant to that value.

- Invite members of your organization to write short pieces for the newsletter responding to a particular key question, welcoming success stories that speak to ethical dilemmas where people know what is legal or right but may be tempted to choose otherwise, or must choose among competing ethical options.

- Include everyone in the process of reflection, from board members and senior staff to the newest entry level employee and volunteer. Everyone has insights to contribute.

- Use these questions as a monthly study group open to all members of the organization. Plan the meeting at a convenient time, such as a brown bag lunch gathering. Think about ways to make the meeting an attractive opportunity to participate in the organization; • nurture such a group as an opportunity to build trust, develop community and move the value of ethical behavior off the pages of documents and into the daily life of the organization.

- Look for multiple ways to reflect. Review all the communication channels within your organization and consider what each may contribute to building an atmosphere that values "everyday ethics."

Appendix C continued

- Be open to learning what ethical practices and policies members of your organization perceive exist. (For example, if an organization has a published code of ethics that the board members all acknowledge, what if few staff or volunteers know such a code exists?) Discrepancies and differences of opinion can be as valuable as areas of agreement.

- Use the information learned from this questioning process to refine the questions, perhaps adding new ones, or streamlining what emerges through consensus as "essential questions" that can form the basis for an ongoing audit of your organization's ethics. One sign that the value of ethics is finding a home in our organizations is when questions and suggestions such as these are adapted and personalized. Each organization will need to determine the balance between privacy, quiet reflection and group discussion around these questions that will promote a climate of trust and engender candid, productive and ongoing dialogue.

The goal is to find ways to live with such questions throughout the year. In other words, we need to give these questions, and the values and behaviors they represent, a home in our organization. They should come to our desks everyday. We should meet them in our corridors, and they should be with us as we begin new journeys.

Independent Sector is a national leadership forum working to encourage giving, volunteering, not-for-profit initiative and citizen action. Copyright © 1997 Independent Sector.

Appendix D

Steps to Take When Faced With an Ethical Challenge

A sound process for evaluation and decision making when an individual faces an ethical challenge.

☐ **Review Your Standards**

Review your organization's mission, values, code of ethics and/or standards to remind yourself of the context for thinking about the issue you face.

☐ **Develop Good Questions**

Develop a list of good questions which will help you to further focus on the specific facts necessary for careful consideration of a specific issue. (Be certain the questions are relevant and thorough to assure that the answers to them will provide sound direction; review recent ethics audit questions, if available, looking for questions useful to include on this list).

☐ **Gather the Facts**

Gather the facts that answer these questions thoroughly and in complete honesty.

☐ **Decide What to Do**

Decide what to do based on the answers to your good questions.

☐ **Decide How to Do It**

Decide how to do it (sometimes this will require another full and careful review of the above steps).

Reprinted with permission from Independent Sector, Washington DC. Independent Sector is a national leadership forum working to encourage giving, volunteering, not-for-profit initiative and citizen action. Copyright © 1997 Independent Sector.

Appendix E

Editor's note: **This document was developed by participants in the 1997 Executive Course in Strategic Management sponsored by the United Way and Community Chest of Greater Cincinnati. Submitted by Lee Reading, former Executive Director, Joy Outdoor Education Center, Clarksville, OH.**

Core Competencies

Core executive competencies include a mix of leadership and business management skills which are interwoven with the effective use of self. This can best be defined as the unique blend of science and art that an individual brings to the job which conveys commitment to mission, compassion, integrity, creativity, style, and a variety of other personal characteristics which energize and inspire others to do their best.

Leadership

1. **Change Management:**
   Recognizes and addresses the complexities of successfully integrating change within the organization.

   A. Spearheads efforts to develop organization vision and maintains tension to facilitate change focused on this vision within the context of agency mission.
   B. Manages change in a thoughtful and well-planned rather than reactive manner.
   C. Considers the organization's culture and capabilities in responding to change.
   D. Introduces change in a way that allows the organization to respond effectively; actively assists others in adapting to change and overcoming barriers.
   E. Makes timely and effective decisions in the absence of perfect information.
   F. Maintains effectiveness in situations marked by a great deal of complexity or ambiguity.
   G. Maintains positive attitude, passion, and commitment in the midst of change.

2. **Communication:**
   Effectively communicates the organization's mission, vision, programs and services to its various constituencies.

   A. Demonstrates effective spoken and written communication with varied audiences, both within and outside the organization.
   B. Possesses the ability to define the audience and simplify information for quick and easy understanding.
   C. Responds appropriately to information needs during a crisis.

3. **Negotiation Skills:**
   Understands the key positions of all parties involved in a given negotiation and works towards agreements that serve the interests of the organization.

   A. Identifies the motivation, needs, concerns, and feelings of the parties involved in a negotiation and can create strategies to reach constructive agreements.
   B. Promotes conflict resolution through effective listening, feedback, exploring options, and gaining closure.
   C. Demonstrates flexibility when seeking solutions in which all parties can benefit.
   D. Stresses common goals when carrying out a negotiation.

4. **Teamwork and Partnership:**
   Collaborates with others in teams or partnerships and supports integrative efforts which enhance organizational effectiveness.

Director's Guide to Best Practices

A. Conveys expectation for staff to collaborate with other functions and departments to find solutions to problems.

B. Employs constructive group problem solving and decision making practices when participating on teams, partnerships, or ventures.

C. Leverages the diverse sets of knowledge and skills of associates to ensure the organization's success.

D. Sets the foundation for building effective teams and creates teams only when indicated.

E. Understands when decisions should be made independently and when to involve others.

F. Employs active listening skills.

5. **Action and Results Orientation**
Demonstrates personal and organizational accountability in order to achieve results.

A. Appropriately defines problems/issues and determines urgency and importance, prior to taking action. Once an issue is defined, clarifies risks involved, and emphasizes the need for speed or cautiousness needed to achieve desired results.

B. Eliminates barriers to fast action and develops processes that support efficient and effective actions.

C. Makes tough decisions in implementing business strategy.

D. Takes active responsibility and accountability for achieving results.

6. **Accurate Self Assessment and Personal/Professional Balance:**
Strives to continually increase self knowledge, awareness of impact on others, takes care of self, and develops plans for improving executive capability.

A. Accurately evaluates own strengths and limitations.

B. Maintains balance between professional and personal life to ensure personal health, well being and vitality; models the way in establishing balance for others.

C. Actively solicits feedback from senior managers, peers, subordinates, suppliers and customers regarding strengths and areas for development.

D. Selects associates/staff and seeks outside resources that have capabilities that compliment own deficits.

E. Changes own behavior to minimize the impact of own limitations; learns from experience.

F. Is appropriately open with others about own capabilities.

G. Understands and manages impact on others.

H. Delegates tasks appropriately in order to remain focused on priority efforts.

7. **Multiple Influence Skills:**
Recognizes the wide variety of players and audiences that must be influenced in order to achieve organizational goals.

A. Has sharp awareness of external political dynamics which guide appropriate individual and coordinated actions to support agency goals.

B. Develops and employs influence strategies that have the greatest chance for success given the audiences and circumstances.

C. Demonstrates a willingness to listen to a diverse range of views and differing opinions.

D. Recognizes influence failures when they occur and employs alternate strategies and actions to meet goals.

E. Demonstrates effective interpersonal communication skills crucial to fostering positive working relationships with others.

F. Instigates/facilitates dialogue amongst organizational associates.

G. Provides appropriate and effective feedback to facilitate organizational improvement.

Appendix E continued

8.   **Cultural Competence:**
Strives to achieve organizational cultural competence in individuals, work groups, and the entire organizational structure within the context of the community.

   A.   Identifies/understands current organizational culture and plans for change.
   B.   Creates and models appropriate culture for the organization.
   C.   Maintains sensitivity to the climate of the organization, the strengths/weaknesses in others, and variety of differences.
   D.   Understands dynamics of difference between dominant and non-dominant groups within the organization and the community. Values cultural diversity.
   E.   Understands key concepts of prejudice, discrimination, "isms", and institutionalized concepts relating to gender and race as illustrated by actions, impacts, and feelings.
   E.   Develops personal, group, and organizational goals to recognize, include, and best utilize individual abilities, skills, and characteristics of individuals, groups, and organizations.
   F.   Practices verbal and behavioral "walking the talk;" advocates and facilitates inclusion of others.

Business Management/Development

1.   **Strategic Focus and Integrated Business Alignment:**
Integrates the organization's mission, strategic direction and objectives into the operations with an understanding of environmental challenges.

   A.   Creates aligned direction with a compelling vision for the organization. Provides consistent application of principles contained in the vision.
   B.   Sets strategic plans that support the direction and integration of different aspects of operations to ensure achievement of long term goals and objectives.
   C.   Allocates resources (time, capital, and human) in accordance with the strategic priorities of the business.
   D.   Takes whatever action is necessary and prudent to reduce costs and free resources for better use; optimizes resources.
   E.   Informs and educates division associates so they can elevate their efforts to a more strategic focus.
   F.   Has a global view of social, economic, and related events and their potential impact on the organization.
   G.   Demonstrates ability to prioritize.
   H.   Possesses the strategic ability to understand the total environment and the ability to see where the agency fits.

2.   **Customer Drive:**
Focuses on customers and their needs as a priority in daily operations and long-term planning.

   A.   Establishes systems and processes which keep the organization customer focused. Responds quickly and effectively to customer feedback and complaints.
   B.   Understands customer requirements, stays up to date with them.
   C.   Understands diversity of constituents.
   D.   Promotes the development of effective working relationships with internal and external customers.
   E.   Seeks ways to continually increase customer satisfaction.

Director's Guide to Best Practices

3. **Performance Management:**
    Manages employee and volunteer performance through a process which clearly identifies performance expectations, delivers timely constructive feedback and appropriate recognition.

    A. Sets challenging but realistic and specific formal/informal performance goals and standards for subordinates.
    B. Holds people accountable for achieving results.
    C. Provides associates with information, training, support and resources for them to successfully carry out their responsibilities.
    D. Actively works to encourage and allow associates to reach their full working potential.
    E. Conducts meaningful performance reviews that are consistent with established objectives.
    F. Uses recognition, praise, and compensation to reward subordinates for excellent performance.

4. **Financial Management:**
    Employs sound financial management.

    A. Analyzes key financial reports, interprets them meaningfully, and makes effective decisions.
    B. Understands the key strategic cost drivers in the organization; creates and executes plans to continually manage the cost structure of operations.
    C. Asks the right questions to test validity of financial data, analysis and recommendations.
    D. Prioritizes capital plan to address short and long term needs.
    E. Influences board through clear explanation of situations which affect financial aspects of the business.
    F. Plans for cost effective utilization of resources.

5. **Board Development:**
    Facilitates the development of the organization's mission, vision, governance and the recruitment of volunteer leadership to achieve the organization's mission.

    A. Articulates and reviews the organizational mission and vision.
    B. Ensures appropriate governance and operational policies.
    C. Provides leadership to the governing board in matters of organizational and volunteer resource development.
    D. Facilitates board education.
    E. Is responsive to the board.

6. **Resource Development:**
    Secures necessary resources to advance the mission of the organization.

    A. Demonstrates the ability to identify and procure human (paid and volunteer) resources necessary to meet organizational goals.
    B. Identifies and secures appropriate sources of funding and other financial resources.
    C. Researches, develops, and shares information and knowledge with others.
    D. Promotes the development of positive relationships and goodwill to further the agency's work.

7. **Operations Knowledge:**
    Understands and is skillful in the key disciplines and technical areas required to manage the organization.

    A. Has enough knowledge and experience in key functions to know what questions to ask to get at the critical components of an operational problem or issue.
    B. Is familiar with critical aspects of operations and contributes successfully to planning and

Appendix E continued

C. Identifies risk factors and manages risk by employing best practices to ensure safety and minimize liability to the organization.

D. Demonstrates the ability to answer questions about key issues in the organization.

E. Utilizes the diversity of the workforce to ensure maximum individual and work unit effectiveness.

8. **Critical/Analytical Thinking:**
Employs a data based approach to identify solutions to issues and opportunities.

A. Identifies causal factors in complex situations.

B. Makes sense out of disparate pieces or sources of information.

C. Understands how to use analytical models and what the results mean.

D. Views situations/problems from a global perspectives taking into account multiple perspectives (e.g. customers, production, finance, quality, government regulation, etc.).

E. Reduces large quantities of information to a useful form.

F. Demonstrates creativity and ability to "think/act" outside the box.

9. **Organization and Job Design:**
Understands the importance of consistently reviewing the organization and individuals to ensure appropriate capabilities are in place or developed to keep the organization viable, relevant, flourishing, and competitive.

A. Periodically conducts organization analysis to develop structures and jobs which keep the organization efficient, effective, and aligned with strategic direction.

B. Consistently looks for ways to employ information technology to help the organization be more effective.

C. Knows core competencies required for key positions in the organization. Uses appropriate selection methods when hiring or promoting within the organization.

D. Makes compensation decisions fairly. Rewards are consistently applied according to performance standards.

E. Conducts an effective succession and career development planning process annually and ensures plans for development are executed.

Director's Guide to Best Practices

Key Customers	Key Outputs Per Customer	Critical Tasks	Skills
		Functions Related	**Basic Skills/Qualities** (All should have in common)
Public		- Leads strategic plan - Tactical planning	- Writing/communication - Strategic planning skills
Clients	- Mission - Receive/assess service - Feedback	- Oversees compliance of policies (govt/agency) - Provides reality check for board	- Do multiple tasks at once - Action/results orientation - Performance management - Appropriate self assessment
Volunteers		- Financial management	- Identifies opportunities
Board	- Develops policy - Fiduciary responsibility - Fund development - Strategic planning/long range planning - Evaluation - Marketing/promotion	- Oversees fund development - Public Relations - Advocacy **Interfaces** - Clarifies the roles/respon. for staff, volunteers, between departments	- Knowledge of local requirements - Upward influence skills - Analytical capability - Understands language/culture of customers - Negotiation - Priority skills
Policy Makers		- Education of board - Interfaces with key customers	- Keeps current in field - Insightful
Funding Agents or Donors	- Contract/terms purchase of service - Funding	- Collaborates/participates in community activities	- High stress tolerance - Takes constructive criticism - Sense of humor
Staff	- Performance (job) - Job description - Goals and objectives - Mission of organization - Represents organization - Provides information/feedback	**Supervisory/Managerial** - Adequate financial and human resources - Development of staff (coach/referee) - Instrument of change - Staff supervision	**Advanced Skills** (Result - superior performance) - Change management - Critical thinking - Manages cultural diversity - Forecasts trends - Changes/adapts to climate and needs
Collaborative Agencies		- Intervenes & sets direction in crisis situations - Sets tone in culture - Conflict resolution	- Command of latest tech. - Stress reduction - Compromiser - Collaboration
National Associations			
Self	- Balance - Family - Health		
Special events/projects			
Others			

Used with permission of Redwood Rehabilitation Center, a United Way Agency.

Appendix F

Adapted Nominal Group Technique
© Corky McReynolds, Ph.D.
Director, Treehaven Education and Conference Center, Tomahawk, WI
Used with permission.

A common problem in strategic planning is not attending to the needs of effective small group facilitation. Most strategic planning resources do not describe the techniques needed to skillfully, fairly and effectively establish or facilitate planning teams. Applying an effective technique for small groups is important to ensure individuals experience a fair and equal process which results in increased participation, creativity, ownership of ideas and consensus. Once people are invited to participate in a planning process it is critical for everyone to gain a sense of confidence and equality through effective techniques.

The Adapted Nominal Group Technique (ANGT) described here sets the stage for fair and equal participation, and is based on other Nominal Group Techniques (Delbecq, et al, 1975 and Fox, 1987). This article describes ANGT while resources attending to effective meetings can be located in the references (Doyle 1976, Frank 1989, Tagliere 1992).

Preparation: The Driving Question

Strategic thinking typically begins with a question. The development of the driving, or key, question is best accomplished through assessment of the needs of the organization and/or the purpose of the session. The driving and subordinate questions should be determined well in advance by key stakeholders and stated in simplest form. Driving questions should not include "and", "or", or other words that end up constructing two or more questions in one. The question, "What are our strengths and weaknesses?" should be rewritten as two separate questions. Do not ask two questions with expected responses at the same time. If the "strengths" are the preferred driving question, then ask for responses to that question separately from "weaknesses" question. The language of the question should be chosen carefully to reduce the confusion over possible multiple interpretations.

Good Examples of Driving Questions

- What are the trends in education for the next 10 years?
- What should environmental education be 20 years from now?
- What should Treehaven become within the next five years?

The driving question should be disseminated to participants one week in advance of the session for any clarification, reflection and participation.

The Technique: Sharing in the Round

The face-to-face technique begins with people situated in a room with tables typically in U-shape, with the facilitator and easel/pads at the open end of the U.

The driving question is reintroduced through a worksheet, and the first five to seven minutes is designated for individual reflection and idea generation. This time is critical, and the facilitator needs to make sure people do not talk loudly. If two or more people finish early and get up for coffee, make sure conversation does not take place. Participants still writing might think "decisions" are being discussed outside of the process. Build the expectation quickly that the creative and critical center of the discussion is through sharing in the round.

To begin sharing in the round, request one idea from one person at a time. Record and number the statement onto the newsprint. Do not change the wording, but the recorder can abbreviate or edit with input and approval from participants. For example, if to the question "What development should we build along the riverfront boardwalk?" the participant responded, "slope seating," do not automatically change the phrase to "amphitheater."

Appendix F continued

Each person offers their ideas in the round, one at a time, until all are finished. One may pass when all of their ideas are offered, but may again offer a new idea their next turn. The process continues until everyone passes in a complete round.

The rules for this stage are:
- No clarification of ideas when presented (this comes next).
- No critiquing, judging or any evaluation of any statement (this will follow clarification).
- Do not allow comments from one participant directed to another — keep all comments directed to the idea.
- If an idea is already offered, the next participant does not offer the same idea, but simply crosses it off and goes to their next idea.

Tips for sharing in the round

- Toward the end of the initial brainstorming, one or two participants may have many more ideas while others have all passed. The mistake would be to turn to those individuals and ask for the rest of their list. This immediately excludes all others from reentering the process with a great new idea! Keep the process in the round until all are offered and pass.
- If a participant suddenly exclaims, "I've got an idea and I can't wait till my turn," the mistake of the facilitator would be to interrupt the process to accept the idea. The facilitator should respond, "Please write your idea down so you don't forget," then continue with the sequence.
- A facilitator takes on the role of taskmaster to ensure the integrity of the process. Firm, but positive, reminders to "unintentional violators" will set a culture within the group to accept and quickly embrace the procedures. Remember the process is designed to guarantee fairness, equality and creativity.
- If there are severe time limits, before you begin sharing in the round, ask participants to circle their top three or four ideas. During "in the round" only those the participants circled are offered to the process.

Clarification

The next step is to clarify any of the ideas on the list. The purpose of clarification is for everyone in the group to have a common level of understanding of the statements.

The Quickround is a time-saving technique while allowing clarification of any idea. Explain the purpose of clarification, emphasizing it is not to critique but simply to define an idea. Begin with statement #1. The facilitator looks "in the round" for a raised hand, eye contact, or a verbal question from the participants. If a participant ask a question, typically the author will define or explain the meaning. Check with the participant for satisfaction. Continue the quickround until all the statements have been covered.

Tips for Clarification

- Do not bypass this stage. If is very important that all participants have an opportunity to ask and check for understanding.
- Do not allow the original author to volunteer an explanation when no other participant asks for clarification. If the facilitator allows one to do this, then soon every author will feel obligated to explain, and the group will become bogged down on each item. Make sure anyone explaining the statement does not begin to justify or lobby the idea.

Focused Pro

At the completion of clarification the next two stages, Focused Pro and Focused Con, allow the participants to critique ideas fairly and efficiently. Depending on time, number of participants or number of ideas, ask each

Appendix F continued

participant to choose two, three, four, or five ideas that they believe would be the best answer to the original driving question. This should be an individual activity, not a discussion among the participants. Ask each person to write the number of the idea on their paper, and prepare a brief statement supporting the idea. After a few minutes, begin the "in the round" again, starting with a new participant. Ask for the number of one of their statements, and their verbal support. Circle the number of the idea on the newsprint. Continue in the round, one person and one supportive statement at a time. All numbered ideas that were supported are now circled on the newsprint.

Tips

- Provide instruction before the round begins for participants to offer supportive statements to all of their self-selected ideas, even if someone has already offered support of that statement. This is very important to begin the consensus building process and avoid making supportive statements to a large number but less important ideas.
- Participants might moan about having so few ideas that they can support, but the facilitator should stick to a number. Don't let the participants choose the number of ideas to support; the facilitator should make this decision based on the previously mentioned criteria.
- Keep the discussion positive, reminding participants that the focused con will follow.
- Some participants will quickly see pattern and relationships among some of the statements, and will look for "combining" or "grouping" before beginning to focus pro. Do not combine at this stage. Better decisions will result with focused pro/con on the more specific statements rather than broad categories.
- The facilitator needs only to circle a selected idea once regardless of how many times participants choose that item. Participants are responsible for keeping their own notes.

Focused Con

Depending on the size of the group, time constraints and number of ideas chosen for focused pro, have the participants choose the same number or one less for focused con. For example, if the instructions for focused pro were to select three from the entire list, then instruct participants to choose three from the CIRCLED numbers (those receiving pro statements), or two if time is a problem. Have participants make their choices and prepare brief statements as to why those are not the best ideas to the answer.

Begin in the round with a new person, requesting one comment. Continue in the round until all statements are provided. The facilitator does not need to make any notations; however, a checkmark to the items selected for con provides a visual aid to the participants. Again the participants are responsible for taking their own notes from the discussion.

Tip

- Participants may verbalize with difficulty in selecting any of the ideas to say anything negative about, but insist they critically look at both sides of any of the ideas that have been circled from focused pro. Better informed decisions will result.

Combining Up - Optional

Now that the self-selected ideas have received focused discussion, some combining may be desirable. Review the circled ideas with the participants and ask if anyone sees a possible combination. Stress that combinations should be only ideas that are so similar as to become better as one. Do not attempt to form categories through combination. Often participants will want to combine, but once the process begins a snowball effect is very likely. For example, a participant suggests #3 and #11 can be combined. Everyone agrees and then someone suggests #27 could also be added, and then another. Participants become tired and often readily agree to the additions, only later to discover the new, larger version has become something that, when asked to vote upon in the final stages, lacks specific meaning or contains one that cannot be supported.

Appendix F continued

If combining is necessary or requested by participants, then use Combining Up. Review the first circled item on the list. Ask participants to offer possible combinations from the remainder of the list to that item. An item can only be combined if everyone agrees. If one person does not believe it should be combined, then it remains separate. No discussion — no debate. Go to the second item circled and look for any circled items below it that could be combined up. Follow the procedure until combinations are complete, or all of the circled ideas have been reviewed.

Tips
- Do not try to rewrite statements (ideas); simply cross out the number — not the statement — and add that number up into its combined number.
- It is not necessary to combine non-circled numbers. Remember, the ANGT process helps focus discussion and sets priorities. Non-circled items, when appropriate to the task, can always be inserted to support the prioritized or circled statements.
- Groups often bog down in combining. As a facilitator, keep it moving and avoid trying to form categories. If a large number of items exist that need to be grouped into categories, use affinity or oval mapping techniques.

Statements — Optional

Occasionally, after focused pro and focused con, there is a need among the participants to summarize their thoughts. The facilitator needs to discern this option and ask if it is desired by the group. If opted, then ask each participant to prepare a verbal statement with a maximum time limit of one to two minutes. The statements must be directed to the idea and not personal statements to or about other participants. Participants may pass.

Tip
- Do not allow grandstanding, personal attacks, or lengthy statements. Keep the statements focused on the ideas.

Setting Priorities/Ranking the Ideas

The final stage is to set some type of prioritization or ranking to the ideas that have been circled. There are many voting techniques, but one called 10/4 is easy to administer and very effective in establishing priorities/ranks. Each participant has 10 votes, but can only place a maximum of four votes on any one item. All of the circle items (pro/con) are eligible to receive voting, but only those circled ideas. An idea selected for focused con has not been eliminated.

Each participant reviews the list, selects and distributes their 10 votes. When participants are finished as a group, individuals place their votes in pen or pencil next to the circled numbers. Votes are tallied and the results are presented to the group.

Tip
- The facilitator should note any obvious statements that emerge towards the top. Typically, two to five items will clearly rise with a cluster of most of the votes. The remaining statements will receive few or no votes. The top vote getters, through ranking, can become the focus of action for the group to pursue. If the voting results in a horizontal or flat vote distribution, then the group has not reached consensus toward its priorities, and those statements receiving votes need to be re-discussed, then re-voted.

Appendix F continued

Summary of ANGT

1. Select a driving question.
2. Distribute the question and a summary of the process to participants one week in advance of the session.
3. At the session, provide orientation to the purpose, process and the question.
4. To begin, allow individuals time to reflect/prepare comments to the question.
5. Begin in the round, recoding ideas one at a time. Continue until all have passed.
6. Conduct focus pro.
7. Conduct focus con.
8. Option — Combine Up
9. Option — Statements
10. Priorities/rank

Tips

- ANGT is designed as an open process which will build trust and encourage open communication among participants. Offering ideas, comments to ideas and voting are open visible processes. If a sensitive topic desiring confidentiality is preferred, see Improved Nominal Group Technique (Fox, 1990). The advantage of the open process is building intentional communication bridges and understandings.
- Do not surprise participants with the technique. Always plan and communicate the technique in advance of the session. Use the written information describing the process/technique as a letter of contract to faithfully participate in the process.

ANGT and other facilitation techniques provide a structured forum to encourage creativity and effectiveness for small group decision making. Quality information can be exchanged, everyone has an equal opportunity to participate and the open process has positive unintended outcomes in addition to focused prioritized results. There is no perfect process; therefore, the facilitator's role needs to be reflective and always open to experimenting with creative improvements.

....

References

Delbecq, Andre L. et al. (1975). *Group Techniques for Program Planning*. Middleton, WI: Green Briar Press.

Doyle, Michael & Strauss, David. (1977). *How to Make Meetings Work*. NY: Jove.

Fox, William M. (1987). *Effective Group Problem Solving: How to Broaden Participation, Improve Decision Making, and Increase Commitment to Action*. San Francisco: Jossey-Bass Publishers.

Fox, William & Glaser, Rollin. (1990). *Improved Nominal Group Technique (Trainer Guide)*. King of Prussia, PA: Organization Design & Development.

Frank, Mil. (1989). *How to Run a Successful Meeting in Half the Time*. NY: Pocket.

Tagliere, Daniel. (1992). *How to Meet, Think, and Work to Consensus*. San Diego: Pfeiffer.

INDEX